Lecture Notes in
Computer Science

Edited by G. Goos and J. Hartmanis

177

Programming Languages and Their Definition

H. Bekič (1936–1982)

Selected Papers edited by C. B. Jones

Springer-Verlag
Berlin Heidelberg New York Tokyo 1984

Editor

C. B. Jones
Department of Computer Science, The University
Manchester M13 9PL, Great Britain

CR Subject Classifications (1982): 0.3, D3.1, F.3

ISBN 3-540-13378-X Springer-Verlag Berlin Heidelberg New York Tokyo
ISBN 0-387-13378-X Springer-Verlag New York Heidelberg Berlin Tokyo

Library of Congress Cataloging in Publication Data. Bekič, H. (Hans), 1936–1982. Programming languages and their definition. (Lecture notes in computer science; 177) 1. Programming languages (Electronic computers) I. Jones, C. B. (Cliff B.), 1944-. II. Title. III. Series. QA76.7.B45 1984 001.64'24 84-14094
ISBN 0-387-13378-X (U.S.)

Printing and binding: Beltz Offsetdruck, Hemsbach/Bergstr.
2145/3140-54321

for:

Sophie, Johannes, Edith, Wolfgang,
Hildegard, Ludwig, Rudolf and Alban

CONTENTS

Selected Papers

Languages

Language Definition

Parallelism

INTRODUCTION

The IBM Vienna Laboratory has made a significant contribution to the work on the semantic description of computer systems. Both the operational semantics descriptions ("VDL") and the later work on denotational semantics ("Meta-IV", "VDM") contain interesting scientific ideas. Partly because of the large scale of the applications tackled, much of the material is difficult to access.

Hans Bekic was one of the key members of the "Vienna Lab". His tragic death in a mountain accident in October 1982 left unpublished an important body of research. (The editorial notes below contain further details of his scientific career; a biographical note has been written by Professors Kuich and Zemanek).

Hans' computer research can be considered under three headings. His work on programming languages took place partly within IFIP WG 2.1 of which he was a member from 1965-1971. He also had an influence on the development of PL/I. Hans was a mathematician and so moved naturally to research on formal language description. Most of his scientific career was spent on this work. Hans was largely responsible for the move by the Vienna Lab from operational to denotational semantics. He was a member of IFIP WG 2.2 from 1969 until his death. Work on the description of parallelism occupied the last years of Hans' life. This was a difficult period in which the laboratory was employed on practical programming tasks: Hans pursued his scientific work in his "spare time".

This book contains a selection of Hans Bekic's papers. Publication of his specific contribution presents special problems. Much of his work was unpublished and even, in some cases, existed only as hand written manuscripts. Sometimes Hans postponed publication because he considered a piece of work to be flawed; in other cases - it must be conceded - his habit of leaving things to the last minute resulted in his missing a deadline for publication. In spite of this, Hans' work has been widely circulated and has influenced others. His untimely death means that he cannot complete the work in the way he would have wished.

After discussions with his family, friends and colleagues, it was decided that it would be valuable to publish a selection of Hans' papers. To alleviate any fear that he would not have wished them to be published in this form, his own reservations - where known - have been included. A list of all known writings and main talks on computer topics is given below (book reviews etc. are not listed); the most important papers are reproduced.

I am one of many people who regard their contact with Hans as having been immensly stimulating and enjoyable. He was also a good friend. I hope that this volume will make some of his scientific work known to a wider community.

Editorial Notes

Because of Hans' interest in music, the items below have been given "Opus" numbers. They have been arranged in order of earliest reference to give coherence to the development - subsequent publication is shown as such. The list contains the title and source of every known "paper" with comments (written by CBJ) in italic fount. These comments attempt to set the background and to record any reservations which HB was known to have had about a piece of work.

Citation research used "Compumath" and "Science Citation" indices. Many of the source documents used the ISO data format (yyyy-mm-dd) - this has been preserved.

The decision was made to retype all of the papers. Apart from the effort and delay this entailed, it has clearly increased the risk of error. It is hoped that the uniformity and style of presentation justify this step.

Acknowledgements

Funding for travel and typing has been provided by the UK Science and Engineering Research Council (Contract SO/261/83) and IBM Austria. The typing of the editorial material was done by Julie Hibbs and of manuscripts themselves by Margaret Barringer. Library research was undertaken by Alison McCauley and translations by Prof. Prachar and Jill Jones.

The following people provided input to the editorial material: Derek Andrews, Egidio Astesiano, Jaco de Bakker, Kurt Bandat, Dines Bjorner, Andrzej Blikle, Manfred Broy, Edsger W. Dijkstra, K. Indermark, Don Knuth, W. Kuich, Peter Landin, Peter Lauer, J. Loecks, Peter Lucas, Robert Milne, Erich Neuhold, Robin Milner, John Nicholls, David Park, Brian Randell, Don Sannella, Dana Scott, Jim Thatcher, Kurt Walk, Fritz Weissenboeck, Niklaus Wirth, Heinz Zemanek.

Most of all, I should like to thank Sophie Bekic for allowing me access to Hans' papers.

Cliff B. Jones

List of Papers and Main Scientific Talks

[Opus 1]
Die Zahl der Symmetrieklassen der Funktionen n Logischer Variabler
H.Bekic
Internal Report, Vienna, December 1960
10 pages, 2 Refs.

[Opus 2]
Extension of the Algorithmic Language ALGOL
V.Kudielka, P.Lucas, K.Walk, K.Bandat, H.Bekic, H.Zemanek
Mailuefterl Vienna, Final Report DA-91-591-EUC-1430, July 1961
200 pages.

See note on this project with [Opus 10].

[Opus 3]
Compilation of ALGOL, Part I - Organization of the Object Program.
P.Lucas, H.Bekic
IBM Laboratory Vienna, LR 25.3.001, May 1962
48 pages, 4 Refs.

[Opus 4]
Ueber die Ausdehnung zweier bekannter Probleme aus der additiven Zahlentheorie auf arithmetische Reihen grosser Differenz
H.Bekic
Dissertation at University of Vienna (Dept. Philosophy) 1963
67 pages, 7 Refs.

Hans Bekic read mathematics at the University of Vienna and this was his Ph.D thesis. The title might be translated as "On the Generalisation of Two Known Problems from Additive Number Theory to Arithmetic Progressions with Large Differences".

[Opus 5]
Some Aspects for a Comparison of FORTRAN and ALGOL
P.Lucas, H.Bekic
IBM Laboratory Vienna, LR 25.3.003, November 1963
23 pages, 13 Refs.

[Opus 6]
An Input-Output Proposal for ALGOL Based on FORTRAN IV Input-Output
H.Bekic
IBM Laboratory Vienna, LR 25.3.005, March 1964
12 pages, 5 Refs.

[Opus 7]
Some Comments on the ACM Committee Proposal on I/O Conventions for ALGOL 60, by D.E.Knuth
H.Bekic
Originally printed as a note:
IBM Lab Vienna, LN 25.3.006, March 1964
5 pages, 3 Refs.
Then as:
ALGOL Bulletin No.18, October 1964
pages 16-19, 3 Refs.

[Opus 8]
Scope of Names in NPL
K.Bandat, H.Bekic
IBM Laboratory Vienna, LR 25.0.002, July 1964
19 pages, 7 Refs.

"NPL" was the first name given to the programming language which eventually became PL/I. This paper refers to scope features which were changed even before the first compiler was built for the language.

[Opus 9]
Block Concept for NPL
K.Bandat, H.Bekic, P.Lucas
IBM Laboratory Vienna, LR 25.0.003, July 1964

9 pages, 5 Refs.

Here again, the discussion relates to features of the PL/I language which changed.

[Opus 10] *see page 1 below*

Note on a Test Example for ALGOL 60 Compilers by D.E.Knuth

H.Bekic

Originally printed as a note:

IBM Laboratory Vienna, LN 25.3.009, September 1964

Then as:

ALGOL Bulletin No.18, October 1964

page 13, 3 Refs.

A group led by Heinz Zemanek left the Technische Hochschule Vienna (now "Technical University") to become the IBM Science group (later "Laboratory") in 1961. This group designed and built the Mailuefterl computer. Zemanek explains the choice of name as follows:

> The name of MAILUEFTERL is derived from a joke I made when I first announced our project at the historic conference in Darmstadt in 1955. "We are not going to have a WHIRLWIND, TAIPHOON, or HURRICANE", I said, "But we shall have a nice Viennese spring time breeze (MAILUEFTERL)", because the transistors we got free of charge were intended for hearing aids and so had a very low cutoff frequency. But my people developed circuits that finally allowed a clock frequency of 133 kHz, and that was not so low for the time.

A project was started to build a compiler for the ALGOL 60 language and the compiler was available in 1961. The language, which had been designed by IFIP Working Group 2.1, included a block concept, recursive procedures and the possibility of procedures passed to parameters. The "ALGOL Bulletin" was the main publication for comments on the language and its implementation. Donald Knuth had earlier published the following program as a test to see whether compilers handled the new features correctly:

```
begin real procedure A(k, x1, x2, x3, x4, x5);
          value k; integer k;
          begin real procedure B;
                    begin k := k - 1;
                          B := A := A(k, B, x1, x2, x3, x4)
                    end;
               if k ≤ 0 then A := x4 + x5 else B
          end;
     outreal(A(10, 1, -1, -1, 1, 0))
end;
```

Hans Bekic had been working on the ALGOL compiler and this brief note shows that the Mailuefterl team had implemented recursion etc. correctly. This note is an interesting "pre-echo" of the discussion relating to PL/I (see [Opus 18]). The Mailuefterl project is described in "Central European Prehistory of Computing" by H. Zemanek, published in "A History of Computing in the Twentieth Century", (eds.) N. Metropolis, J. Howlett and Gian-Carlo Rota, Academic Press, 1980; and the ALGOL 60 compiler is discussed in [Opus 3].

[Opus 11] *see pages 2 - 3 below*
The Assignment to a Type Procedure Identifier in ALGOL 60
H.Bekic
Originally printed as a note:
IBM Laboratory Vienna, LN 25.3.010, September 1964
2 pages, 2 Refs.
Then as:
ALGOL Bulletin No. 18, October 1964
pages 14-15, 2 Refs.

This discussion of the implementation consists of technical details but the introduction is characteristic of Hans Bekic's style. It should be remembered that ALGOL 60 is not "fully typed": procedure formal parameters were not, in general, fully specified. The "w" used in the text was probably intended to be a Greek "ω".

[Opus 12] *see pages 17 - 25 below*
Defining a Language in its Own Terms
H.Bekic
IBM Laboratory Vienna, TN 25.3.016, 22nd December 1964

12 pages, 4 Refs.

The Vienna Laboratory decided to apply the ideas on formal definition to PL/I - [Opus 27] includes the following comments:

History

This Technical Report, called "Formal Definition of PL/I" (Universal Language Document No.3: 'ULD 3'.), describes PL/I as gathered from the SRL - Manual Form C28-6571-3. It formally describes the programming language, but not a specific implementation in a specific environment.

The project was initiated by a formal proposal made by members of the Hursley Laboratory, of the Poughkeepsic Laboratory, and of the Vienna Laboratory in October 1965 /1/. This proposal was accepted by the PL/I manager and the Vienna Laboratory was committed subsequently to prepare the document by end of 1966 in the form of a technical report.

The early ideas of the Vienna group on the method are documented in the "Tentative Steps" /2/ and have been discussed with responsible and interested IBM advanced programming specialists on many occasions. There was a frequent exchange of working documents and there were regular working meetings between the Hursley language definition group, the Poughkeepsie language evaluation group, and the Vienna language definition group. K.BANDAT represented the Vienna Laboratory in the Language Resolution Board and served as liaison to the other IBM PL/I groups.

The method of defnition and its application to PL/I have been presented at various occasions internally in IBM to groups involved in PL/I and at the IBM Programming Symposium in Skytop in November 1965 /3/, to SHARE representatives in Vienna in October 1966, and to language committees outside IBM /4/.

Remark

This first version of the document contains essentially the formal description as such, with a minimum of reading aids. It certainly is not a teaching device or a kind of text-book. But some additional work will yield a considerable improvement in this direction.

We believe that formal definition is a necessary step in the development of the art of programming. This document on PL/I not only removes the ambiguities that no informal description can avoid. It also establishes the way of discussion and asking questions in precise terms. It constitutes a ground for the future development of PL/I.

We hope that this document and its coming improved versions will be a good service for IBM and IBM's customers

H.Zemanek, Vienna, 30th December 1966.

References

/1/ Unambiguous Definition of PL/I. - Memorandum in response to a Telex of Dr. M. de V.ROBERTS signed by K.BANDAT, E.F.CODD, R.A.LARNER, P.LUCAS, J.E.NICHOLLS, and K.WALK, dated 8th October 1965.

/2/ K.BANDAT (ed.): Tentative Steps Towards a Formal Definition of PL/I. - IBM Laboratory Vienna, Technical Report TR 25.065, July 1965.

/3/ P.LUCAS: On the Formalization of Syntax and Semantics of PL/I. - IBM Laboratory Vienna, Technical Report TR 25.060, November 1965.

/4/ P.LUCAS, K.WALK: Formal Definition of PL/I. - Presented at ASA X3.42C - Meeting, New Yrok, 28th July 1966.
K.BANDAT: Formal Definition of PL/I. - Presented at ECMA TC10 Meeting, Madrid, 12th October 1966.

The group acknowledged the influence of Elgot, Landin and McCarthy. The approach (cf. note on [Opus 27]) was "operational". This first paper by Hans Bekic on semantics shows his distinctive style. It is particularly interesting to note how section 4 indicates an awareness of an alternative, more denotational, approach.

It should be remembered that a conference had been held in Baden bei Wien in September 1964. This conference led to the formation of IFIP's working group on Formal Description (WG 2.2). The proceedings of this conference are published as "Formal Language Description Languages" (ed) T.B.Steel, North-Holland, 1966 and include key papers by, among others, Peter Landin and Christopher Strachey.

[Opus 13]

Comment on "Cleaning up ALGOL 60"

H.Bekic

Originally printed as a note:

IBM Laboratory Vienna, LN 25.3.018, January 1965

2 pages, 2 Refs.

Then as:

ALGOL Bulletin No.19, January 1965

page 58, 2 Refs.

[Opus 14]

The Meaning of Identifiers in ALGOL and in "Generalized ALGOL"

H.Bekic

Originally printed as a note:

IBM Laboratory Vienna, LN 25.3.019, February 1965

2 pages, 1 Ref.

Then as:

ALGOL Bulletin No.20, July 1965,

pages 29-30, 1 Ref.

[Opus 15]

Bibliography on Formal Language Description Languages

H. Bekic, F. Schwarzenberger

IBM Laboratory Vienna, TR 25.052, February 1965

34 pages.

[Opus 16]

Mechanical Transformation Rules for the Reduction of ALGOL to a Primitive Language *M* and their Use in Defining the Compiler Function

H.Bekic

IBM Laboratory Vienna, TR 25.051, February 1965

77 pages, 4 Refs.

[Opus 17]

Assignment to Formal Procedure Identifier, or How to Cite the Bible

H.Bekic

Originally printed as a note:

IBM Laboratory Vienna, LN 25.3.034, March 1965

3 pages

Then as:

ALGOL Bulletin No.20, July 1965

pages 30, 45-46, 4 Refs.

[Opus 18] ***see pages 4 - 16 below***

The Meaning of Names in PL/I

H.Bekic

IBM Laboratory Vienna, LR 25.3.025, June 1965

23 pages, 6 Refs.

The formal definition of PL/I was produced as a series of Vienna Laboratory technical reports. The term used by the group was "Universal Language Document No.3" ("ULD"). (The index reflects the existence of the natural language description of PL/I and a semi-formal description developed in the IBM Hursley Laboratory). The more widely used term "Vienna Definition Language" ("VDL") was coined by J.A.N. Lee.

Based on the ALGOL experience (cf. note on [Opus 11]), Hans Bekic was quick to spot an inconsistency in the way recursion was described for the PL/I language. His point was not just that PL/I differed from ALGOL 60 but, as he saw it, the language designers were ignoring mathematical convention and properties. Hans Bekic spearheaded a crusade (cf. [Opus 19], [Opus 20], [Opus 21]) for a language change. Although the first version of the PL/I "F" compiler stuck to the old interpretation, this crusade resulted in a change to both language and compiler. To many PL/I programmers the examples which are cited might appear rather esoteric - even the implementors were reluctant to see the importance of the change and there was often reference to "Bekic recursion". (A letter from the chairman of the PL/I Language Control Board contains: "The first release of the F-level Compiler will indeed contain an implementation of a special kind of recursion. In the second release, however, recursion will be implemented as defined in Dr. Bekic's report".)

For obvious reasons, notes on language changes were treated as confidential when written. It now seems reasonable to publish this history: although of no great depth, Hans Bekic's contribution to this debate may have prevented a widely used programming language disseminating a strange form of recursion. It is also interesting to see Hans Bekic's preference for compact notation.

(The PL/I term "AUTOMATIC" describes normal ALGOL-like stack variables; "STATIC" was PL/I's version of "own" variables and "CONTROLLED" had heap-like properties - among others. The topic of variable reference was subsequently studied in connection with compiler justification - see, for example "Proving Correctness of Implementation Techniques" by C.B.Jones and P.Lucas in "Symposium on Semantics of Algorithmic Languages", (ed) E.Engeler, Lecture Notes in Mathematics, No.188, Springer Verlag).

[Opus 19]
Recursive Procedure Interpretation
H.Bekic
IBM Laboratory Vienna, LN 25.3.027, September 1965
8 pages.

[Opus 20]
Recursion
H.Bekic
LDV 1, IBM Laboratory Vienna, 22nd October 1965
4 pages, 4 Refs.

The "LDV" file consisted of points concerning the PL/I language. They were essentially questions and proposals about the language which were sent to the Hursley Laboratory. This is the change proposal which led to the correction of the error discussed in the note on [Opus 18].

[Opus 21]
Questions on BASED, POINTER CELL
H.Bekic
LDV 3, IBM Laboratory Vienna, 6th December 1965
2 pages.

[Opus 22]
Pointers, BASED reference class, area
H.Bekic
LDV 6, IBM Laboratory Vienna, 14th January 1966
5 pages.

[Opus 23]
Two Notes on Syntax
H.Bekic
LDV 9, IBM Laboratory, Vienna, 9th Febraury 1966
5 pages, 3 Refs.

[Opus 24]
Correspondence between Concrete and Abstract Syntax
H.Bekic
LDV 12, IBM Laboratory Vienna, 21st February 1966
6 pages.

[Opus 25] *see pages 26 - 29 below*
Note on some Problems Concerning the PL/I Manual and its Rewriting
H.Bekic
26 May 1966
55 pages, 1 Ref.

This note is self-explanatory. Although it is written in PL/I terms, it is of wider relevance. It is reprinted here to show Hans Bekic's desire for precision even when not being "formal".

[Opus 26]
The Main Features of van Wijngaarden Report on ALGOL X
H.Bekic
IBM Laboratory Vienna, LN 25.3.042, November 1966
8 pages.

IFIP's working group 2.1 had, after the publication of ALGOL 60, moved on to design a new language which eventually became ALGOL 68. Hans Bekic was a member of and contributor to WG 2.1. This report was written to convey the status of the work.

[Opus 27]
Formal Definition of PL/I (Universal Language Document 3)
PL/I - Definition Group of the Vienna Laboratory
IBM Laboratory Vienna, TR 25.071, 30th December, 1966
4 cm!, 4 Refs.

This is the first version of the "ULD" (cf. [Opus 32], [Opus 33]). Hans Bekic's contribution is shown as writing sections 4.8 Interpretation of Pseudo-Variables and 5.11 Built-in Functions, and as having read the whole (4cm!) document. The definition is definitely operational (for a description of styles of language definition see "Main Approaches to Formal Specifications" by Peter Lucas in "Formal Specification and Software Development" by D.Bjorner and C.B.Jones, Prentice-Hall International, 1982.)

[Opus 28]
Ueber die Anzahl der Zahlen a^2+b^2 in einer arithmetischen Reihe grosser Differenz.
H.Bekic
Journal fuer die reine und angewandte Mathematik, Berlin 1967
Band 226, pages 120-131, 5 Refs.

Summary of one of the results from [Opus 4] - the title might be translated as: "On the Number of Integers of the Form $a^2 + b^2$ in Arithmetic Progressions with Large Differences".

[Opus 29]
Modelling ULD 3's Abstract Objects by Infinite Trees
H.Bekic
LDV 27, IBM Laboratory Vienna, April 1967

This document has not been traced.

[Opus 30]
A Notation for Instruction Definitions in ULD 3
H.Bekic
IBM Laboratory Vienna, LN 25.5.024, July 1967
17 pages, 3 Refs.

On his working version of this report, there is an undated note which states:

> "Once this metalanguage *L* has been introduced, it would seem better to <u>map</u> PL/I progs into expressions of that language, instead of writing an interpreter in that language".

[Opus 31]
PL/I Arithmetic
H.Bekic
Note to G.W. Bonsall of 16 April 1968
14 pages.

[Opus 32]
Abstract Syntax and Interpretation of PL/I
K.Walk, K.Alber, K.Bandat, H.Bekic, G.Chroust, V.Kudielka, P.Oliva, G.Zeisel
IBM Laboratory Vienna, ULD Version 2, TR 25.082, 28 June 1968
590 pages, 8 Refs.

This document represents the core of the second version of the formal description of PL/I (which was printed as 6 reports). Hans Bekic's contribution is shown as writing chapter 8 "Data, Operations and Conversions" and revising chapter 11 "Built-in Functions". Partly because of his QMC visit to work with Peter Landin, Hans Bekic is not shown as a contributor to the widely known third version of the ULD: clearly his earlier input did have an influence.

[Opus 33]
Informal Introduction to the Abstract Syntax and Interpretation of PL/I
P.Lucas, K.Alber, K.Bandat, H.Bekic, P.Oliva, K.Walk, G.Zeisel
IBM Laboratory Vienna, ULD Version 2, TR 25.083, 28 June 1968
205 pages, 8 Refs.

This document provides a (much-needed) introduction to the remaining (3cm of) reports.

[Opus 34]
The Description of Programming Languages
H.Bekic
Fortnightly seminars given at Queen Mary College, London
November 1968 onwards.

No information has been traced on these talks

[Opus 35]
Strong Logical Connectives and ALGOL 68
H.Bekic
IFIP W.G. 2.2 Bulletin No. 2, 25 August 1969.

[Opus 36] *see pages 30 - 55 below*
Definable Operations in General Algebras, and the Theory of Automata and Flowcharts
H.Bekic
IBM Laboratory Vienna, 8th December 1969
29 pages, 15 Refs.

The importance of fixed points in reasoning about recursive functions and iterative programs is now recognized. It would appear that the idea had (at least) three independent discoverers: Dana Scott, David Park and Hans Bekic. The references are "A Theory of Programs: an outline of joint work by J.W. de Bakker and Dana Scott" (these notes were presented in August 1969 at the Vienna Laboratory - Hans Bekic was at this time still in the UK so no discussion took place until the WG 2.2 meeting) and "Fixpoint Induction and Proofs of Porgram Properties", D.M.R.Park, pp. 57-78 of "Machine Intelligence 5" (ed) B.Meltzer and D.Michie, Edinburgh Univ. Press, 1970.

This work was mainly done during Hans Bekic's time with Peter Landin at QMC (November 3 1968 - November 2 1969). He presented his work at the 1979 AI conference (September 14 - 20 1969). Characteristically, he was too late submitting his paper and it was not published. (There was some subsequent correspondence about publication in the journal "Artificial Intelligence" but the material did not really fit the interests of its readership.) In spite of receiving no formal publication, this is a widely cited paper (e.g. Indermark, Goguen, Harel, Lescarme, Scott and Wagner). Hans Bekic attended the fourth meeting (Colchester September 1969) of IFIP WG 2.2 as an observer and presented his material on fixed points.

The report which is reprinted here describes the results in terms of automata theory. This makes it less readable than it might otherwise have been, but clearly the firm mathematical base appealed to Hans Bekic. Landin's influence may have been responsible for the algebraic flavour of the paper. The case of simultaneous recursion is covered.

Although this paper is often referenced, it has never been formally published. Hans Bekic appears to have considered that his work was subsumed by "A Concrete

Approach to Abstract Recursive Definitions" by M.Wand, AI Lab, MIT, January 1972. (Jaco de Bakker and Andrzej Blikle have also pointed out that a related reference is Leszczylowski,J., "A Theorem on Resolving Equations in the Space of Languages", Bull. Acad. Pol. Sci., Ser. Sci. Math. Astr. Phys., 19, pp 967-970, 1971.)

[Opus 37]
Universelle Algebra und die Theorie der Programmierung
H.Bekic
Seminar series in Vienna Laboratory, from 1970-01-26.

Only Hans Bekic's preparatory notes have been found.

[Opus 38] *see pages 56 - 85 below*
Formalization of Storage Properties
H.Bekic, K.Walk
Originally printed as a note:
IBM Laboratory Vienna, LR 25.5.034, July 1970,
43 pages, 7 Refs.
Then in:
Symposium on Semantics of Algorithmic Languages, Edited by E. Engeler,
Lecture Notes in Mathematics, Vol.188,
Springer-Verlag, 1971,
pages, 28-61.

The definition of PL/I presented a number of problems concerned with storage mapping. Concepts like sub-locations were necessary because of structured types (arrays etc.); the property of storage being "connected" was relevant to overlay defining; various changes occurred on assignment which could affect the available locations. A different set of features were present in ALGOL 68, flexible locations being especially relevant.

The ULD had taken an axiomatic approach. Here, a more constructive view is presented. Even so, Hans Bekic commented later "The storage model is a little more abstract, in fact better, than the one used in TR 139" *(here [Opus 55]). See also [Opus 50]).*

An attempt was made to persuade Hans Bekic to revise this paper for "Formal Specification and Software Development" D.Bjorner and C.B.Jones, Prentice-Hall International 1982. When he decided he could not complete the work in time, Hans

Bekic wrote (to Jones 1981-12-20):

"Let me say briefly what I was trying to do.

Starting as in LNM 188, I would introduce values and ranges, but as domains: V is a domain, each R is a subdomain (Same ⊔, not necessarily same ⊥), built from elementary ranges by a finite number of Π's and Σ's:

composite R: $R = \Pi \langle R_i \mid i \in I \rangle$

flexible R: $R = \Sigma \langle R^{(i)} \mid i \in I \rangle$

Locations have ranges and are elem/composite/flexible accordingly. There is a bijection $l \leftrightarrow \langle l_i \mid i \in I$, the l_i independant $\rangle$ for composite l's, and a mapping $l \mapsto \langle l^{(i)} \mid i \in I \rangle$ for flexible l's. Independence is defined axiomatically, with a view to express "having no parts in common". Given $f_o\colon L_o \to V$, $f_o(l) \in rg(l)$, L_o independent, we can "close" f_o w.r.t.
$(l,V) \leftrightarrow \langle (l_i,V_i) \mid i \in I \rangle$ for composite l,
and $(l, (i, v^{(i)})) \mapsto (l^{(i)}, v^{(i)})$ for flexible l. Again, given an independently-based, closed $f\colon L \to V$ and $g\colon M \to l'$ with M independent, $M \subseteq L$, we can define f + g in terms of a similar closure operator. (For g = (l,v), i.e. M = {l}, this is assignment). Of course, these closure operations make heavy existence/uniqueness assumptions, and I have gone some way towards proving those (where LNM 188 had at most plausibility arguments) - there are still problems of notation/presentation.

Now the problems. first, locations "of length zero" (e.g. A CHRAR(C), or SUBSTR(B, length (B) + 1, 0) in PL/I): completely ignored in LNM 188, ignored or wrong in TR 139. Second, and more important: the model is quite implicit, to certifiy that it is sound and "works", I would have to apply it to define - at least the storage related part of - a nontrivial language - which I cannot and will not do in the near future. Sure, the book will define Pascal; but only little of the storage model will be used, and in different notation, presumably different presentation of locations, etc. Thirdly, when I orginally "invented" the model, its scope as envisaged then was quite small: I wanted to give a simple and coherent presentation of some apparently complicated features of Algol 68. If, more than ten years later, no sufficiently different or new application of the model have been worked out, rewriting of LNM 188 can hardly be justified, even if more precise etc. Now I think there ought to be new applications: data base, ADA's variant parts. Unfortunately, I don't have time to work out those applications now, quickly - so maybe all the book should do is to refer in an appropriate place, like Foundations or your Modelling Concepts of PLS, to the existing ideas in LNM 188 and TR 139; someone starting to formulate a (next) language can then apply them, modifying/extending them as needed."

[Opus 39]
States Belong to Names, not to Multiple Values
H.Bekic
Note of 29 July 1970
2 pages

A brief note on ALGOL 68.

[Opus 40]
ALGOL Status Report
H.Bekic, V.Kudielka
IBM Laboratory Vienna, LR 25.2.021, October 1970
8 pages, 2 Refs.

[Opus 41]
Assemblersprachen
H.Bekic
Vorlesungen TH Wien, 1970-71.

In spite of the modest theme of this course ("Assembler Languages"), Hans Bekic managed to bring in ideas on program proofs.

[Opus 42] *see pages 86 - 106 below*
On the Formal Definition of Programming Languages
H.Bekic
Originally printed as a note:
IBM Laboratory Vienna, November 1970
30 pages, 20 Refs.
Then in:
Proceedings of the International Computing Symposium 21-22 May 1970 of the German ACM Chapter in Bonn (Ed. Wolf. D. Itzfeldt),
pp 297-315 Gesellschaft fuer Mathematik und Datenverarbeitung, Birlinghoven,

November 1973.

In late 1972 the Vienna group was charged with a project which concerned the implementation of PL/I. This was seen (by some) as an opportunity to show that a formal definition of a language could be used as a basis for the design of a compiler. The question was which definition? Attempts in the late 1960's to use ULD definitions had shown that many of the operational features complicated proofs in a gratuitous way. The joint ECMA/ANSI committee were working on a new standard document. This had a formally described state but the state transitions were described in natural language. But, worst of all, the basis was again operational and in many respects the state was unnecessarily baroque (cf. treatment of END - the final standard document is "Programming Language PL/I", American National Standard ANSI X3.53-1976). Somewhat to the dismay of management, the decision was made to begin the compiler project by writing a new definition! The aim was to produce a denotational definition of PL/I (see [Opus 55]).

Section 4 of this paper can be seen as the logical continuation of [Opus 12]. Hans Bekic rather modestly writes:

> If you have compared Vienna I (ULD) to Vienna II (TR 25.139) you will have noticed the shift from operational to denotational, and I feel somewhat responsible for that shift.

He was certainly most insistent that we stay within the denotational style.

[Opus 43]
Rapport d'Evaluation ALGOL 68
J.C.Boussard, J.J.Duby (Eds.), J.Andre, H.Bekic, M.Berthaud, S.Brehinier, M.Griffiths, Ph.Jorrand, C.H.A.Koster, M.Nicolas, J.C.Paillard, C.Pair, D.Peccoud, M.Sintzoff, P.Wodon
Revue Francaise d'Informatique et de Recherche operationnelle
RIRO 5e annee, B-1, 1971
pp 15-106, 124 Refs.

[Opus 44]
An Introduction to ALGOL 68
H.Bekic
Originally printed as a note:
IBM Laboratory Vienna, TR 25.118, February 1971

51 pages, 1 Ref

Then as:

Annual Review in Automatic Programming, Vol.7 part 3, 1973

pages 143-169, 5 Refs.

Hans Bekic wrote in a letter (to Jim Thatcher):

> [this] was written because I liked the language but not its official description; it [Hans Bekic's report] emphasizes (informally) the denotational point of view.

This is an interesting description of ALGOL 68 but, since it was published, is not reproduced here. A number of changes were made between the technical report and final versions. These improvements were largely a response to a review by Fraser Duncan.

[Opus 45]

A Simple Algorithm for Partitions of Natural Numbers with Summands Bounded Above

H.Bekic

IBM Laboratory Vienna, LN 25.6.025, October 1971,

4 pages, 1 Ref.

[Opus 46] *see pages 168 - 206 below (see also pages 207 - 214 below)*

Towards a Mathematical Theory of Processes

H.Bekic

IBM Laboratory Vienna, TR 25.125, December 1971,

55 pages, 17 Refs.

In 1970 the Vienna laboratory as a whole became involved in projects relating to parallelism. Hans Bekic's work on parallelism grew naturally out of his earlier work. PL/I had parallel features which gave rise to the control trees of the ULD. The desire to move to a denotational semantics created a serious difficulty: it was not clear how the denotational method could be applied to parallelism. Certainly, the choice of denotations as functions could not be maintained. This problem occupied the scientific part of the remaining years of Hans Bekic's life.

Although this report is widely cited, it would not have been correct to publish the report without Hans Bekic's own comments. Basically, after writing the technical report, he found an error ("the element-wise ordering of the powerset is not an

ordering".) However, the paper contains one of the early attempts at solving the problem of providing a denotational semantics for parallelism; it is widely referenced; and it sets the stage for Hans Bekic's later work on the topic (cf. [Opus 60], [Opus 61] [Opus 62]). Manfred Broy points out that other people are still "discovering" this approach and not spotting the error! Robin Milner describes this work as a "pre-echo" of his own.

Also of interest is the discussion in section 6.1 of a proposed change to ALGOL 68. The text here is typed from a copy of the report on which Hans Bekic had marked a number of minor corrections. Some of his own comments on this paper have been traced and are printed after the text of the report. The paper was submitted to and accepted by IBM's "Journal of Research and Development". Two of the comments come from correspondence with the editor of that Journal. Hans Bekic eventually withdrew the paper.

[Opus 47]
Formal Semantics of Programming Languages: Theory and Applications
H.Bekic
Lecture given in Amsterdam
June 1972

Hans Bekic appears to have lectured from [Opus 46]. He afterwards wrote a note which summarized his general approach and commented on errors in his Actions paper - the latter material is reproduced below on pages 207 - 210.

[Opus 48], [Opus 49]

These two internal reports relate to a project which IBM would prefer to remain confidential. Although Hans Bekic was occupied on this work for some time, these (multi-authored) reports contain no essential scientific material.

[Opus 50]
Storage-related Concepts in PL/I
H.Bekic
Notes for the PL/I Seminar 3-5 January 1973 (for Workbook Chapter 3.1.3).

This was a (manuscript) working document which eventualy led to the storage part of [Opus 55].

[Opus 51]
Axioms for 'for'
H.Bekic
Note of 15 March 1973
2 pages.

Tony Hoare's "An Axiomatric Basis for Computer Programming" had been published in 1969. It clearly evoked strong interest in the Vienna group and, after some seminars, Hans Bekic wrote this brief note.

[Opus 52]
Impl. Beispiel
H.Bekic
(undated) probably 1973/4
Manuscript 5 pages

When the PL/I implementation was being considered in later 1972, it was decided to sketch a small example of specification and design justification. This was to be the basis of many notational experiments. Because of the first schedule, it became known as the "Weihnachts Beispiel". This manuscript presents one of many attempts at the problem - in essence, it is contained in [Opus 58].

[Opus 53] – *see pages 215 – 229 below*
The Semantics of Parallel Processing
H.Bekic
In: Formal Aspects of Computing Science, Proceedings of the Joint IBM University of Newcastle upon Tyne Seminar 3–6 September 1974 (B.Shaw, Ed.) University of Newcastle upon Tyne Computing Laboratory 1975
pp 105–123.

This is the transcript of a series of lectures given by Hans Bekic at the Newcastle seminar on "Formal Aspects of Computing Science". He comments in a letter (Milne 1975-12-17) that the transcripts are "just terrible" but takes the blame on himself ("missed my chance to correct ...") - it must also be recognized that the creation of such a transcript is extremely difficult.

The notes are published here since they show one possible way of correcting the error in [Opus 46]: the use of an "infinite tape of choice values" (oracle) is considered.

Edsger Dijkstra's reaction to the talks by Hans Bekic and Dana Scott at this conference sparked off a written discussion on the use of the denotational semantics. Considerably more heat than light was generated and no scientific purpose would be furthered by its publication.

[Opus 54]
Freitag der 13
H.Bekic
Friday, 13 September 1974
3 pages.

This very brief note (in German) is a humorous comment on the choice of Friday 13th September 1974 as the date for a Laboratory social gathering. Hans Bekic credited van Wijngaarden with the observation that the 13th falls (very slightly) more often on a Friday than any other day of the week.

[Opus 55] *see pages 107 - 155 below*
A Formal Definition of a PL/I Subset
H.Bekic, D.Bjorner, W.Henhapl, C.B.Jones, P.Lucas
IBM Laboratory Vienna, TR 25.139 (Part I and II), December 1974
201 pages.

The implementation project mentioned in the comments on [Opus 42] was terminated when the target machine was cancelled. It was, however, decided to salvage some of the scientifically interesting material. One part of this was the denotational description of PL/I. These reports contain a description of PL/I as in the ECMA/ANSI standard except for the Input/Output part (this was written by Walter Pachl but it was not included since the notation was not up-to-date). The undertaking was made simpler by the decision of the standardization committee to remove the (anachronistic) Tasking features of PL/I.

It would probably not be worth publishing the whole of this definition even though it is far shorter than the ULD definitions. Nor is the portion published exactly Hans Bekic's contribution. The complete index is given along with the whole of the Abstract Syntax and States part of the report. In an attempt to make these intelligible, appropriate parts of the commentary and notation are included. The discussion of exits (N4.3) and non-determinism (N4.4) are of particular interest. (Deletions are marked - Ed.)

It was felt that the use of a name for the meta-language might put a mistaken focus on irrelevant concrete syntax questions (cf. "Introduction"). The overall approach of using a formal description as the basis of a step-wise, justified, design was christened the "Vienna Development Method" - the abbreviation "VDM" was confusingly close to "VDL". The first book ("The Vienna Development Method: The Metalanguage" (eds.) D.Bjorner and C.B.Jones, Lecture Notes in Computer Science No.61, Springer-Verlag) was sometimes referred to as though it were still VDL based. This completely lost the point of the change from operational to denotational semantics. Eventually the name "Meta-IV" (!) was used in an attempt to distinguish the new metalanguage from that of the ULD.

One characteristic of the VDM metalanguage is its much more frequent use of "combinators" than the Oxford style denotational semantics. Peter Mosses acknowledges that this is a step towards his "abstract semantic algebras".

Hans Bekic commented in 1975:

> TR 139 I don't send because Dines Bjorner tells me you have (and even read) it. One of our (at least my) objectives in working on it was to describe "transformations" (i.e. functions from states to states or to states x values), which are the "denotations" involved, in a "variable-free" way, i.e. without using a variable for the state, hence the "combinators" like the familiar ";" and the less familiar "let x:e;g(x)". That the family of int/eval definitions amounts to a (parametric) homomorphism is slightly blurred by some recurring uses of int-xxx with identical arguments, but N.5 points out how this can be remedied in a purely formal way. More serious is our cavalier treatment (or rather non-treatment) of $\perp$, $\subseteq$, lim, but we hope to fill the gap soon. (For the most part, this only requires adaptation of existing work, the one really new point is non-determinism which TR 125 attempted to solve unsuccessfully.)

[Opus 56]
Formale Semantik
H.Bekic
Manuscript
Linz, 26 May 1975.

These notes (in German) are of a seminar given in Linz.

[Opus 57] *see pages 156 - 167 below*

Mathematical Semantics and Compiler Correctness

H.Bekic

Presented at the Meeting of IFIP WG 2.1 in Munich, 25 August 1975

12 foils.

The set of foils from which this contribution was typed was probably also used at the Pont-a-Mousson talk which Hans Bekic gave to WG 2.2 in September 1975. They provide a brief overview of Hans Bekic's view of compiler correctness proofs at that date.

[Opus 58]

Some Experiments with Using a Formal Language Definition in Compiler Development

H.Bekic, H.Izbicki, C.B.Jones, F.Weissenboeck

IBM Laboratory Vienna, LN 25.3.107, December 1975

54 pages, 7 Refs

See comment on [Opus 52].

[Opus 59]

Mathematische Semantik von Programmiersprachen

H.Bekic

Vienna 1975/76

Manuscript.

In the academic year 1975/6, Hans Bekic again taught a series of lectures at the Technical University. These notes, in German, were given to the students - broadly, they follow "Denotational Semantics: The Scott-Strachey Approach to Programming Language Theory" J. E. Stoy, MIT Press, 1977.

[Opus 60] *see pages 230 - 239 below*

Nondeterministic Functions and the Semantics of CSP

H.Bekic

Lecture at the Second Workshop on Semantics of Programming Languages, Bad Honnef, 17 March, 1981

Foils

Abstract in: Bull EATCS 14 (1981)

This talk (the foils of which are reproduced below) appears to be the first time that Hans Bekic spoke publicly about the use of indexed sets to model non-determinism. The introductory foil lists some problems with Power domains and gives an example which relies on unbounded non-determinacy. After developing indexed sets, the idea is applied to some problems of modelling Hoare's CSP language.

In order to understand the basic idea it is probably easier to study the note [Opus 61] below. The foils from Bad Honnef are reproduced here because of the application to CSP.

In notes made in May 1982, Hans Bekic observed that the CPO should be a domain (with an appropriate limit operation). This change is reflected in [Opus 61]. The notes also suggest the use of "diagrams" and this is pursued in [Opus 62].

[Opus 61] *see pages 240 - 247 below*
Nondeterministic Programs: An Example
H.Bekic
Presented in Garmisch-Partenkirchen, March 1982,
Manuscript.

This note contains the most lengthy explanation of the indexed set idea. The version here has been typed from a manuscript corrected in May 1982. The example (provided by E. Astesiano) is one which involves the fairness issue.

[Opus 62] *see pages 248 - 254 below*
A Model of nondeterminism: Indexed Sets and their Equivalence
H.Bekic
talk to IFIP WG 2.2, June 5-8 1982 Germany
7 foils.

The move to a category theory framework is clear from a number of manuscript notes. These working notes, however, are difficult to follow and, since they predate these foils, no attempt is made to reproduce the less organized material.

These foils were written just four months before Hans Bekic's death. As such, they must remain his last words on the semantics of parallelism.

AB18.3.4 Note on a test example for ALGOL60 compilers by D.E. Knuth

H. Bekić

There seem to be three reasons why the test example, given by D.E. Knuth [1] to separate man-compilers from boy-compilers, could upset the latter ones:

1. The example contains procedures with free variables, and recursive calls of such procedures.
2. It contains the call of a type procedure in a statement context.
3. It contains "unusual" assignments to type procedure identifiers, i.e. assignments occurring within, but not on the outermost level of the corresponding procedure body.

The problems connected with point 1 are well known and are properly solved by several of the existing compilers. An implementation technique for point 2 has been described by Dijkstra [2]. Point 3 has been shown in [3] to make no serious difficulties. So there is no reason why there should not exist man-compilers; at least the Mailüfterl Compiler (Vienna 1962) is one of them.

References

[1] Knuth, D.E.: Man or boy ? - AB17.2.4, July 1964.

[2] Dijkstra, E.W.: An ALGOL60 translator for the X1 - AB Supp. 10, 1962.

[3] Bekić, H.: The assignment to a type procedure identifier in ALGOL60 - AB18.3.5, October 1964.

IBM Laboratory Vienna,
September 1964

AB*18.3.5* The assignment to a type procedure identifier in ALGOL*60*

H. Bekić

Within an ALGOL program, a reference of a type procedure identifier P can have two different meanings. In a "value" position it denotes activation of the corresponding procedure body; in an "address" position it is interpreted as a simple variable. A third kind of occurrence is that in an "undefined" position, i.e. as an actual parameter, where the interpretation depends on the eventual use of the parameter.

A more precise definition is the following: For each type procedure identifier P, declare an additional variable P' local to the corresponding procedure body; replace each reference of P, according to the three kinds of position of the reference, by

P, P', *(*P,P'*)* *(1)*

respectively. Execution of P, then, means execution of the body *(*together with returning the value of P' to the calling expression in the case that the reference of P occurred in an expression-context rather than a statement-context*)*. Execution of *(*P, P'*)* is equivalent to execution of P or of P' according to the position of the formal parameter causing that execution. The scope of P' is the procedure body associated with P, and is therefore a proper subregion of the scope of P. In order to detect illegal cases, references of P outside the scope of P' should be replaced by

P, w, *(*P, w*)* *(2)*

respectively, rather than by *(1)* where w is a symbol denoting "undefined". Whenever, on execution of an assignment statement, a left part turns out to have the value w, an error indication should occur.

Implementation

We use the notions of the procedure number PN and of the display D[ ] as introduced in [*1*] *(*treating, however, blocks and procedures differently, i.e. counting the procedure depth, not the block depth, by PN, see [*2*]*)*. Each reference of a type procedure identifier P will be represented by a vector P*, which, besides some class and type information and the starting address of the procedure body, contains the procedure number PN_p of the level to which P is local, and a logical value t_p indicating whether or not the particular reference occurs within the scope of P'. An operation corresponding to an address- position and having the eventual argument P* should actually calculate the address of P'. Assuming that P' is mapped into a storage cell which has an arbitrary but fixed distance c from the beginning of the storage area to which it is local (i.e. a distance not depending on the specific procedure body), this address can in fact be calculated out of P*. If t_p is false, there exists no P', and an alarm occurs; otherwise, the address of P' is

$$D[PN_p + 1] + c$$

since, in this case, $D[PN_p + 1]$ points to an activation of the procedure P. (It is assumed of course, that, whenever P* has been reached via formal parameters, the display has been updated correctly according to an accompanying environment information).

Apart from the w-check, which does not affect the execution of correct programs, this is the technique which has been used in the Vienna Mailüfterl Compiler [2].

References

[1] Dijkstra, E.W.: Recursive Programming - Numerische Mathematik 2 (1960).

[2] Lucas, P. and Bekić, H.: Compilation of ALGOL, Part 1 - Report No. LR 25.3.001, IBM Laboratory Vienna (1962).

IBM Laboratory Vienna
September 1964

THE MEANING OF NAMES IN PL/I

H. BEKIĆ

ABSTRACT

Recursion as defined in PL/I is essentially different from recursion in existing languages (ALGOL, LISP, common mathematical notation). This difference follows from the specific explicit rules by which recursion, instead of resulting implicitly from a dynamic block concept, is defined in PL/I, particularly from the intermixture of recursion and storage allocation. On the other hand, there is a number of arguments which seem to prove that this difference has not been intended.

LABORATORY REPORT
LR 3.025
June 2, 1965

CONTENTS

1. INTRODUCTION

There are many concepts in the New Programming Language PL/I that leave open questions: The block concept; the concept of explicit storage allocation; label variables- structures and their relation to arrays; expressions having side-effects; "computed" names (procedure identifiers that may be represented by string expressions); asynchronous operation; compile time activity. Each of these concepts requires careful investigations, as to which extent it has been included and in which way it has been defined.

Among this list, the block concept deserves particular interest: governing the rules how names have to be introduced into the language and how meaning can be associated with them, it stands on a higher level than most of the other concepts; more important for the discussion of PL/I, it is the only concept which is common to other languages (ALGOL /3/, LISP /4/, customary mathematical notation) and has been incorporated within these languages in a most general and satisfactory way.

It is the purpose of the present study to show:

(1) That the block concept as defined in PL/I is essentially different from the block concept in those other languages; so that an PL/I program containing only features that are also present in LISP or ALGOL will, in general, not be equivalent to the corresponding LISP or ALGOL program.

(2) That this concept fails to possess some properties which one would accept as intuitively true.

(3) That these differences to known languages as well as to the intuitive meaning of block concept do not seem to result from the desire to reach a specific effect or to gain some advantage in other parts of the language.

This is not the first time we deal with the problem; see /5/, /6/, which relate to earlier versions of PL/I. Meanwhile, the concepts of scope and of storage class, which originally were intermixed, have been separated (see /1/, /2/); also, it has become more apparent that a general concept of recursion is intended (e.g. labels are qualified now by the level of recursion). But the proper reason for all the troubles still persists: recursion is defined by explicit additional rules, instead of resulting automatically from a general block concept; moreover, these explicit rules intermix the concept of recursion with that of storage allocation.

The plan of the subsequent sections is as follows: After a short discussion of the block concept in current languages, its PL/I-definition is analysed. An example for the difference of the two interpretations is given. Then, some unexpected properties of the PL/I-interpretation are derived. Finally, relations to other parts of PL/I as well as to questions of implementation are briefly investigated.

2. THE BLOCK CONCEPT IN EXISTING LANGUAGES

(a) In Descriptive Languages

In customary mathematical notation, arbitrary names can be introduced for two purposes: to denote the argument positions of a function, or to make auxiliary definitions. Consider the following definition of a function:

f(x) = [...x...]

Here, the occurrence of x on the left hand side of "=" serves as a declaration; the block which is qualified by that declaration (or to which the declaration is local) is the formula included by "[" and "]". The scope of the declaration is this block, diminuished by subblocks that are qualified by a re-declaration of the same name x. Each occurrence of x within the scope of the declaration denotes the thing associated to x by the declaration, i.e., in this case, the argument position of the function f. - Next, consider the following example for the use of an auxiliary definition:

{[...g...] where g(x) = [...x...]}

Here, a name g is declared to stand for a certain one-place function; the block qualified by that declaration is the entire formula between "{" and "}".

The x of the first example has of course no relation what so ever to the x of the second, even if the formulas occur as subparts of one bigger formula. But still more: Also the two x's of two different activations of the function f(x) (by two calls f(a) and f(b), say) must be considered as two different things, each one denoting the argument place within a specific activation of the function (and each one associated, by the rules of function evaluation, with a specific argument a or b). This suggests the following dynamic definition of the block concept:

On d namic entrance into a block B, each declaration D local to B gives rise to the creation of a new thing. Each occurrence of the name N, declared by D, within the scope of D denotes that new thing.

This dynamic definition is particularly important if one wants to include recursion. Conversely, this dynamic definition yields, without any additional rules, the inclusion and correct interpretation of recursion. To see this, consider the following function definition:

$$f(n) = [n = 0 \to a;\ T \to b(n,\ f(n-1))]$$ [1]

To evaluate $f(1)$, we have to associate, in a first recursion, the name n with the integer 1, and get $b(1,\ f(0))$; thus, we must enter a second recursion, associating the argument position of the second recursion with the integer 0, and obtaining finally $b(1,a)$. - As a more complicated example, consider

$$f(n,g) = \{[n = 0 \to a(g);\ T \to b(n,g,f(n-1,g'))]$$

$$\underline{\text{where}}\ \ g'(x) = c(n,g,x)\}$$

and evaluate $f(1,g)$. The thing associated with g' at the first recursion is the function of x, $c(1,g,x)$, call it g_1'; therefore it is this thing g_1' which has to be transmitted to the second recursion $f(0,g_1')$; therefore, this second recursion, though associating with g' a new function g_2' (namely the function of x, $c(0,g_1',x)$), yields $a(g_1')$, not $a(g_2')$. - This second example illustrates the fact, that not only names denoting argument positions, but also names introduced by auxiliary definitions (here the name g') stand for different things in different recursions.

(b) In Command Languages

The dynamic definition of block concept is the same: only the class of things which can be denoted by names of the language is larger than in descriptive languages. We have not only formal parameters denoting argument positions and procedure identifiers denoting functions or subroutines, but also variable identifiers denoting variables and labels denoting program points. Here, a variable (contrary to the use of this term in some parts of mathematics) is a thing to which, by an explicit command, a value can be assigned; on machine language level, one would call this thing a storage cell.

Again, the things denoted by names are associated to these names dynamically, on entrance into the block to which the declaration of the name is local. Notice, in particular, that a variable is not a statical thing, but that a variable identifier denotes different variables in different recursions.

3. THE DEFINITION OF BLOCK CONCEPT IN PL/I

For compactness and easier readability, we use the notations of the previous section, especially the notation for conditional expressions, and the brackets "[" and "]" for block boundaries. Instead of using the "where"-clause of the previous section, we will sometimes write

---

1) We use the notation $[p_1 \to e_1;\ \dots\ ;\ p_n \to e_n]$ for conditional expressions, where the p_i are propositions and the e_i are expressions; T denotes the truth-value true.

p(f) ∿ [...]

for procedure and function definitions. Where declarations are implied contextually, we will not write explicit declarations: procedure identifiers, formal parameters, labels. Only in the case of variable identifiers, an explicit declaration is necessary; we will indicate it, without giving attributes, by an underlined occurrence of the name to be declared on the beginning of the block to which the declaration is local:

[$\underline{v}$; ...] .

The Block Concept Itself

Occurrences of PL/I -names may have different meanings, if the occurrences belong to the scopes of different declarations. Consequently, PL/I knows at least a statical block concept. - If this concept were to be interpreted dynamically, then each declaration would give rise to the dynamical creation of a new thing, each time the containing block is entered. This would particularly be true for the kind of thing which we would like to call a stack and which is represented in PL/I by names declared CONTROLLED. However, as we will make explicit below, the meaning of CONTROLLED names (and therefore also the meaning of AUTOMATIC names, which, in PL/I, are treated as special cases of the former) has not been defined this way in PL/I.

The Explicit Definition of Recursion

As we have seen in section 2, the possibility and the meaning of recursion would result automatically from the dynamic interpretation of the block concept. On the contrary, recursion is considered in PL/I as an additional concept, and its meaning is defined by additional explicit rules- e.g. the rule that, on assignment and on parameter transmission, "labels are qualified by the current level of recursion".

Its Intermixture with the Allocation Concept

CONTROLLED names represent stacks; the number of elements of a stack (these elements being storage locations in PL/I-terminology, variables in the terminology of current programming languages) can be increased and decreased dynamically by ALLOCATE and FREE statements; there are rules which determine for each kind of occurrence of a CONTROLLED name, whether it stands for the entire stack, or for the last element of the stack. AUTOMATIC and STATIC names are special cases; the stacks corresponding to them consist of a single element, which is allocated to or freed from the stack on entering or leaving the declaring block, or the whole program. - The dynamic block concept would be applicable also to names representing stacks, creating a separate stack on each dynamic entrance into a block containing such a name among its locals.

(The stack would be of variable length in the case of CONTROLLED; of length 1 in the case of AUTOMATIC or STATIC. Moreover, declarations of STATIC names had to be transferred into the outermost block of the program).

But among the explicit rules concerning recursion there is one which identifies the different things, associated to an AUTOMATIC name by different recursions, with a stack of storage cells allocated to some global thing. This global thing, represented by the AUTOMATIC name V, exists independently from any activation of the block B to which the declaration of V is local; it exists, so to speak prior to the execution of the program. And a new activation of block B does not create an entirely new thing, but only increases the pre-existing global thing by a new storage cell. On the other hand there are kinds of occurrences of V which, as we shall see below, stand for the global thing, i.e. for the whole stack. <u>It is the very difference between the thing created by the activation of a declaration, and the thing represented by some occurrences of the name in the scope of the declaration, which causes the dynamic block concept not to be valid in PL/I.</u>

If V is CONTROLLED, the situation is similar. Again, V is thought to represent some global stack, independently from activations of the declaring block. This stack can be increased and decreased by the execution of ALLOCATE and FREE statements; but an activation of the declaring block will not create a new thing to be associated with V, nor even change the thing already associated.

<u>Note</u>: Only from this concept of pre-existing things, the EXTERNAL concept as defined in PL/I becomes possible: two equal names declared in two different declarations denote the same pre-existing thing if and only if they are declared EXTERNAL. The meanings of the notions INTERNAL, EXTERNAL on the one hand, and of the notions STATIC, AUTOMATIC, CONTROLLED on the other hand, have been defined independently from each other; therefore, each of the 6 possible combinations is well defined, though the combination AUTOMATIC EXTERNAL has been forbidden in PL/I by an explicit rule.

<u>Names in On-Line Positions</u>

We say that a non-declarative occurrence of a name N is in <u>on-line position</u> if it is contained in the declaring block, but in no smaller procedure; otherwise, it is an <u>off-line</u> position. In the example

[<u>v</u>; p(f(∿ [...v...]; ...v...]

(where we assume that there are not contained other blocks or procedure declarations) the second v occurs off-line, the third v occurs on-line.

A <u>label</u> is "qualifed by recursion level" on assignment and parameter transmission (and we believe sincerely that it is qualified also if appearing as the argument of a GOTO statement). An AUTOMATIC name - we do not discuss CONTROLLED names in this context - denotes, in on-line positions, the last element of the associated allocation stack, and one might say, therefore, that it also is qualified by recursion. But what about procedure names in actual parameter positions? Contrary to labels, there is no rule stating that they are qualified; and, due to the intermixture of allocation and recursion, it would also be difficult to imagine how such a qualification of the procedure identifier, i.e. a qualification of the corresponding subroutine or function, should be defined.

Names in Off-Line Positions

Consider

[v; p(f) ∿ [...v...]; ...]

If v is CONTROLLED, then the occurrence of v in the inner block certainly denotes the stack associated with v, not a specific element of the stack. Subsequent allocations of v may change the stack, and only during the eventual execution of the procedure associated with p the name v will refer to that element of the stack which then is the topmost element.

In the case of v AUTOMATIC, the inner occurrence of v again denotes the stack, not a specific element of it. (There is no rule in PL/I which would cause another interpretation). This time, the stack cannot be changed by explicit allocations; but it can be changed by subsequent recursive activations of the outer block, and from this fact we will derive, in the next section, an example which yields different results under the present interpretation and the interpretation of section 2. For the present, it suffices to state, that an off-line occurrence of an AUTOMATIC name designates another thing (namely the allocation stack, subject to further changes) than the thing created dynamically by the corresponding declaration (namely that storage cell that had been added to the stack on dynamic entrance into the block containing the declaration). Moreover, the same is true for off-line occurrences of other kinds of names. Consider

[...; p(f) ∿ [...n...]; ...]

where n is a label, a procedure identifier, or a formal parameter, local to the outer block. Then, the meaning of the inner occurrence of n is determined again only "up to recursion", i.e. this occurrence does not necessarily represent the thing which had been associated with n on entrance into the outer block.

Conclusion

We have seen that recursion, instead of resulting automatically from a dynamic block concept, is defined in PL/I by explicit additional rules. Moreover, these rules are such, that they destroy the dynamic block concept altogether; for there are occurrences of names (namely the off-line occurrences), which do not denote the thing that was associated to the name dynamically by the corresponding declaration.

4. THE DIFFERENCE OF THE TWO CONCEPTS

It has become clear that the block concept as defined in PL/I is conceptually different from the dynamic block concept as described in section 1. There exist, of course, examples which, though revealing the conceptual difference, do not produce different results under the two interpretations. Consider, e.g.

[v; q ∿ [...v...]; ...q...]

where v is AUTOMATIC. After an entrance into the outer block, the inner occurrence of v denotes in the one interpretation the entire allocation stack, in the other interpretation a specific variable created by that entrance (where "variable" is used in the ordinary sense, i.e. for "storage cell" rather than for "stack of storage cells"). But since the allocation stack in the moment of the eventual call of q is still the same that it was after entrance into the outer block, no effective difference results.

So, what we have to do is to enforce a new recursion of the outer block prior to the eventual use of the q that was declared in the old recursion. Consider

{p(f) ∿ [v;q ∿ [...v...]; ....p(q) ....f....]; ...p(a)...}

Assume, that the first recursion of p (activated by p(a)) runs through that branch that contains p(q), while the second recursion runs through that branch that contains f.

According to the dynamic block concept: On the first recursion, the local names v and q are associated with a variable v_1 and a procedure q_1 containing a reference to v_1; the q in p(q) refers to q_1. On the second recursion, p(q_1), f is associated with q_1, which refers to v_1 (though, meanwhile, there have been introduced, by the second recursion, two new things v_2 and q_2).

According to PL/I: The first recursion augments the allocation stack of v by a new storage cell v_1. The second recursion associates f with the name q and furthermore augments the allocation stack of v by another storage cell v_2; execution of f causes execution of q; within this execution, the name v refers to the topmost element of its allocation stack, i.e. to v_2.

Thus, the variable name v within the eventual call of the procedure q refers to a variable of the first recursion level in the one interpretation, to a storage cell of the second recursion level in the other interpretation. We have thus constructed an example which yields different results under the two different interpretations.

5. SOME CONSEQUENCES OF THE PL/I-DEFINITION

In this section we want to make still more explicit the fact that the block concept as defined in PL/I leads to consequences, which contradict both common mathematical notation and properties which one would require from a procedure concept.

Definition of Recursive Functions

Consider the "prototype" of a one-place recursive function:

$$f(n) = [n = 0 \rightarrow a; \quad T \rightarrow b(n, f(n-1))] \quad .$$

Let f depend from a second parameter, g, which itself is a one-place function:

$$f(n,g) = \{[n=0 \rightarrow a(g); \; T \rightarrow b(n,g,f(n-1,g'))] \; \underline{\text{where}} \; g'(x)=c(n,g,x)\} \quad .$$

According to ordinary mathematical notation, this defines, for each natural $n \geqslant 0$ and for each one-place function g, a certain value f(n,g). We shall show that under the PL/I-interpretation, this definition yields quite different function values: Specializing a and b, we obtain

$$f(n,g) = \{[n=0 \rightarrow g(0); \; T \rightarrow f(n-1,g')] \; \underline{\text{where}} \; g'(x) = c(n,g,x)\} \quad .$$

Using arguments analogous to those of the previous section, one obtains f(1,g) = c(1,g,0), whereas, under the PL/I-interpretation, f(1,g) = c(0,g,0). Thus we see, that the definition of recursive functions is not expressible in a straightforward manner in PL/I, although PL/I is intended to permit recursion.

Some Identities not valid in PL/I

Let Π be a program that contains the definition of a procedure p(f), and furthermore contains only direct calls of p, i.e. no occurrences of p as an actual parameter. Then we prove the following:

(1) Let f only occur in expression-positions, i.e. not in a position to the left of an assignment operator or in an actual parameter position. Let Π contain only such calls p(v) of the procedure p, where the actual parameter v is an unsubscripted variable. Execute, for each such call p(v), the replacement

p(v) => [q ∿ v; p(q)] . [1)]

Then the resulting program Π' will in general not be equivalent to (i.e. have the same effect as) the original program Π.

(2) Let f only occur in the context GOTO f. Let Π contain only such calls p(l) of the procedure p, where the actual parameter l is a label. Execute, for each GOTOf and for each p(l), the replacements

GOTOf => f; p(l) => [q ∿ GOTOl;p(q)] . [1)]

Then again the resulting program Π' will in general not be equivalent to the original program Π.

A counter-example for case (1) is a p(f) of the form

p(f) ∿ [x;....p(x)... f ...];

similarly, a counter-example for case (2) is a p(f) of the form

p(f) ∿ [...m: ...p(m)...GOTOf...] .

These counter-examples are quite similar to the example of section 4, and the proof that they are indeed counter-examples uses the same arguments that were used there.

The result obtained could be formulated as follows:

Even for programs that satisfy some restrictive conditions - conditions that are necessary on account of the restricted call-by-name concept in PL/I, and of the fact that functions may assume as values only constants but not arbitrary names - even under these restrictions the introduction of auxiliary definitions does, in general, not preserve equivalence.

6. CONNECTION WITH OTHER PL/I-CONCEPTS

(a) The Concept of Storage Allocation

We have seen that names denoting stacks could be present in a language without affecting the general dynamic block concept. (See section 3). The only reason why this is not the case in PL/I is, that the definition of recursion has been based par-

---

1) q is an arbitrary name not present in Π.

tially on the concept of allocation. -Moreover, one can consider such stacks that are increased and decreased dynamically by the execution of explicit or implicit statements. Consequently, the concept of storage allocation could be incorporated into a language containing the dynamic block concept of section 2.

(b) The Concept of EXTERNAL Names

The way this concept has been defined in PL/I supposes, as we have remarked in section 3, the existence of some global thing that is associated to a name independently of, and prior to, any activation of the declaring block. This supposition is contrary to the dynamic block concept.

On the other hand, the usefulness of the EXTERNAL concept, and the motivation for its introduction, lie in the fact that it permits to use a name with the same meaning in separated parts of a program, so-called compilations: these parts are connected to a single program only during a later stage. But this could be achieved also by a modified form of the EXTERNAL concept: to specify a name EXTERNAL simply could mean that its declaration should stand in an outermost block surrounding the whole (still unknown) program. The scope of an EXTERNAL name then would be the whole program, i.e. the set of all compilations making up the program. -This modified form of the EXTERNAL concept clearly would not contradict the dynamic block concept.

7. A REMARK ON IMPLEMENTATION

In discussions on the dynamic block concept versus the PL/I-block concept (more precisely, the block concept as defined in older versions of PL/I) it has been argued that the implementation of the former raises almost insuperable difficulties or, at least, does not permit the design of efficient compilers.

First of all, this objection is not true; the wide use of languages like ALGOL and LISP has enforced the design of various good and general compilers, some of which possess a considerable degree of efficiency.

Second, the objection is irrelevant, at least for the versions /1/ and /2/ of PL/I. For, since labels are "qualified by recursion level", all the dynamic difficulties which arise from the fact that a newer level of recursion may have access to a piece of program of an older recursion level are present also in PL/I.

Therefore, the difference of the two block concepts cannot be defended by the claim that one of them results in easier implementation.

8. CONCLUSIONS

(1) We have seen, that the block concept as defined in PL/I is conceptually different from the dynamic block concept as used in common mathematical notation, or,

e.g., in ALGOL and LISP. This conceptual difference is caused by the fact that, within PL/I, recursion is defined by explicit rules and that these rules connect the concept of recursion with that of storage allocation.

(2) This conceptual difference results in an effective difference: we have constructed an example of a program that, under the two different interpretations, produces different results. This proves that PL/I-programs, that contain only concepts which are present also in other current high level programming languages, will in general not be equivalent to the corresponding programs of these languages, i.e. to their literal translations.

(3) Furthermore, we have derived properties of PL/I-programs which, in fact, give rise to the question whether PL/I (which clearly is intended to contain recursion) can really be considered as a recursive language: We have shown that recursively defined functions are not, at least not immediately, translateable into PL/I; and that the procedure concept in PL/I has some hardly accpetable properties.

(4) Finally, we have seen that this different block concept does not result in a gain concerning other concepts with which, in PL/I, it has been intermixed (the allocation concept and the EXTERNAL concept), nor in a gain concerning implementation.

(5) From all that, we would like to draw the conclusion that the differences of the PL/I-block concept from the known and accepted version of this concept is not a result of the desire to achieve some specific new effect, but rather seems to be an unforeseen consequence of the complicated definition given in PL/I.

REFERENCES

/1/ NPL Technical Report -
IBM Hursley, Dec. 1964.

/2/ IBM Operating System/360. PL/I: Language Specifications -
C 28-6571-0, 1965.

/3/ P. NAUR, Revised Report on the Algorithmic Language ALGOL 60 -
The Comp. J., Jan. 1963.

/4/ J. McCARTHY, LISP 1.5 Programmers Manual -
M.I.T. 1962.

/5/ K. BANDAT, H. BEKIĆ, Scope of Names in NPL -
LR 25.0.002, July 1964.

/6/ K. BANDAT, H. BEKIĆ, P. LUCAS, Block Concept for NPL -
LR 25.0.003, July 1964.

IBM LABORATORY VIENNA, Austria

DEFINING A LANGUAGE IN ITS OWN TERMS

H. BEKIĆ

ABSTRACT

The technique of expressing the semantics of a mechanical language in terms of the language itself is considered; an attempt is made to give a description that is independent of the specific language to which the technique is applied. The main investigation is restricted to expression languages, i.e. languages whose meaningful terms are expressions denoting constants. Lisp is used as an example, and some remarks how to extend the technique to programming languages are added.

TN 25. 3. 016
22 December 1964

DEFINING A LANGUAGE IN ITS OWN TERMS

CONTENTS

Locator Terms for IBM Subject Index

Semantics
Mechnaical Definition
Metalanguage
Mechanical Languages
21 Programming

1. INTRODUCTION

While there are many examples of mechanizing the definition of syntax of mechanical languages, the corresponding problem for semantics is extremely difficult. Most of mechanical languages have their semantics defined in natural language; others use a second mechanical language for the definiens, thus transferring the problem to this language. In Lisp [1] the language itself is used to express its semantics; this kind of definition has some advantages; it reduces the problem, though, being circular, it does not solve it.

The present paper gives a short description of this latter technique of self-definition. The languages under consideration will be expression languages, i.e. mechanical languages whose meaningful terms are expressions denoting constants (as opposed to programming languages which contain statements denoting actions). Only at the end of the paper some comments on the corresponding technique for programming languages will be given.

We have used here the term mechanical language because we are interested in a language together with its interpretation. Otherwise, i.e. if we were considering a language as a set of strings, apart from its possible interpretations, the term formal language would be more appropriate.

2. SELF-DEFINITION OF EXPRESSION LANGUAGES

2.1. To describe the language $\mathcal{L}$ which we will consider, we distinguish three different levels:

(I) The set C of constants of $\mathcal{L}$.

(II) The set L of expressions of $\mathcal{L}$. Each expression $l \in L$ denotes a unique constant $c \in C$, the value of l. Especially we assume that the constants are expressions and that they denote themselves. Thus

$$C \subset L.$$

(III) A metalanguage $\mathcal{M}$ (being e.g. the English language augmented by some mathematical means of expression) within which we can talk about $\mathcal{L}$. For instance we may describe in $\mathcal{M}$ a mapping

$$w: \ L \to C$$

from L into C, which maps each expression $l \in L$ into its value $w(l)$.

A definition of the language $\mathcal{L}$ then consists of the definitions of the set C, the set L, and the function w.

Note 1. By the notion of constant we do not mean the most general one; we mean individuals (as opposed to operators or functions). A more general notion would consider individuals as constants of a specific type, say of type i; a constant of type $(a_1, \ldots, a_n; v)$ would then be a functions having arguments of types $a_1, \ldots a_n$, respectively, and a value of type v. We will not use this general notion in the following, and therefore the class of languages L will only be a subclass of the class of all expression languages.

2.2. Since, within L, each use of an expression l refers to the value of l rather than to l itself, it is not possible to speak within L about the expressions of L. We now introduce a one-to-one mapping

$$* \; : L \to C$$

from L into C, which associates with each expression $l \in L$ a constant $l^* \in C$. Since $l_1^* \neq l_2^*$ for $l_1 \neq l_2$, we can use in L the constant l^* as a unique name for the expression l, i.e. the function * allows us to quote l in L. We therefore call * the quote function.

Note 2. Since $C \subset L$, c^* is defined also for all $c \in C$. Moreover we have

$$c^* \neq c$$

at least for such constants c for which there exists an $l \notin C$ with $c = l^*$; otherwise the two different expressions l and c would have the same name c, contrary to the one-to-one assumption.

Note 3. $C \subset L$ together with the one-to-one property of * implies that the sets C and L have the same cardinality. This condition is, however, not a severe restriction; it can be reached by adding to C an appropriate number of constants which then will serve the only purpose to name elements of L.

2.3. With the aid of the functions w and *, we can define a partial function

$$\text{val} : \quad C \to C$$

from C into C as follows:

$$\text{val}\,(l^*) = w\,(l) \qquad \text{for } l \in L \tag{1}$$

(val is a partial function because not any $c \in C$ must necessarily be an l^*). This function maps the constant, which is the name of an expression l, into the constant denoted by l, i.e. into the value of l. Writing

$$l_1 \sim l_2$$

to express that two expressions $l_1, l_2 \varepsilon$ L have the same value, i.e. that

$$w(l_1) = w(l_2),$$

we can describe the function val as follows: For any expression $l \varepsilon$ L, val (l^*) is the unique constant $c \varepsilon C$ satisfying

$$\text{val}(l^*) \sim l. \qquad (2)$$

We say that a function f from C into C is <u>definable in L</u>, if there exists a string F such that, for each $c \varepsilon C$ for which f(c) is defined, F [c] is a string belonging to L and satisfying

$$F\,[c] \sim f(c).$$

(In making this definition we had to assume that there exists in L a notation N (F,c) which is interpreted by the function w as denoting application of the function denoted by F to the constant c; without loss of generality we have chosen this notation to be F [c]). - The string F is called an <u>L-definition</u> of the function f.

According to equation (1), val is the functional product of the functions $(*)^{-1}$ (the inverse of *) and w. While none of these two functions, mapping C into L, and L into C, respectively, is definable in L, it may very well be the case that the function val is definable in L, i.e. that there exists a string VAL satisfying

$$\text{VAL}\,[c] \sim \text{val}(c)$$

for all $c \varepsilon C$ for which val (c) is defined. Because of (2), such a string VAL satisfies

$$\text{VAL}\,[l^*] \sim l \qquad (3)$$

for all $l \varepsilon$ L.

A <u>self-definition</u> of L consists of

(I) A quote function *, i.e. a one-to-one function from C into C.

(II) A string VAL satisfying (3), i.e. a L-definition of the function val defined by (1).

We do not investigate here the conditions under which, for a given language and a given quote-function *, there exists such a string VAL.

Note 4. By the function * the relation

$$w\ (l) = c$$

is mapped into a relation

$$w'\ (l^*) = c^*$$

and one might think it useful to take as function val this more symmetrically defined function w' instead of the function (1). However, val would then cease to fulfill (2), i.e. the corresponding VAL would cease to fulfill (3). On account of (3), replacing an expression l by VAL [l^*], or by VAL [e] where e is an expression having the value l^*, does not change the value of l; thus the function val as defined by (1) can be used to express in L the process of computing at first the name of an expression and evaluating it afterwards.

Note 5. A self-definition of L does by no means eliminate the necessity of defining the semantics of L in some other language, e.g. in natural language. However it is sufficient to provide such a definition for the function represented by VAL, rather than for the entire set of expressions of L.

3. AN EXAMPLE : LISP

By Lisp we mean that language which is defined in the first chapter of [1]. This language is an expression language in the sense of section 1, and is capable of self-definition. - Using the terminology of [1], we make the following definitions.

(I) The set C of constants is the set of S-expressions.

(II) The set L of expressions is the set of M-expressions containing no free variables.

(III) The metalanguage M is the English language.

(IV) The relation "∿" denoting the property of two expressions to have the same value is represented by "=".

(V) Application of a function f to the arguments $a_1,\dots,a_n$ is represented, within M-expressions, by $f[a_1;\dots a_n]$.

The quote-function * mapping each M-expression into a unique S-expression is defined in [1] by some explicit rules; e.g.

s* = (QUOTE s)   for S-expressions s ,

var* = VAR   for identifiers var

(where VAR is the result of replacing in var all small letters by the corresponding capital letters), and so on. * is also defined for M-expressions containing free variables, and for substrings of M-expressions representing functions.

Using this quote function, a function val satisfying

$$\text{val}\ [m^*] = m \qquad \text{for all M-expressions } m \tag{1}$$

can be defined in terms of M-expressions. (This corresponds to equation (3) of section 2, and in accordance with the notation of that section we should write VAL instead of val; this would violate however the syntactic rules for M-expressions). The definition given in [1] uses an auxiliary function

$$\text{evalquote}\ [n;l]$$

where n is the name of a function f and l is a list of already evaluated arguments; the value of evalquote $[n;l]$ is the result of the application of f to these arguments. Thus

$$\text{evalquote}\ [f^*;\text{list}\ [s_1;\ldots;s_n]] = f\ [s_1;\ldots;s_n] \tag{2}$$

for S-expressions s_i (where list is a function yielding a list of its arguments) and

$$\text{val}\ [\{f[m_1;\ldots;m_n]\}^*] = \text{evalquote}\ [f^*;\text{list}\ [\text{val}[m_1^*];\ldots;\text{val}[m_n^*]]] \tag{3}$$

for M-expressions m_i.

In fact, the definition given in [1] uses instead of the functions

$$\text{val}\ [n],\ \text{evalquote}\ [n;l]$$

the functions

$$\text{eval}\ [n;a]\ ,\ \text{apply}\ [n;l;a].$$

These are applicable also to names of M-expressions containing free variables and have as an additional parameter an association list a. We have

$$\text{val}\ [n] = \text{eval}\ [n;\text{NIL}]$$
$$\text{evalquote}\ [n;l] = \text{apply}\ [n;l;\text{NIL}]$$

(where NIL is the null list), and, corresponding to the relation (3) between val and evalquote

$$\text{eval}\ [\{f[m_1;\ldots;m_n]\}^*;a] = \text{apply}\ [f^*;\text{list}[[\text{eval}[m_1^*;a];\ldots;\text{eval}[m_n^*;a]];a] \qquad (4)$$

Note 1. Actually Lisp programs must not be written as M-expressions, but as S-expressions representing M-expressions. This is no essential restriction and seems to have only the historical reason that at the time when the Lisp Manual was written there did not exist a machine program performing the evaluation of the function *. Of course anyone using Lisp will write a program as an M-expressions and will translate it afterwards (by hand or by machine) into an S-expression.

Note 2. A Lisp program must not be an arbitrary S-expression representing an M-expression, but must be a pair consisting of a function name f^* and a list of argument values $(s_1 \ldots s_n)$. This is the reason why [1] defines the function evalquote (which according to equation (2) is directly applicable to this case, and uses eval and apply as auxiliary functions), but does not need the function val.

4. NOTE ON THE EXTENSION TO PROGRAMMING LANGUAGES.

Contrary to expression languages, the meaningful terms of programming languages (the statements) do not denote constants of the language, but rather denote actions. Therefore the method of section 2 cannot directly be applied to such languages. In the following we sketch very briefly two different ways how to overcome this difficulty.

The first way uses the fact that a statement can be interpreted as a function mapping states into states. (We do not give here a general definition of the notion state; it may be considered as the set of current assignments of values to the variables of the program, or, in the case of a machine language, as the set of contents of the machine store cells). With this interpretation, the programs of a programming language P may be rewritten as expressions, and the language may be considered as an expression language L. The set C of constants of L is the set C_o of constants of the original programming language, augmented by a suitable set of states. The expressions of L denote states and are applications of functions to states or to expressions denoting states. In defining the quote function * it will be useful to restrict the range of this function to C_o. - This method of interpretation of a programming language has for instance been used by McCARTHY [2], not for the purpose of self-definition, but for defining the semantics of a programming language in terms of a more simple expression language.

The second way is a more direct approach that avoids the - somewhat artificial - reinterpretation of *P* as an expression language. We consider the set C of constants of *P*, and the set S of statements of *P*. Like in section 2, we introduce a relation "∿", holding now between statements; $s_1 \sim s_2$ is true if and only if the statements s_1 and s_2 have the same meaning, i.e. denote the same action. Again we use a quote function *, which is a one-to-one mapping from S into C. Instead of a function val (c) satisfying condition (2) of section 2, we define a statement execute (c), containing one free variable c, such that

$$\text{execute } (s^*) \sim s$$

for all $s \in S$. Again execute may be definable in *P* itself, and in this case we call the quote function * together with the *P*-definition of execute a self-definition of *P*. - Examples for this kind of self-definition are the Universal Machine of TURING [4] and the Universal Algorithm of MARKOV [3].

REFERENCES

[1] McCARTHY, John: Lisp 1.5 Programmers Manual - Massachusetts Institute of Technology (1962).

[2] McCARTHY, John: Towards a Mathematical Science of Computation - In: C. M. Popplewell (editor), Proceedings of IFIP Congress 1962 - North Holland Publishing Company, Amsterdam (1963).

[3] MARKOV, A.A.: The Theory of Algorithms - Am. Math. Soc. Transl. Ser. 2, vol.15 (1960).

[4] TURING, A.M.: On computable numbers with an application to the Entscheidungs problem - Proc. London Math. Soc., vol.42 (1936); vol.43 (1937).

Note on some Problems Concerning the PL/I Manual and its Re-writing

There seems to be agreement that the present SRL is not easy to read and to use; it is not even complete, nor unambiguous (see below). Here some few thoughts on points that would be important when re-writing the manual. Of course, both the list of points and the treatment of each of them as given here are very sketchy and incomplete. Also, no comments on the language itself are given, but only its presentation is discussed.

1. Organisation of material

In the SRL treatment of one subject is scattered usually over many places; e.g. essential information concerning procedures is contained in ch. 1,4,5,6,8,10. In particular there are chapters of a more introductory nature, and others which seem to be intended for complete reference (ch. 4,8); but the latter ones are far from being complete and the first ones cause more duplication than seems necessary or desirable.

Of course, it is rather difficult to arrange the material in a really satisfactory manner. Roughly speaking, there seems to exist two possibilities, namely a semantical approach where there is one chapter for each of the semantical concepts that can be expressed in the language and a structural (or syntactical) approach, where the main arrangement is according to the main syntactical categories of the language. For example, call-statement, procedure block, and entry name attributes would all be contained in a chapter "Procedures" according to the first approach, whereas with the second they would be included, respectively, in a "Statements"-chapter and in two different parts of the "Declarations" -chapter (See below for the sense in which "statement" and "declaration" are used here).

A tentative listing within the first method would be (not necessarily in this sequence):

1. Data: types; constants; variables (simple variables, arrays, structures) and their attributes, naming.
2. Expressions:scalar, array, structure; operators; evaluation (including specifications when and which conversion functions are invoked, but not description of the functions themselves).
3. The most simple statements: assignment, goto, null.
4. Compound statements: conditional, do-group, block ("beginblock" only).
5. Storage allocation: storage class attributes; allocate/free; pointer; area; PACKED; ALIGNED; SECONDARY.
6. Procedures: procedure declarations (SRL: = "procedure blocks"; including primary and secondary entry points, return statement, formal parameters, prologues); procedure references (including argument-parameter, correspond-

ence); entry name attributes (including abnormality).

7. Defined
8. Tasks
9. Interrupts
10. I/O
11. Declarations: including scope, implicit, contextual, default, factoring; not including descriptions of attributes themselves.
12. Programs
13. Compile-time

Appendix: Collection of built-in functions, pseudo-variables, conversion functions, conditions, etc.

An obvious arrangement with the second method is:

1. Characters, key-words, identifiers, numbers, strings
2. Expressions (including variables)
3. Statements
4. Declarations
5. Programs
6. Compile-time (listed separately from other statements and declarations because of its constituting a pre-pass).

There remain some difficulties with either approach. The first arrangement would perhaps be better suited for the beginner; it would require a separate chapter giving the complete syntax, and, if to be used as a good reference manual, an extensive index. The second arrangement is probably the better one; it would be the better reference manual for one who uses it during program writing; precise syntax descriptions can be included naturally into the text. (Incidentally, the second approach corresponds to the one taken by the Algol authors, and indeed their report is a good reference manual but difficult for most beginners).

2. Terminology

The SRL would have gained much in clarity and facility of expression: if, instead of the overall term "statement", the more differentiating terminology, as introduced by the designers of other languages, had been used (see, for example, /1/):

statement for "executable statement",

declaration for all kinds of notations that introduce a name and associate properties with it,

specification for associating properties with names that have been introduced elsewhere (for examples see below),

clause for notations that are not themselves statements, but modify the meaning of a statement, e.g. IF - THEN, DO V = __, punctuation mark or bracket for the "statements" BEGIN, END, DO, PROCEDURE, ENTRY, and for ELSE.

For example, the DECLARE-" statement" would be a declaration, DO__END and BEGIN__END would be single statements. P : PROCEDURE (F):__END would be a declaration, namely it introduces a name P and declares it to denote that procedure whose formal parameter part is F, and whose body is BEGIN__END. The differentiation between specification and declaration would be particularly useful for parameters: e.g. a parameter specified CONTROLLED behaves quite differently than a variable declared CONTROLLED, the former not having any storage class at all; probably the distinction would be useful also for external "declarations", and for explicit entry name "declarations".

3. Method of definition

The most serious difficulty with the SRL is its lack in concise, unambiguous and exhaustive definitions. Here, the most important requirements seem to be the following:

1. Do not enumerate a list of single cases (even if the list is exhastive) where it would be possible to give one general principle. (Examples: passing the address represented by the argument, or a dummy argument, to the parameter; definition of abnormality). It should be avoided that there is a "general rule", followed by "special cases" that supply information that was not implicitly contained in the rule itself. Logical consequences of a rule should be separated clearly by clauses like "in particular ...", "for example ...", etc. (often it would be better to give them into an appendex, or to omit them altogether).

2. If semantics of a certain piece of notation is to be defined, the definition should be given in one place only, but in this place completely. (Multiple definitions are likely to contradict each other: e.g. definition when a dummy is created). Describe clearly the constituent parts of the notation and their arrangement (by specifying the syntax, or at least the structure, if precise syntax is given in an appendix), and give cross reference to the definitions of meanings of these parts; then define meaning of compound text as unique function of those meanings.

3. Some terms (e.g. variable, scalar variable, array, generation) are used again and again. Give most careful definition of these terms, even if their meaning seems to be obvious. Only then one will be sure that "variable" really means variable (and not scalar variable, or unsubscripted variable, as it does in many places in the SRL). For example, the general definition of "variable" should include the pointer-qualified variable, whereas in the

SRL one is told only later on that "a variable may be qualified by a pointer". With such complete definitions, many semantical rules could be formulated much more concise. Thus, the rule for passing a defined variable as an argument could simply state that the generation represented by the corresponding base (and not its value, or the piece of program evaluating to that generation) is passed. Also it would be avoided that technical terms are used without having been defined: e.g. "qualification by recursion".

4. Selfcontainedness

There are cases in which the effect of a PL/I program depends on information that must be specified by the programmer somewhere outside the program. One example is the correspondence title-external medium, which must be communicated to the operating system on a DD-card. Another example is the notion "program" itself: Somehow the programmer has to specify which are the external procedures constituting the program, and which is the one to start with. The SRL should contain an explicit enumeration of such cases and give the necessary information for each of them.

Reference

/1/ P. LUCAS: Unification of Statement Formats in PL/I
LN 25.3.028, September 1965, IBM Lab Vienna.

DEFINABLE OPERATIONS IN GENERAL ALGEBRAS, AND THE THEORY OF AUTOMATA AND FLOWCHARTS [1)]

Hans Bekić, IBM Laboratory, Vienna

Abstract. We study the class of operations definable from the given operations of an algebra of sets by union, composition, and fixed points; we obtain two theorems on definable operations that give us as special case the regular-equals-recognisable theorem of generalised finite automata theory. Definable operations arise also as the operations computable by charts; by translating into predicate logic, we obtain Manna's formulas for termination and correctness of flowcharts.

To be published in Machine Intelligence 5, Edinburgh

Vienna, 8 December, 1969

---

1) Work carried out at Queen Mary College, London, under Research Grant B/SR/5987 of the S.R.C.

INTRODUCTION

The regular-equals-recognisable theorem of generalised (i.e. tree) automata theory can be viewed as asserting that the sets of terms, or trees, definable by equation systems in a certain normal form are the same as those obtainable from the empty set and unit sets by union, a kind of composition, and a kind of iteration. In the attempt to arrive at a better understanding of this theorem and its proof, it appeared that one could start from an arbitrary algebra rather than just from the algebra of terms. Given the operations of an algebra, it is usual to consider a larger set of operations, namely those "derivable" from the original ones by permutation of variables and composition. If we raise the given algebra to the set level (f applied to set = set of results of applying f to the elements), then we can use two other ways of extending the class of our operations: union, and (simultaneous) fixed points, i.e. definition by an equation system. It turns out that our original theorem can be gained as special case of the combination of two simple theorems on the class of "definable" operations so obtained. The first theorem asserts that in fact we can do with simple recursion. The second asserts that each definable operation can be defined by an equation system in normal form.

Conventional, i.e. string automata used to be represented by transition charts. Hence it is not surprising that normal operations - which where those giving us the recognisable sets - are precisely those computable by charts, also if the chart is not interpreted just in the algebra of strings (and also if we go to the generalised case, i.e. to arbitrary instead of unary algebras, generalising the notion of chart appropriately). Remaining for a moment at the unary case, i.e., at conventional flowcharts, we observe that the normal operation associated with the chart asks us to find the smallest system of sets satisfying certain mutual closure relationships. This is a typical second order problem, like e.g. the problem of defining the natural numbers, i.e. the smallest set containing 0 and closed under successor. It is second order, because, as we well know from the fifth Peano axiom, such definitions can be expressed in predicate logic only speaking about all properties, or all sets, of elements. Expressing our operation computed by a chart in predicate logic, we thus get second order formulas - or, since the formulas have only one kind of second order quantifier, validity or satisfiability of first order formulas; so here are Manna's conditions on termination and correctness of flowcharts.

It may be difficult enough to discover just a mechanism for telling precisely what a programming language means. It is still more difficult to find a formalisation that keeps describing a language, i.e. preserves the structural similarity between expressions and meanings. Expressions in conventional mathematics, like arithmetic expressions, can easily be defined as an algebra and their meaning as a homomorphism from the algebra of expressions to the algebra of numbers. Can we do something similar for charts? Conventional automata are charts, generalised automata have been defined as (finite) algebras. So it is only one step to an idea of P. Landin to define a chart as a finite algebra (plus entries and exits). Executing the chart in an other algebra then means following equal paths in the two algebras; so the computation of the chart becomes the algebra generated in the direct product of the two algebras from the assignment of initial values.

In the first part of the paper (sections 1 to 3) we develop the theory of definable operations; instead of the set of subsets of a given set, partially ordered by set inclusion, we consider an arbitrary set with an arbitrary partial ordering. In the second part (sections 4 to 6) we return to algebras, automata, and flowcharts.

Notation. We use familiar notation from set theory, e.g. $\cup$ and $\bigcup$ for union, { } or Ø for the empty set. $\mathcal{B}A$ is the set of subsets of A; $A_1 \times \ldots \times A_n$ is the Cartesian product of the sets A_i, i.e. the set of n-tuples $(a_1,\ldots,a_n)$ with $a_i \in A_i$; A^n is the set of n-tuples of elements of A. A (total) function $f: A \to B$ is a mapping from A to B; $A \to B$ denotes the set of all such functions. A relation from A to B is a subset of $A \times B$. In the last section, we use propositional connectives and quantifiers from predicate logic.

1. DEFINABLE OPERATIONS IN COMPLETE LATTICES

In this section, we consider a set M partially ordered by a relation $\leqslant$, a set θ of operations on M with certain "good", i.e. order-preserving, properties, and certain functionals, i.e. operations on operations, that preserve goodness. As indicated, M in our applications will become $\mathcal{B}A$, the set of subsets of A, $\leqslant$ will become $\subseteq$, i.e. set inclusion, and θ will result from raising to the set level a given set of operations on A. One of our functionals is concerned with the construction of fixed points and is applicable only to good operations. Therefore we will start with discussing good functions and fixed points, and will then introduce our functionals and show that they preserve goodness. Our aim is to define a class $D\theta$ as the smallest class containing θ and closed under the functionals.

Some lattice-theoretic definitions (cf.e.g. Cohn [4] chapter I.4 and II.4). A set M is partially ordered by a binary relation $\leqslant$ on M, if $\leqslant$ is reflexive ($a \leqslant a$), transitive (if $a \leqslant b$ and $b \leqslant c$ then $a \leqslant c$), and antisymmetric (if $a \leqslant b$ then not $b \leqslant a$). For a subset L of M, $a \in M$ is the least upper bound (l.u.b.) of L, if a is an upper bound of L, i.e. $a \geqslant x$ for all $x \in L$, and if for every upper bound b of L we have $b \geqslant a$. (We write $b \geqslant a$ for $a \leqslant b$). Lower bound and greatest lower bound (g.l.b.) are defined similarly. We write $\bigcup L$, or, in the case $L=\{b,c\}$, $b \cup c$ for the l.u.b. of L; similarly $\bigcap L$ or $b \cap c$ for g.l.b.s; these notations are borrowed from the special case of $\mathcal{B}A$ ordered by $\subseteq$, where $\bigcup$ and $\bigcap$ become union and intersection. M is called a lattice, if $b \cup c$ and $b \cap c$ exist for all $b,c \in M$; a complete lattice, if $\bigcup L$ and $\bigcap L$ exist for all $L \subseteq M$.

Now let M be partially ordered by $\leqslant$. We will gradually introduce assumptions on the existence of l.u.b.s (assumptions 1,2,3 below) which together will be only slightly weaker than postulating M as a complete lattice.

Good functions, minimal fixed points

From the theory of production systems and context-free languages we are familiar with definitions like (after translation into set notation) the following:

$$x = a \cup gxy$$
$$y = b \cup hjy$$

Here, a and b are sets of strings, gxy is the set of strings starting with the letter g, followed by a member of x followed by a member of y. This definition by "simultaneous recursion" is intended to describe x, y as the smallest sets x and y that satisfy the indicated equalities. Of course we know how to find x, y: Denoting by f the function which the pair $a \cup gxy$, $b \cup hxy$ is of x,y we start with the pair of empty sets: $x_0 = \emptyset$, $y_0 = \emptyset$, and iterate the process of applying $f: x_{i+1}, y_{i+1} = fx_i y_i$; then the x_i , y_i form an ascending chain, i.e. $x_i \subseteq x_{i+1}$, $y_i \subseteq y_{i+1}$, and the required pair x,y is the limit, or union, of the chain.

In the theorem below, we describe and justify this construction in the abstract. We start with two assumptions on M :

1. M has a minimal element 0, i.e. $0 \leqslant x$ for all $x \in M$.
2. Any countably infinite ascending chain $a_0 \leqslant a_1 \leqslant \dots$ in M has a l.u.b. $\bigcup_i a_i$.

Definition: A function $f: M \to M$ is called good if it is monotone, i.e. $fa \leqslant fb$ for $a \leqslant b$, and continuous, i.e. $f \bigcup_i a_i = \bigcup_i fa_i$ for countable ascending chains a_i.

(In fact, monotonicity follows from continuity, but it is convenient to consider the two properties separately.) Note, that, by monotonoicity, the fa_i are ascending if the a_i are.

Theorem (Construction of minimal fixed points, "recursion theorem"). Let M be partially ordered with minimal element and l.u.b.s for countable ascending chains; let $f: M \to M$ be a good function. Then there is a minimal solution a of

$$x \geqslant fx$$

which is given by $a = \bigcup_i f^i 0$ and in fact satisfies $a = fa$, i.e. is a fixed point of f.

Proof. $0 \leqslant f0$, hence by monotonicity $f0 \leqslant f^2 0$, $f^2 0 \leqslant f^3 0, \ldots$, i.e. the $f^i 0$ are ascending. Now $fa = \bigcup_i f^{i+1} 0$ by continuity, i.e. $fa = a$. Further, $b \geqslant fb$ implies $b \geqslant fb$ implies $b \geqslant 0$, $b \geqslant fb \geqslant f0$, $b \geqslant fb \geqslant f^2 0, \ldots$ thus $b \geqslant \bigcup_i f^i 0$, i.e. $b \geqslant a$.

Notation. We call a the minimal fixed point of f and write $a = \mu x.fx$.

There are several well-known applications of this theorem. One is the recursion theorem in recursive function theory, where M is the set of partial recursive functions of natural numbers, partially ordered by "being an extension of "; the theorem justifies recursive definitions like the familiar one for the factorial function. Another application is the construction of sets closed under given operations, i.e. minimal subalgebras. This is the one we are interested in, and it will be discussed (using a slightly modified version of our theorem, see end of this section) in section 4.

If we were interested only in the existence of fixed points, not in the particular construction, we could use also the following theorem, which gets away with weaker assumptions on f (through stronger ones on M):

Theorem (Tarski's fixed point theorem, see Tarski [14]). Any monotone mapping of a complete lattice into itself has fixed points. In particular, $\bigcap\{x \mid x \geqslant fx\}$ is the minimal fixed point.

Note that the set of partial recursive functions in the previous example does not form a complete lattice.

Functionals preserving goodness

We add a third assumption on M:

3. M has l.u.b.s for pairs, i.e. if $a,b \in M$ then $a \cup b \in M$.

Thus we have now l.u.b.s for finite subsets (by 1 and 3; note that $0 = \bigcup\{\ \}$) and for countable ascending chains. By assuming l.u.b.s for every subset, we would in fact have a complete lattice (see e.g. Cohn [4] I.4).

Extending $\leqslant$ to tuples. For any $n \geqslant 0$, we consider the set M^n of n-tuples of elements of M and extend $\leqslant$ to a partial ordering of M^n defining

$$(a_1,\ldots,a_n) \leqslant (b_1,\ldots,b_n) \qquad \text{if } a_i \leqslant b_i, \ldots, a_n \leqslant b_n$$

Thus $\leqslant$, and therefore $\bigcup$, are defined component-wise; conditions 1 to 3 extend to M^n, in particular, $(0,0,\ldots.0)$ is the minimal element.

Operations on M. Instead of functions f: M → M, we want to consider more generally operations on M, i.e. functions $f{:}M^n \to M^p$ $(n \geq 0,\ p \geq 0)$. We also write $f \in [n \to p]$ and say that f is of arity $n \to p$; sometimes we write $[n\to]$ for $\bigcup_p [n \to p]$, $[\to p]$ for $\bigcup_n [n \to p]$.

For $f{:}M^n \to M^p$ we define good component-wise, i.e. f is good if it is monotone and continuous under the ordering $\leq$ in m^n and M^p.

Notation for tuples. If $a = (a_1,\ldots,a_n)$, $b = (b_1,\ldots,b_m)$, we write (a,b) for $(a_1,\ldots,a_n,b_1,\ldots,b_m)$. (This notation is unambiguous, since we will only consider tuples of elements, not tuples of tuples). The 0-tuple is denoted by (). We will in general use unindexed letters a,b,...x,y for tuples, indexed letters for elements. In $(a_1,\ldots a_n)$ or (a,b), parantheses and commas may be omitted, in particular in the context $f(a_1,\ldots,a_n)$ or f(a,b).

The list of functionals. We now give our list of functionals, i.e. operations on operations on M. Actually, the list contains an element of M (namely 0), and operations on M (namely $e_i^n, 0^n$); these may be viewed as constant, i.e. 0ary, functionals. n, p etc. ≥ 0 unless otherwise stated.

1.a. components: $e_i^n \in [n \to 1]$; $e_i^n x_1 \ldots x_n = x_i$ $(1 \leq i \leq n,\ n \geq 1)$

b. producing (): $0^n \in [n \to 0]$; $0^n x = ()$

c. tupling: for $f \in [n \to p]$, $g \in [n \to q]$:

$$(f,g) \in [n \to p+q]; \quad (f,g)x = (fx,gx)$$

2.a. the minimal element 0 (considered as operation $\in [0 \to 1]$).

b. union: for $f,g \in [n \to p]$: $f \cup g \in [n \to p]$; $(f \cup g)x = fx \cup gx$

3. composition: for $f \in [m \to p]$, $g \in [n \to m]$:

$$f \circ g \in [n \to p]; \quad (f \circ g)x = f(gx)$$

4. fixed points: for $f \in [n + p \to p]$, good: $f^\dagger \in [n \to p]$; $f^\dagger x = \mu y.fxy$

Thus 1 is concerned with tupling and untupling, 2 with finite unions, 3 with functional composition, 4 with fixed points, or definition by simultaneous recursion, relative to the last components (this is no restriction, since permutations are included by 2).
4 is justified by observing that M^p satisfies the assumptions of the recursion theorem and that, for given x, the function $g{:}M^p \to M^p$, $gy = fxy$, is good if f is good.

Lemma (preservation of goodness). Functionals 1 to 4, applied to good gunctions, yield good functions.

Proof (Note: for 0ary functions, i.e. operations, this means that the operation is good.)

1.abc : Goodness is defined component-wise.

2.a. : any constant (i.e. 0ary operation) is good.

b. : if $fb \geqslant fa$, $gb \geqslant ga$ then $fb \cup gb \geqslant fa \cup ga$;

also, $\bigcup_i (fa_i \cup ga_i) = \bigcup_i fa_i \cup \bigcup_i ga_i$.

3. If $b \geqslant a$ then $fb \geqslant fa$, hence $g(fb) \geqslant g(fa)$;

$\bigcup_i g(fa_i) = g \bigcup_i fa_i = g(f \bigcup_i a_i)$.

4. For $b \geqslant a$, we have $fby \geqslant fay$, i.e. each $y \geqslant fby$ is also $\geqslant fay$, thus $\mu y, fay \geqslant \mu y.fby$. To prove continuity we put $a = \bigcup_i a_i$, $y_i = \mu y.fa_i y$ and have to show $\mu y.fay = \bigcup_i y_i$. Now for $y \geqslant fay$, we have $y \geqslant fa_i y \geqslant y_i$, thus $y \geqslant \bigcup_i y_i$; conversely, $y = \bigcup_i y_i$ satisfies $y \geqslant y_i = fa_i y_i$, thus $y \geqslant \bigcup_i fa_i = fay$.

The set Dθ

Definition. Let a set θ of good operations over M, i.e. good functions $\in \bigcup_{n,p} M^n \to M^p$ be given. The set Dθ of operations definable from θ (or of definable operations, if θ is understood), is the smallest set containing θ and closed under functionals 1-4.

This definition is justified by the previous lemma: since we never leave the set of good operations, † is always applicable. By closed under a given function, e.g. $\circ$, we mean that $f \circ g$ is in the set whenever f and g are in the set and satisfy the conditions on their arities as stated in the definition of $\circ$. In particular, for a 0ary functional we mean that the operation denoted by it is in the set. Thus we could also say that Dθ is the smallest set containing θ and the operations 1a, 1b and 2a and closed under 1c, 2b, 3 and 4.

where-where rec-notation

In discussing definable operations, we will often find it more convenient to use a notation that provides for variables and auxiliary definitions, rather than to use explicitly the functionals introduced in 1-4. If E and F are expressions denoting after assignment of elements or tuples of elements of M to their free variables, elements or tuples of elements of M, then, denoting by $\lambda x.E$ the function which E is of x, we will write

$$E \ \underline{\text{where}} \ x = F \qquad \text{for} \qquad (\lambda x.E)F$$
$$\underline{\text{rec}} \ x = F \qquad \text{for} \qquad x = \mu x.F$$

Thus E where rec x = F for E where rec $x = \mu x.F$, i.e. for $(\lambda x.E)$ $(\mu x.F)$. Note that a x which occurs free in F is not bound by the where-clause in E where x = F, but is bound by the where-rec-clause in E where rec x = F. Thus our use of where corresponds to that formalised in Landin [7] rather than to that in most of informal mathematics (which is nearer to where rec). Again our use of rec is that introduced in [7]: there rec x = F was explained as Y $(\lambda x.F)$, where Y is a fixed point finder; we are lucky to be in the special situation where we know precisely what Y is.

Translating from functional notation to where - where rec-notation

Our expressions in where-where rec-notation will be built up from 0 and variables by tupling, symbols denoting operations in θ, and auxiliary definitions. Given an operation $h \in D\theta$ by a derivation using functionals 1-4, we can find an expression whose value, as a function of its free variable x, is hx by using the rules $(f \circ g)x = f(gx)$ and $g^{\dagger}x = (y$ where rec $y = gxy)$, together with obvious rules for $(f,g)x$, $0^n x$, $e_i^n x_1 \dots x_n$ (other uses of e_i^n can be reduced to this one by introducing auxiliary definitions).

Translating from where - where rec-notation to functional notation

To find,
conversely, a derivation for the function which a given expression is of x, we can use (again together with a few more trivial rules)

$$(fxy \ \underline{\text{where}} \ y = gx) = f(x,gx) = (f \circ (I,g))x$$

where I is the identity on x , i.e. $I = (e_1^n, \dots e_n^n)$ if y ranges over M^n, and

$$(fxy \ \underline{\text{where rec}} \ y = gxy) = (fxy \ \underline{\text{where}} \ y = g^{\dagger}x)$$

where the right hand side is to be transformed further by the first rule.

Example. Suppose $a,f \in \theta$. The (0ary) operation $\mu y.a \cup hay$ is written y where rec y = $a \cup hay$ in where - where rec-notation , $[a \circ 0^1 \cup h \circ (a \circ 0^1 \ , e_1^1)]^{\dagger}$ in functional notation.

Cumulative iteration vs. fixed points

The minimal fixed point $\mu x.fx$ was defined as $\bigcup_i f^i 0$. This suggests the question whether we could have used iteration, i.e. the functional * defined by $f^*x = \bigcup_i f^i x$, instead of μ (and hence iteration with respect to the last components instead of †) in building up $D\theta$. The answer to this question should be no (even under the necessary existence assumptions on $\bigcup_i$), but we will show that we can use cumulative iteration $^{\cup *}$ defined by $f^{\cup *}x = \bigcup_i (I \cup f)^i x$, where I is the identity function on the domain of f, i.e. $I = (e_1, \ldots, e_n)$ for $f \in [n \to]$. We note $(I \cup f)x = x \cup fx \geqslant x$, i.e. the $(I \cup f)^i x$ are ascending (whereas the $f^i x$ in general are not). The following lemma expresses $^{\cup *}$ in terms of μ (and in fact gives the recursion theorem for $x = 0$).

Lemma. For M satisfying the assumptions of the recursion theorem, and good $f: M \to M$:

$$f^{\cup *}x = \mu y.x \cup fy$$

Proof. Let $a = f^{\cup *}x$. We have $a \geqslant x$ and also $a = (I \cup f)a \geqslant fa$, thus $a \geqslant x \cup fa$. For $b \geqslant x \cup fb$, we have $b \geqslant x$, $b \geqslant (I \cup f)x$, $b \geqslant (I \cup f)b \geqslant (I \cup f)^2 x \ldots$, thus $b \geqslant \bigcup_i (I \cup f)^i x = a$.

Conversely, $\mu x.fx = \bigcup_i f^i 0 = \bigcup_i (I \cup f)^i 0 = f^{\cup *}0$, i.e. μ is expressible in terms of $^{\cup *}$. Thus $^{\cup *}$ would be as good as μ in building up $D\theta$; this result will be used in section 5 for comparing two definitions of regular set.

2. THEOREM I: ELIMINATION OF SIMULTANEOUS RECURSION

We have included in our list of functionals the use of μ with respect to several variables, because it is convenient to have an operator solving simultaneous equation systems, e.g. in the definition of recognisable set in automata theory. We will now prove that we could have done as well with μ on single (element) variables, hence that simulaneous recursion † can be defined by simple recursion $†_1$ i.e. by the restriction of † to operations in $[n+1 \to 1]$.

Given the equation system $x = fxy$, $y = gxy$, we can first solve the equation for y (with x as parameter), then substitute the solution in the equation for x and solve it for x. This is expressed by the following lemma:

Bisection lemma. For good f,g [p+q p] , [p+q→q] , respectively:

$$\mu xy.(fxy,gxy) = x_\circ , y_\circ$$

where

$$x_\circ = \mu x.f(x,\mu y.gxy)$$
$$y_\circ = \mu y.gx_\circ y$$

(with certain tacit assumptions on the ranges of x and y.)

Proof. We have $x_\circ = \mu x.f(x,g^\dagger x)$, $y_\circ = g^\dagger x_\circ$. Now $y_\circ = gx_\circ y_\circ$, $x_\circ = f(x_\circ ,g^\dagger x_\circ) = fx_\circ y_\circ$, i.e. $x_\circ ,y_\circ$ is a fixed point of (f,g). Conversely, if $x,y \geqslant fxy,\ gxy$, then $y \geqslant g^\dagger x$, $x \geqslant f(x,g^\dagger x)$, thus $x \geqslant x_\circ , y \geqslant g^\dagger x_\circ = y_\circ$; hence $x_\circ ,y_\circ$ is the minimal fixed point.

In where - where rec-notation, the lemma reads

(x,y where rec x,y = fxy, gxy) =
= x, (y where rec y = gxy) where rec x = f(x,(y where rec y = gxy)).

We note the special fxy = hx:

(x,y where rec x,y = hx,gxy) =
= x, (y where rec y = gxy) where rec x = hx

Theorem I (elimination of simultaneous recursion). † can be defined in terms of $^{\dagger 1}$ and the remaining functionals.

Proof. For $f \in [\rightarrow 0]$, i.e. fx = (), we have $f^\dagger x = ()$, i.e. $f^\dagger = f$. For $h \in [\rightarrow p+q]$, there are $f \in [\rightarrow p]$, $g \in [\rightarrow q]$ such that h = (f,g) (and f and g are in Dθ if h is). It follows from the lemma that $h^\dagger$ can be expressed in terms of $f^\dagger$ and $g^\dagger$ (the actual expansion is

$$(f,g)^\dagger = (f \mathbin{\acute{\circ}} g^\dagger)^\dagger \ ,\ g^\dagger \mathbin{\acute{\circ}} (f \mathbin{\acute{\circ}} g^\dagger)^\dagger$$

where $f \mathbin{\acute{\circ}} g$ is $f \circ (I,g)$ with suitable identity function I). Thus † on $\bigcup_{p>1} [\rightarrow p]$ can be gradually reduced to $^{\dagger 1}$.

3. THEOREM II : NORMAL FORM

In this section we define a normal form for operations on M and show that each operation in Dθ is representable in normal form. Operations in normal form arise (in the case m = *BA*) as the operations computed by charts, and we will introduce and use charts informally below for illustration. (A formal treatment of chart and operation computed by a chart is given in section 4). Our proof of the normal form theorem can be viewed as introducing operations on representations in normal form, or charts, corresponding to the functionals 1-4 on operations and as showing that the mapping "operation computed by a chart" is a homomorphism from the algebra of charts to the algebra of operations.

Assumption. We assume $\theta \subseteq [\to 1]$, i.e. the $f \in \theta$ produce elements rather than tuples. (This assumption is for convenience only; without it we had to base our definition of normal form on components of $f \in \theta$ rather than on $f \in \theta$.)

Normal form

Consider the following definition of a (0ary) operation (the example at the beginning of section 2, with changed names of variables, written in where - where rec-notation with the licence of splitting up definitions of tuples into definitions of their components):

$$y_1, y_2 \ \underline{\text{where rec}} \ y_1 = a \cup g y_1 y_2 \qquad \text{(Fig. 1)}$$
$$y_2 = b \cup h y_1 y_2$$

We have associated a chart with it by generalising the usual notion of chart (e.g. transition chart in conventional automata theory): we allow "polyarcs", like the ones labelled g and h in the example, i.e. arcs leading from tuples of nodes to nodes, rather than from nodes to nodes. (In fact also the nullaries a and b give rise to polyarcs, namely to ones joining a 0-tuple of nodes to a node).

In this example (and in anyone of a 0ary operation for which there is a similar chart), the right hand side of each auxiliary definition consists of alternatives each of which is an operation $\in \theta$ applied to a tuple of variables (corresponding to an arc in the chart); the main clause is a tuple of variables (corresponding to a tuple of nodes marked as "exits" in the chart).

More generally, for an operation $\in [n \to p]$, we need a tuple $x_1, \ldots x_n$ of argument variables (corresponding to a tuple of nodes marked as "entries" in the chart):

$$y_1, x_2 \ \underline{\text{where rec}} \ y_1 = g x_1 y_2 \qquad \text{(Fig. 2)}$$
$$y_2 = x_2 \cup f y_1$$

Like the y_j we allow the x_i as components of the main part (exits) and as arguments to $f \in \theta$. Unlike the y_j, we have to allow the x_i as alternatives on the r.h.s. (giv-

giving rise to an unlabelled arc); otherwise we could not even define e_1^1. Another difference is that we want the x_i to be free, i.e. not to appear as the left-hand side of a definition (thus no arc leading into them), whereas the y_j are bound (if only by a definition with no alternatives, i.e. 0 on the r.h.s.). (We treat the x_i as variables translating into nodes, rather than as (variable) nullaries translating into (nullary) arcs; in our formal treatment of charts we will choose the latter alternative, whereas here we prefer the slightly greater freedom of the former.)

To give now our definition of normal form, we call an operation on M degree 0, if it can be obtained by functionals 1 a,b,c alone, i.e. is a permutation with gaps and repetitions; degree 1, if it is $f \circ e$, where $f \in \theta$ and e is degree 0.

Definition. An operation f on M is normal if it can be represented in normal form, i.e. in the form

$$fx = e(x, \mu y.dxy)$$

(thus $f = e\circ(I,d^\dagger)$), where e is degree 0, $d = d_1,d_2,\dots,d_m)$, $d_j \in [\to 1]$, with each d_j a finite union of operations each of which is either degree 1 or is degree 0 in x, i.e. $e'xy = e'x$ with e" degree 0 (thus e" is some e_i^n).

The normal form theorem

Clearly each normal operation is in $D\theta$. We want to show the converse.

Theorem II. (normal form theorem). Each operation in $D\theta$ is normal

Normal form with spontaneous moves. Our proof of the theorem will produce as intermediate results representations in normal form with spontaneous moves; these are defined like representations in normal form, except that the e' may now be arbitrary degree 0 operations. They correspond to allowing the y_j as alternatives on the r.h.s. of a definition (thus to allowing "spontaneous moves" i.e. unlabelled arcs from y_j, in the chart). Spontaneous moves are familiar from conventional automata theory. Perhaps we should use the term more properly for any unlabelled arc; however we needed a name for the restricted case; for nullary operations i.e. when no x_i are present, the two uses coincide.

Some identities. We prove some simple identities on where - where rec-expressions, which we will use without explicit reference.

1. (y where rec y = a) = a

Proof: the l.h.s. satisfies y = a by definition.

2. (distribution:) f(x where rec x = gx) = fx where rec x = gx)

Proof: by definition of where, f(x where x = a) = fa = (fx where x = a) ;
put a = μx.gx.

3. ("moving right":) (fx where rec x = gx) where rec y = hy
= fx where rec x,y = gxy,hy

Proof: From the bisection lemma (special case), we have

(x,y where rec x,y = gxy,hy) =
= (x where rec x = gxy),y where rec y = hy

Apply to both sides λxy.fx, using 2.

4. ("moving left":) (fx where rec x = (gxy where rec y = hxy)) =
= (fx where rec x,y = gxy, hxy)

Proof: similar.

Note. 3. and 4. (as well as the bisection lemma) become intuitively obvious if one remembers that the "scope" of a where rec-definition is the expression qualified by the definition, plus the definiens.

Proof of theorem II (up to spontaneous moves).

We show that f $\in$ θ is normal, and that each of the functionals 1-4, when applied to operations in normal form, yields an operation representable in normal form with spontaneous moves. The corresponding operations on charts are very simple, e.g. joining exits of one chart with the corresponding entrances of the other for composition, with the last entrances of itself for †. To complete the proof of the theorem, we will show how eliminate spontaneous moves.

0. For f θ, we have fx=(y where rec y = fx). (Note θ [$\to$1], i.e. f [$\to$1]).

1a. $e^n_i x_1 \ldots x_n = x_i$ (Note that in e(x, μy.dxy), y may be (), i.e. we may have no auxiliary definitions at all).

1b. $0^n x$ = ()

1c. (exy **where rec** y = dxy, e'xz **where rec** z = d'xz)

= (exy, e'xz) **where rec** y,z = dxy, d'xz

= $(e\circ c, e'\circ c')$xyz **where rec** y,z = $(d\circ c, d'\circ c')$xyz

where cxyz = xy, c'xyz = xz. If e and e' are degree 0, then so are $e\circ c$, $e'\circ c'$; if the components of d and d' are unions of operations which are degree 1, or degree 0 in x, then so are the components of $(d\circ c, d'\circ c')$. (In other words, dxy etc. continue to satisfy the assumptions if viewed as functions of more variables).

2a. 0 = (y **where rec** y = 0)

2b. (exy **where rec** y = dxy) $\cup$ (e'xz **where rec** z = d'xz)

= exy $\cup$ e'xz **where rec** y,z = dxy, d'xz

= u **where rec** u,y,z = exy $\cup$ e'xz, dxy, d'xz

(In this and the following two cases, we may get spontaneous moves).

3. (exy **where rec** y = dxy) **where** x = (e'x'z **where rec** z = d'x'z)

= exy **where rec** y,x,z = dxy, e'x'z, d'x'z

4. z **where rec** z = (exzy **where rec** y = dxzy)

= z **where rec** z,y = exzy, dxzy

(This gives us a representation for $\mu z.fxz$, i.e. for $f^{\dagger}x$, if we have one for fxz).

Elimination of spontaneous moves

Assume we have a representation of f in normal form with spontaneous moves:

fx = exy **where rec** y = dxy

Choose some index k. To eliminate spontaneous moves from y_k, i.e. alternatives y_k in the $d_j$xy, proceed as follows: For each j, decompose the equation $y_j = d_jxy$ into

$$y_j = d'_jxy \cup \delta_j y_k$$

where $\delta_j z$ is either z or 0, and d'_jxy does not contain an alternative y_k, and replace it by the equation

$$y_j = d'_jxy \quad \ldots \text{ for } j = k$$

$$y_j = d'_jxy \cup \delta_j(d'_kxy) \quad \ldots \text{ for } j \neq k$$

Thus we delete an alternative y_k in the equation for y_k, and substitute the modified r.h.s. for alternatives y_k in the other equation, thereby eliminating all alternatives y_k. Clearly, $z \geqslant gz \cup z$ is equivalent to $z \geqslant gz$; therefore the modification to the equation for y_k does not change the set of solutions of the system of inequations, in particular it preserves the minimal solution (of the inequations, hence of the equations). Modifying now the other equations produces an equivalent system even of equations, since we substitute according to an equation which remains in the system.

4. ALGEBRAS, CHARTS, THE OPERATION COMPUTED BY A CHART

We proceed now to the application of our results to the theory of automata and flowcharts and specialise our system M,θ to BA, the set of subsets of a given set A, together with a set of fully additive operations on BA, i.e. to a raised algebra (see below). We find it convenient to present first a generalised notion of chart (corresponding, with small variations, to the charts used informally in the previous section) and of the operation computed by a chart; these notions will cover the conventional flowchart and the transformation denoted by it, but also the (generalised) automaton and the set recognised by it. Our formalisation of charts is essentially due to P. Landin (see Landin [8]): it defines a chart as a finite (partial, nondeterminate) algebra plus entries and exits, and considers the computation of the chart in a second algebra as the process of generating pairs of elements with corresponding derivations, i.e. as generating the smallest subalgebra of the Cartesian product of the two algebras that contains the pairing of the entries with given initial values.

We start with a short survey of the necessary concepts from algebra. For a fuller treatment we refer the reader to Cohn [4] and in particular to Burstall and Landin [3] which contains many examples from programming; specifically for partial, nondeterminate algebras (usually called relational algebras) also to Grätzer [6] and Eilenberg-Wright [5].

Nondeterminate functions

By a nondeterminate function f from A to B, we mean a mapping $f: A \to BB$, i.e. equivalently, a relation $f \subseteq A \times B$. We write fa for $\bigcup_{x \in a} fx$. By a nondeterminate element of A, we mean a subset of A, except that we include elements, i.e. identify elements with unit sets.

Basic definitions from algebra

Partial nondeterminate algebras. Let Ω be a set of operators with arity, i.e. Ω is the union of disjoint sets Ω_n, $n \geqslant 0$; we say ω has arity n if $\omega \in \Omega_n$. (More generally we consider arities $n \to p$; our restriction, which is the usual one, corresponds to the restriction on θ from the beginning of last section).

A partial nondeterminate Ω-algebra (for short: an Ω-algebra) is a set A together with a mapping that associates with each $\omega \in \Omega_n$ a nondeterminate function ω_A from A^n to A. The set A is called the carrier of A; we usually do not distinguish in our notation between the algebra and its carrier. Also we usually write ω for ω_A, if the underlying algebra is understood. We speak of a total, determinate algebra if the ω_A are (total, determinate) functions $\in A^n \to A$.

Raising. The raised algebra $\hat{A}$ is the (total, determinate) algebra with carrier $\mathcal{B}A$ defined by

$$\omega a_1 \ldots a_n = \bigcup_{x_i \in a_i} \omega x_1 \ldots x_n \qquad (\omega \in \Omega_n)$$

(i.e. $\omega a = \omega(\Pi a)$, where Πa is the Cartesian product of the tuple of sets a).

$\hat{A}$ as a good system: $\mathcal{B}A$, ordered by $\subseteq$, is a complete lattice. The $\omega_{\hat{A}}$ are completely additive, i.e. $\omega(\bigcup a) = \bigcup(\omega a)$, hence monotone and continuous. Thus βA, $\{\omega_{\hat{A}} | \omega \in \Omega\}$ satisfy the assumptions an M, θ in section 1.

Subalgebras. $A' \subseteq A$ is a subalgebra of A if $\omega_{A'} : A'^n \to \mathcal{B}(A')$ is the restriction to A'^n of $\omega_A : A^n \to \mathcal{B}A$, i.e. $\omega_{A'} a = \omega_A a$ for all $a \in A'^n$.

Therefore a subset $A' \subseteq A$ can be made into a subalgebra (and then uniquely so), if and only if A' admits the $\omega \in \Omega$, i.e. $\omega_A a \subseteq A'$ for all $a \in A^n$. The subalgebra generated from a subset $x \subseteq A$ is the smallest subalgebra containing x.

The existence of this subalgebra follows from the fact that subalgebras form a complete lattice. Existence and particular construction also follow from our lemma at the end of section1 if we take for $f : \mathcal{B}A \to \mathcal{B}A$ the function $fy = \bigcup_n \bigcup_{\omega \in \Omega_n} \omega y^n$. (We would have to prove yet that f is good; in our applications, Ω will be finite and hence f definable, thus good).

The minimal algebra of A is the algebra generated from the empty set.

Direct product. The direct product A×B of algebras A and B is the algebra whose carrier is the Cartesian product A×B of the carriers and whose operations are

$$\omega_{A\times B}(a,b) = \omega_A a \times \omega_B b$$

Homomorphism, isomorphism. For these definitions we consider only total, determinate algebras, though a more general definition would be possible. Thus for total, determinate algebras A and B : A mapping $f : A \to B$ is a homomorphism from A to B if $\omega(fa_1 \ldots, fa_n) = f(\omega a_1 \ldots a_n)$, i.e. defining $f(a_1,\ldots a_n)$ as $fa_1, \ldots fa_n$:

$$\omega \circ f = f \circ \omega \ .$$

An isomorphism is a homomorphism that is one to one and onto.

The free algebra. The total, determinate algebra T is called the free Ω-algebra if for every total, determinate Ω-algebra A there is a unique homomorphism from T to A.

We say the free algebra because any two of them are isomorphic. To see that there is a free algebra, we take from T the algebra of terms: $\omega \in \Omega_o$ is a term; if $t_1, \ldots t_n$ are terms and $\omega \in \Omega_n$ $(n \geqslant 1)$, then $\omega t_1 \ldots t_n$ is a term. We define $\omega_T(t_1, \ldots t_n) = \omega t_1 \ldots t_n$. (More formally, we take the set of tuples over Ω, define it as Ω-algebra by $\omega t_1 \ldots t_n =$ $(\omega, t_1, \ldots, t_n)$ and define T as the minimal subalgebra.)

Charts

We assume from now on that Ω is finite. Given a finite Ω-algebra B, we can draw a chart like the ones used in section 3 (without entries and exits) as follows: Take as nodes the elements of the algebra. If $b \in fb_1 \ldots b_n$ in the algebra, draw a polyarc, labelled with the operator f, that joins the n-tuple of nodes $b_1, \ldots b_n$ with the node b. Conversely, given the chart, we can interpret its nodes as the elements of an algebra and the polyarcs as describing the extension of the operations of the algebra. Providing for entries and exits, we define therefore:

Definition. A chart is a finite Ω-algebra B, together with a n-tuple r of nondeterminate elements of B called entries, and a p-tuple s of nondeterminate elements of B called exits.

Example: In the following chart, there are four elements $b_1, \ldots, b_4$; there is one operation f defined by $fb_2b_1b_3 = b_4$, $fx_1x_2x_3 = \emptyset$ otherwise (there may be other operators in Ω, but in this algebra they would produce everywhere $\emptyset$) ;

(Fig.3)

r is $(\{b_1, b_3\}, b_2)$; s is b_4. (In drawing the chart, we have numbered the entrances and exits; similarly a numbering of components of polyarcs, or else some suitable convention, would be necessary).

Note that there are some differences to our informal charts concerning entries and exits, for example we did not provide there (and in our definition of normal form) for multiple exits.

The operation computed by a chart

Given a chart (B,r,s), we want to interpret it in a second algebra A. Like of B we may also think of A as given by a set of nodes connected by polyarcs describing the graphs of the operations. (This set will in general be infinite). Given a n-tuple x of initial values in A, we pair these with the corresponding entries in r; for nondeterminate x_i or r_i, we pair each element of the one with each of the other. We follow then polyarcs with equal labels to get further pairings and are interested in the p-tuple of sets of those elements of A that can in this way be paired with the corresponding exits in s. This suggests the following definition:

Definition. The operation computed by the chart (B,r,s) in the algebra $\hat{A}$ is the function $f : (\mathcal{B}A)^n \to (\mathcal{B}A)^p$ given by

$$fa = R_a s$$

where R_a is the subalgebra generated from $r \times a$ in $B \times A$. (Remember that we can consider $R_a \subseteq B \times A$ as $R_a : B \to \mathcal{B}A$.)

Notation. For fixed Ω, we take some fixed set $\{x_1, x_2, ..\}$ of nullaries disjoint from Ω. Given an Ω-algebra A and an n-tuple $(a_1, \ldots a_n)$ of nondeterminate elements of A, we write $A\,[a_1, \ldots, a_n]$ for the $(\Omega \cup \{x_1, \ldots, x_n\})$ - algebra A' with carrier A and operations

$$\omega_{A'} = \omega_A \qquad \text{for} \qquad \omega \in \Omega$$

$$\omega_{A'} = a_i \qquad \text{for} \qquad \omega = x_i$$

The subalgebra R_a can then also be described as the minimal subalgebra of $(B \times A)\,[r \times a]$, i.e. of $B[r] \times A\,[a]$.

Lemma. Let P be the minimal subalgebra of $B \times A$. The sets Pb, for $b \in B$, are the smallest sets satisfying the conditions

$$\underline{\text{if}} \quad b \in \omega b_1 \ldots b_n \quad \underline{\text{then}} \quad Pb \supseteq \omega(Pb_1, \ldots, Pb_n)$$

for all $n \geq 0$, $\omega \in \Omega_n$, $b, b_1, \ldots, b_n \in B$.

Proof. As minimal subalgebra, P satisfies $P \supseteq \omega P^n$. This is equivalent to the condition in the lemma: both conditions express

$$\underline{\text{if}}\ \ b \in \omega b_1 \dots b_n,\ a \in \omega a_1 \dots a_n,\ (b_i, a_i) \in P\ \ \underline{\text{then}}\ \ (b,a) \in P.$$

Also, for $P \subseteq P'$ the sets Pb, P'b satisfy $Pb \subseteq P'b$ and conversely. Hence the minimal solutions coincide.

In our charts, we can view the entries as additional nullaries. This suggests the following slightly modified definition of normal operation on $\hat{A}$: An operation f on $\hat{A}$ is normal-1 if fa is a normal nullary on $\hat{A}[a]$ for all $a \in \hat{A}^n$. Clearly, for nullary f our two definitions of normal operation coincide. It is not difficult to show that they coincide for arbitrary f (but we will not use this result). We get now as corollary to the lemma our characterisation of the operations computable by charts:

Corollary: An operation on $\hat{A}$ is computable by a chart if and only if it is normal-1.

Proof. We use the lemma with $B[r] \times A[x]$. A normal-1 operation f has the form fx= e(μy.dxy). Given such an f, we can immediately find a finite B[r] (by "reading" y = dxy as an algebra) such that, by the lemma, the $R_x b$ are the minimal solutions of y = dxy; ey gives us the p-tuple of exits. Conversely, given (B,r,s), we find by the lemma an equation system y = dxy for the $R_x b$. Then the operation f is

$$fx = (uy\ \underline{\underline{\text{where rec}}}\ y = dxy)$$

where the components of uy are unions of components of y. Now

$$\begin{aligned} fx &= (z\ \underline{\underline{\text{where rec}}}\ z = uy,\ y = dxy) \\ &= (z\ \underline{\underline{\text{where rec}}}\ z = u(dxy),\ y = dxy)\ . \end{aligned}$$

The components of u(dxy) are unions of components of dxy and hence satisfy the conditions on normal form. (Here we have done some simple spontaneous move elimination "by hand").

5. AUTOMATA : KLEENE'S THEOREM

The theory of generalised automata arose from the observation that a conventional automaton, i.e. string automaton, can be regarded as a special algebra (one operator nullary, the rest unary), and the suggestion to extend the study to arbitrary algebras.

Definition (1). An automaton is a finite algebra B, together with a subset b_F.

Definition (2). An automaton is a chart (B, (), b_F) with no entries and one (nondeterminate) exit.

Let val : $T \to \hat{B}$ be the unique homomorphism from the free algebra T to $\hat{B}$. If we view val as a relation, val $\subsetneq$ T×B, it is easy to prove (by induction on T) that val is the minimal subalgebra of T×B; therefore $val^{-1} \subsetneq$ B×T is the minimal subalgebra of B×T.

Definition (1). The set recognised by an automaton (B,b_F) is the set of terms $t \in T$ for which val $\in$ t b_F, i.e. the set val^{-1} b_F.

Definition (2). The set recognised by an automaton (B, (),b_F) is the (0→1) ary operation on, i.e. subset of, $\hat{T}$ computed by the chart (B,()b_F) in $\hat{T}$.

According to the preceding characterisation of val^{-1}, the two definitions are equivalent.

Definition. A subset of T is recognisable if it is recognised by some automaton.

It follows that the recognisable subsets of T coincide with the (0→1) ary operations on $\hat{T}$ computable by a chart, hence, by the result of last section, with the (0→1) ary normal-1, i.e. the (0→1) ary normal, operations on $\hat{T}$.

Call an operation $definable_1$ if it is definable under our list of functionals 1-4, but with † replaced by $^{\dagger 1}$ (see section 2).

Definition. A subset of T is regular if it is a (0→1) ary $definable_1$ operation on T.

Now $definable_1$ = definable (theorem I), definable = normal (theorem II), hence in particular $definable_1$ (0→1) ary = normal (0→1) ary, thus:

Theorem (Kleene-Thatcher-Wright). The regular and recognisable subsets of T coincide.

Thatcher-Wright's definition of regular set. In Thatcher-Wright [15], regular sets are defined as the sets that are Ω'-regular for some $\Omega' = \Omega \cup \{x_1,..,x_n\}$, where the x_i are additional nullaries. A subset of the free Ω'-algebra $T_{\Omega'}$ is Ω'-regular if it belongs to the smallest system containing all the finite subsets and closed under $\cup$, $\mathring{\varepsilon}$, $^{\varepsilon}$ (for all $\varepsilon \in \Omega'_o$), where

$u \underset{\varepsilon}{\circ} v$ = set of all terms obtainable from terms $t \in u$ by replacing all occurrences of ε in t by terms in v,

$$u^{\varepsilon} = \bigcup_i \{\lambda y.y \cup u \underset{\varepsilon}{\circ} y\}^i \{\varepsilon\}.$$

To relate this definition to ours, we associate with each Ω'-regular set u an expression E such that the value of E (interpreted in $\hat{T}$) under the assignment of sets $v_1,\ldots,v_n$ to variables $x_1,\ldots,x_n$ is $u \; x_1,\ldots\overset{\circ}{,}x_n \; (v_1,\ldots,v_n)$, where $x_1,\ldots\overset{\circ}{,}x_n$ is simultaneous substitution. It is clear how to deal with $\emptyset$, $\{x_i\}$, $\{fx_1\ldots x_n\}$ (for $f \in \Omega_n$), and $u \cup v$. For $\underset{y}{\circ}$ and ^{y} we use the translation

$$u \underset{y}{\circ} v \qquad u \text{ \underline{where} } y = v$$

$$u^y \qquad (\mu y.z \cup x) \text{ \underline{where} } z = y$$

(see the lemma at the end of section 1). The resulting expression denotes a definable$_1$ operation of its free variables. Conversely, given such an operation, we may assume that we have a where - where rec - expression for it that has variables for elements only, no simultaneous definitions, and no composite terms (like f(gx)). Then we get the corresponding set by the same rules, except that for where rec we translate into μ-notation and use

$$u^y \underset{y}{\circ} \emptyset \qquad \mu y.u \; .$$

6. FLOWCHARTS : MANNA'S FORMULAS

In the present section we consider charts with all operators unary. By a straightforward translation, we show how the operation computed by a chart can be expressed in second order logic, thus obtaining Manna's formulas for termination and correctness of flowcharts (see Manna [9], [10]).

A flowchart in usual notation contains both operations and predicates. We can eliminate the latter by introducing for each predicate p the partial identity functions I_p and $I_{\neg p}$ on the ranges of p and not p, respectively. Thus $I_p x$ is x if px holds, undefined otherwise; similarly for $I_{\neg p}$.

Now let (B,r,s) be a chart with all operators unary. We assume that there is one entry and one exit only and that both are determinate, i.e. that r and s are elements of B. Let A be the algebra in which we want to interpret the chart. According to the results of section 4, the operation f computed by the chart in A is

$$fx = y_m \text{ \underline{where rec} } y = dxy$$

(assuming that the chart has m nodes, associating y_m with the exit, and writing y for $(y_1,\dots,y_m)$). The components $d_i xy$ of dxy are unions of terms that are either x or hy_j $(h \in \Omega)$.

<u>Termination, partial correctness, correctness.</u> We say that the chart <u>terminates</u> (under the given interpretation) for a given element $a \in A$, if $fa \neq \emptyset$; that it is <u>partially correct</u> for subsets x, $x' \subseteq A$, if $fx \subseteq x'$; that it is <u>correct</u> for x, $x' \subseteq A$, if $fa \cap x' \neq \emptyset$ for all $a \in x$.

Thus termination expresses that for each $a \in A$ there will be at least one result; partial correctness expresses that <u>if</u> there are results for an $a \in x$, then they are in x'. The definition of correctness is obvious for <u>determinate</u> interpretations, i.e. for interpretations for which fa is either $\emptyset$ or a single element. In the general case, it expresses only that <u>some</u> result is in x' for $a \in x$. (For a different definition in the nondeterminate case, which however can <u>not</u> be expressed in terms of f alone, see Manna [11].)

<u>Translation into logic.</u> We assume that the operations $h \in \Omega$ on A are (partial) determinate, i.e. $ha = \emptyset$ or $\in A$ for $a \in A$. For each $h \in \Omega$, we assume that we have a predicate p testing for the domain of h, i.e. $pa = (ha \neq \emptyset)$.

The system of sets $y = (y_1,\dots,y_m)$ is the smallest solution of $y \supseteq dxy$; therefore $a \in A$ is in fx if it is in y_m for <u>every</u> y satisfying $y \supseteq dxy$. Thus we get the following translations:

$a \in fx$	$(\forall y)\ (y \supseteq dxy \rightarrow a \in y_m)$
$fa \neq \emptyset$	$(\forall y)\ (y \supseteq day \rightarrow y_m \neq \emptyset)$
$fx \subseteq x'$	$(\exists y)\ (y \supseteq dxy \wedge y_m \subseteq x')$
$(\forall a)\ (a \in x \rightarrow fa \cap x' \neq \emptyset)$	$(\forall y)\ (\forall a)\ (a \in x \wedge y \supseteq day \rightarrow y_m \cap x' \neq \emptyset)$

Now $y \supseteq dxy$ is a conjunction of conditions $y_i \supseteq hy_j$, $y_i \supseteq x$, for which we get the translations $(\forall a)\ (a \in y_j \cap pa \rightarrow ha \in y_i)$ and $(\forall a)\ (a \in x \rightarrow a \in y_i)$, respectively. Also $\emptyset$ and $\cap$ can easily be eliminated by first order formulas in ε. Finally, $a \in x$ becomes qa if we use predicates q of sets x. Therefore we have the result that termination, partial correctness, correctness can be expressed respectively as validity, satisfiability, validity of certain first order formulas.

<u>Example 1.</u> Consider the program (in Algol-like rather than in flowchart notation):

g;L:h;M:j; <u>if</u> p <u>then</u> (k; <u>goto</u> L); l; <u>if</u> q <u>then</u> (m; <u>goto</u> M); n .

The operation f computed by this chart is

$$
\begin{aligned}
fx = y_6 \ \underline{\underline{\text{where rec}}}\ y_1 &= x \\
y_2 &= gy_1 \cup k(p \rightarrow' y_4) \\
y_3 &= hy_2 \cup m(q \rightarrow' y_5) \\
y_4 &= jy_3 \\
y_5 &= l(\neg p \rightarrow' y_4) \\
y_6 &= n(\neg q \rightarrow' y_5)
\end{aligned}
$$

where we have written $p \rightarrow' a$ for $I_p a$. By substitution we can simplify this to

$$
\begin{aligned}
fx = (\neg q \rightarrow' y_5) \ \underline{\underline{\text{where rec}}}\ y_4 &= j(h(gx \cup k(p \rightarrow' y_4)) \cup m(q \rightarrow' y_5)) \\
y_5 &= l(\neg p \rightarrow' y_4)
\end{aligned}
$$

Note that we could eliminate also y_5 at the cost of duplicating some of the operators. Also, we could use * (iteration as familiar from regular expressions, see also end of section 1) and thus avoid any auxiliary definition, but at the cost of even more duplication. The formula whose validity expresses termination, i.e. $fa \neq \emptyset$, becomes

$$
\begin{aligned}
& q_1 a \wedge \\
& (\forall b)[(q_1 b \rightarrow q_2(gb)) \wedge (q_2 b \rightarrow q_3(hb)) \wedge (q_3 b \rightarrow q_4(jb)) \wedge \\
& \quad (q_4 b \wedge pb \rightarrow q_2(kb)) \wedge (q_4 b \wedge \neg pb \rightarrow q_5(lb)) \wedge \\
& \quad (q_5 b \wedge qb \rightarrow q_3(mb)) \wedge (q_5 b \wedge \neg qb \rightarrow q_6(nb))] \\
& \rightarrow (\exists b)(q_6 b)
\end{aligned}
$$

(Note that in the last formula we "collected arcs" with the same source, whereas for writing the equation system we had to collect arcs with the same target.)

Example 2. Consider the "count-down" program

L: $\underline{\underline{\text{if}}}$ b=0 $\underline{\underline{\text{then}}}$ (n:=pn; $\underline{\underline{\text{goto}}}$ L)

where p is the predecessor function $\lambda n.n-1$. The operation computed by this program is

$$
\begin{aligned}
fx = y_2 \ \underline{\underline{\text{where rec}}}\ y_1 &= x \cup p(I_{\neq 0} \rightarrow' y_1) \\
y_2 &= I_{=0}\, y_1
\end{aligned}
$$

Termination becomes validity of

$$q_1 n \wedge (\forall m)[(q_1 m \wedge m \neq 0 \rightarrow q_1(pm)) \wedge (q_1 m \wedge m=0 \rightarrow q_2 m)] \rightarrow \exists m. q_2 m$$

i.e. equivalently of

$$q_1 n \wedge (\forall m)\ (q_1 m \wedge m \neq 0 \rightarrow q_1(pm)) \rightarrow q_1 0$$

i.e. the condition that every subset containing n and closed under p must contain 0. (To appreciate this result, recall that in fact we are asking which condition an arbitrary interpretation, with arbitrary constant 0 and function p, must satisfy in order that the above program terminates for argument n.)

CONCLUSION

We have obtained the regular-equals-recognisable theorem of generalised automata theory as a special case of two theorems on definable operations in general algebras. Definable operations arise from the familiar concept of derived operations by adding union and definition by recursion as rules for forming new operations. Our proofs consist in simple and intuitively obvious transformations on expressions allowing recursive definitions.

Definable operations are the operations computed by (generalised) flowcharts. Even for conventional flowcharts, the use of simultaneous recursion allows for a formulation of that operation which is simpler, and more directly tied to the structure of the flowchart, than the usual formulation obtained by the iteration operator*. By translating into predicate calculus, we obtained Manna's formulas for termination and correctness of flowcharts, thus showing a connection to what may have seemed an isolated technique.

It would be interesting to extend the study to the context-free case, i.e. to stack-automata on the automata side, to procedures on the programming language side. (De Bakker - Scott [1] give already results on procedures, also Manna's technique has been extended to deal with procedures by Manna-Pnueli [12].) Other relevant and interesting topics are parallel computation and Landin's generalised jumping operator J.

Relation to other work

The relevance of fixed point theorems to the theory of flowcharts has been realised by several authors at about the same time (see de Bakker - Scott [1], Park [13]). Scott also has the μ-operator and the elimination of simultaneous recursion.

Kleene's generalised theorem and its proof are due to Thatcher-Wright [15]. The motivation to replace their definition of regular set by something using derivable (and going from there:definable) operations came at least partly from the use of "theories" in Eilenberg-Wright [5]; their paper also contains a theorem (theorem 2) that is essentially our lemma in section 4 on the minimal subalgebra of B×A (with A = T).

As mentioned earlier, our treatment of charts is due to ideas of Landin [8]. There are many other relationships to that paper. Perhaps the main difference in approach is that there is a homomorphism from formal objects (algebras, charts) to operations denoted by them is established, whereas our theorem II talks on operations only and confines the use of where - where rec - expressions to the informal level.

Acknowledgements. This is a report on research that I carried out while working for Peter Landin at Queen Mary College, London, under a Research Grant of the S.R.C. I would like to thank P. Landin for innumerably many suggestions and discussions. I would also like to acknowledge an early discussion I had with Malcom Bird on the subject.

REFERENCES

[1] J. W. de Bakker, D. Scott: A theory of programs. - IBM Seminar Vienna, August 1969 (unpublished).

[2] M. R. Bird: Binary relations and flow-diagrams. - Memorandum No.11, Sept. 1969, Computer and Logic Research Group, University of Swansea.

[3] R. M. Burstall, P. Landin: Programs and their proofs: an algebraic approach. - Machine Intelligence 4, (B. Meltzer, D. Michie Eds.), Edinburgh University Press 1969.

[4] P. M. Cohn: Universal algebra. - Harper Row. New York - London 1965.

[5] S. Eilenberg, J. B. Wright: Automata in general algebras. - Information and Control 11, 4, Oct. 1967.

[6] G. Grätzer: Universal algebra. - Van Nostrand, Princetown - London 1969.

[7] P. Landin: The mechanical evaluation of expressions. - Comp. Journal Jan. 1964.

[8] P. Landin: Minimal subalgebras and direct products - a scenario for the theory of computation. - Machine Intelligence 5.

[9] Z. Manna: Properties of programs and the first order predicate calculus. - JACM 16, 2, April 1969.

[10] Z. Manna: The correctness of programs. - J. Comp.Syst. Sciences 3, 1969.

[11] Z. Manna: The correctness of nondeterministic programs. - A. I. Memo No.95, Stanford University, 1969.

[12] Z. Manna, A. Pnueli: Formalisation of properties of recursively defined functions. - A. I. Memo No.82, Stanford 1969.

[13] D. Park: Some metatheorems for program equivalence proofs. - Machine Intelligence 5.

[14] A. Tarski: A lattice-theoretic fixpoint theorem and its applications. - Pacific J. Math. 5, p. 285-309, 1955.

[15] J. W. Thatcher, J. B. Wright: Generalised finite automata theory with an application to a decision problem of second-order logic. - Math. Syst. Theory, 2, 1, 1968.

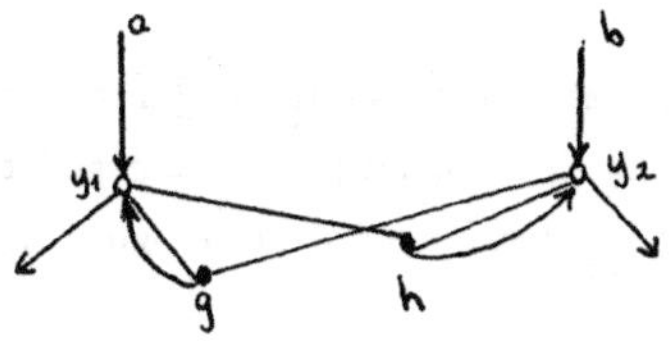

Fig.1.

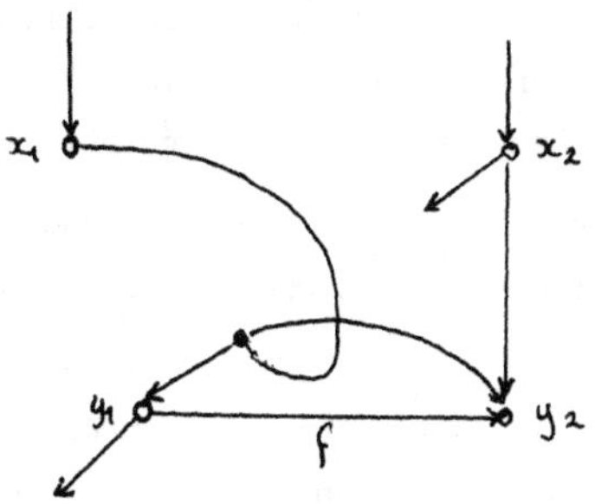

Fig.2.

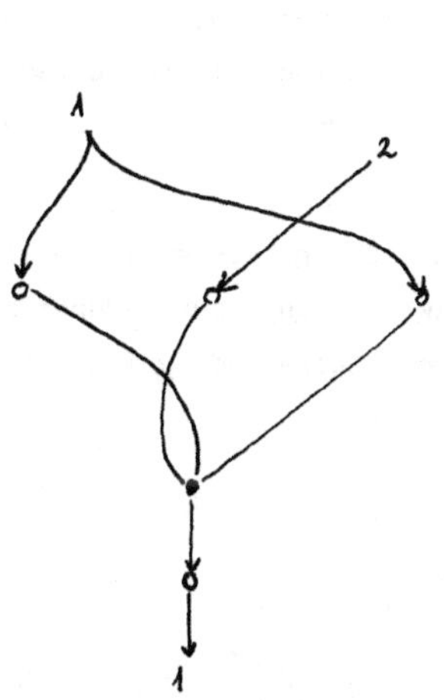

Fig.3.

FORMALIZATION OF STORAGE PROPERTIES

by

H. Bekić and K. Walk

INTRODUCTION

This paper is a contribution to the design of abstract machines for the interpretation of programs. It is concerned with a particular component, the storage component, of the states of abstract machines interpreting programs written in languages like ALGOL 68 and PL/I.

The aim of the paper is to present a model of storage which avoids any special constructions not implied by the languages to be modelled. The design followed closely the informal descriptions of the languages. Notions present in informal descriptions like ALGOL 68 "names" and "modes", PL/I "pointers", etc., will have their formal counterpart in the model. In some cases, however, certain informal notions, like "instances of values" in ALGOL 68, appeared to be unnecessary. They were avoided in the design of the model, making it conceptually simpler than the informal description.

A general storage model is described in section 1. It serves as the common basis for sections 2 and 3, which present the specific storage properties of ALGOL 68 and PL/I, respectively.

The scope of the paper is confined to the investigation of the properties of the storage component of abstract interpreters, i.e., that component which is changed by assignment and allocation of variables, and which represents a (partial) mapping from "locations" to "values". Locations are entities which, during program interpretation, become associated with identifiers of variables. For the languages under consideration, this intermediate step between identifier and value of a variable is mandatory. It introduces the possibility that different variables share their values in the sense that their identifiers are associated with the same location. In these languages locations, or a derivative of locations like the PL/I pointers, also occur as values of variables.

No regard is given in this paper to the problems of the scope of identifiers and the life-time of allocations. "Identifier" will always mean unique identifier. "Storage" will mean internal storage, excluding any devices addressed by input or output operations.

NOTATION

$\neg$	not
&	and
$\vee$	or
$\supset$	implication
$\equiv$	equivalence
$(\exists! x)(\ldots)$	there is exactly one x such that ...
$(\exists! x\in X)(\ldots)$	there is exactly one $x\in X$ such that ...
$\in$	element of
$\cup$, $\bigcup$	set union
$\subseteq$	subset or equal
$\{\}$	empty set
$\{x \mid \ldots\}$	the set of elements x such that ...
$(x_1, x_2, \ldots)$	list of elements $x_1, x_2, \ldots$
$\frown$	concatenation of lists
$f:L\to V$, $(f:L\overset{p}{\to}V)$	f is a (partial) mapping from L to V, L = domain f, V = range f

1. A GENERAL STORAGE MODEL

The storage model to be described in this section originally arose from a study of value classes and storage in ALGOL 68. It then proved possible to generalize some of the underlying postulates in such a way that the model could also be used for reflecting the more machine-like properties of PL/I storage.

Like other models (e.g., in Elgot and Robinson (1964), Strachey (1966)), this one views storage as a "contents"-function from "locations" (called, in different programming languages, "variables", "left-hand values", "generations" of variables, "names") to "values". The main objective in setting up the model was to cover the following two phenomena (exemplified by fixed and flexible arrays in ALGOL 68):

(a) Composite locations. The contents of a location ("the value referred to by a name", in ALGOL 68 terminology) may be allowed to vary over all values of a fixed given structuring, e.g., all one-dimensional arrays with given bounds and given element attributes. This induces a corresponding structure on the location which is preserved by the contents-function: contents of i-th component = i-th component of contents.

(b) Flexible locations. More generally, the contents of a location may have any of a prescribed set of structurings; e.g., it may vary over arrays with arbitrary upper bound. Then assignment of a value to a location will affect not only the contents of the location but also the existence of component locations.

Thus we model storage as a function from a (changeable) set of "active" or "allocated" locations to the set of values satisfying certain consistency conditions; this function will be partial, to mirror allocated locations that have not yet been assigned to.

Each location has associated with it a "range", the set of values over which its contents may vary; in programming languages, these sets are usually denoted by "attributes". Thus our notion of location contains more information than that of PL/I-"pointer", which can be characterized as location minus attributes.

We proceed by isolating properties of values and value classes that affect storage structure. We then introduce the set of locations, the notion of storage, and finally allocation and assignment as operations on storages.

1.1. Values

We assume a set V of values, with a partition into two disjoint subsets, elementary and composite values. Composite values will have a structure that induces a corresponding structure on locations containing such a value; with elementary values, we are not interested in any further structure.

Elementary values

We do not assume any further properties of elementary values. Examples for elementary values would be reals, or intergers, or pointers (even pointers to composite values).

Composite values

A composite value v has:

$$\text{an index-set} \quad I=\text{indexset}(v) , \qquad (1.1)$$

$$\text{components} \quad v_i=\text{compval}(v,i), \text{ for } i \in I .$$

Here compval(v,i) , for given v , is a partial function of $i \in I$, i.e., v_i may be undefined; if v_i is defined, it shall again be a value.

Examples for composite values in conventional programming languages are arrays, where the index-set is the set of n-tuples of integers within given bounds, and structures, where the index-set is a set of identifiers or selectors. Also the storages to be introduced below, and in particular PL/I-areas, can be regarded as composite values.

The value v need not be uniquely determined by its index-set I and its components v_i (see, however, the postulate (1.6) on composite ranges below). Examples are again provided by PL/I-areas, which are additionally characterized by their "size"; also by the difference of the two sets union(struct(int,int,int),struct(int,int,real))

and

struct(int,int,union(int,real))

in ALGOL 68 (assuming some standard selectors for the structure components), which forces the component ranges to be included in the characterization of multiple and structured values (see section 2.1).

Finite nesting assumption

A component v_i may itself be composite and thus have components v_{ij} . We assume that this process cannot be iterated indefinitely, i.e., that $v_{ij\ldots}$ eventually yields elementary or undefined. This excludes, for example, infinitely nested structures, though not self-referential structures: a pointer to a structure would count as elementary.

1.2. Ranges

We assume a set of ranges, i.e., of sets of values. Ranges arise as ranges of locations, i.e., as the sets of values over which the contents of a location may vary. We assume that each value is in some range

$$V = \bigcup \text{ ranges} . \qquad (1.2)$$

Since one of the operations for forming new ranges is set union, ranges will, in general, not be disjoint.

In programming languages, ranges are described by "types", or "modes", or "attributes". These may include dynamic information, like array bounds.

Ranges fall into three disjoint sub-classes: elementary, composite, and flexible ranges.

Elementary ranges

Again, we make no further assumptions on elementary ranges R , except of course,

$$v \in R \supset v \quad \text{is elementary.} \qquad (1.3)$$

Composite ranges

A composite range R has:

an index-set I=indexset(R) , (1.4)

component ranges R_i=comprange(R,i) , for $i \in I$;
the R_i are again ranges.

The elements of R shall be composite values v with indexset I and with components in the corresponding component range:

$$v \in R \supset v \text{ is composite, } \operatorname{indexset}(v)=I ,\quad v_i \text{ , if defined, } \in R_i \ . \qquad (1.5)$$

In R , each system of components shall uniquely determine a composite value: for any system $v^{(i)}$, $i \in I$, such that $v^{(i)} \in R_i$ or undefined:

$$(\exists ! v)(v_i = v^{(i)}) \qquad (1.6)$$

(strong equality: both sides undefined, or both defined and equal).

Examples of composite ranges are: the set of arrays of given dimension, bounds, and elements in a given range (here, the R_i are all equal); the set of structures with given selectors and elements in given component ranges. The last postulate above is used to express that, e.g., the contents of an array location is uniquely determined by the contents of its components.

Flexible ranges

A flexible range R is uniquely decomposable into a union

$$R=R' \cup R'' \cup \ldots \qquad (1.7)$$

of disjoint, non-flexible ranges R',R",..., the alternatives of R. We also write $R= \bigcup$ alternatives(R) , where alternatives(R) is the set of ranges {R',R",...} .

Thus, taking examples from ALGOL 68, the alternatives of the set union(int,real) would be the sets int and real . The alternatives of [1:flex]real would be the sets [1;0]real , [1;1]real , [1;2]real , ... , and the alternatives of union(int,[ ]real) would be the set int and the infinite number of sets [i:k]real . In PL/I, an example for a flexible range is the set of areas of given size.

We have assumed that elementary, composite, and flexible ranges are mutually different. Therefore, if we disregard the empty set, a flexible range has at least two alternatives. Our assumption of unique decomposition proved to be satisfied in the cases we wanted to model. The assumption could be weakened by introducing a flexible range as a set together with a decomposition rule.

Given a value $v \in R$, we can define the current alternative of R as the alternative that contains v :

$$\operatorname{curralt}(R,v) = \text{the range } R' \in \operatorname{alternatives}(R) \text{ such that } v \in R' \ . \qquad (1.8)$$

1.3. Locations

We assume a set L of locations, with a partial relation l indep l' on L, called independence (which expresses "having no common parts").

Each location $l \in L$ has a range, R=range(l) , and is correspondingly classified as elementary, composite, or flexible.

Components of locations

Corresponding to the components of composite values, we introduce components of composite and flexible locations, i.e., of locations that can contain composite values. Different components of a composite location, or different components "under the same alternative" of a flexible location, can be assigned values independently and hence are postulated to be independent; on the other hand, nothing is assumed concerning the relation between components of flexible locations under different alternatives.

For composite l , R=range(l) :

$$\begin{aligned} &l \text{ has components} \\ &l_i = \text{comploc}(l,i) \quad \text{for } i \in \text{indexset}(R) \text{ , with:} \\ &l_i \in L, \quad \text{range}(l_i)=R_i \text{ , } l_i \text{ indep } l_j \quad \text{for } i \neq j \text{ .} \end{aligned} \tag{1.9}$$

For flexible l , R ∈ alternatives (range(l)) , R composite:

$$\begin{aligned} &l \text{ has components} \\ &l_i^R = \text{compflexloc}(l,R,i) \quad \text{for } i \in \text{indexset}(R) \text{ , with:} \\ &l_i^R \in L, \quad \text{range}(l_i^R)=R_i \text{ , } l_i^R \text{ indep } l_j^R \quad \text{for } i \neq j \text{ .} \end{aligned} \tag{1.10}$$

We define sub-location as the reflexive transitive closure of the relation component, i.e., l' is a sub-location of l if it is either l itself or a sub-location of a component of l .

Super-locations

Sometimes it is necessary to construct a composite location from its components. Examples for this situation are provided by "cross-sections" of arrays, e.g., taking a row or a column of a matrix, and by "rowing", i.e., constructing an array location whose only component is a given location, in ALGOL 68. The latter example shows that the "super-location" so obtained need not be a part of a previously introduced location. For simplicity, we are quite liberal in postulating the existence of unique super-locations: our assumption below could be weakened by restricting it to some ranges R and systems of components $l(i)$. On the other hand, there is no need to postulate the construction of flexible super-locations.

For composite R , and a system of locations $l^{(i)}$, $i \in \text{indexset}(R)$, with $\text{range}(l^{(i)})=R_i$, $l^{(i)}$ indep $l^{(j)}$ for $i \neq j$:

$$(\exists ! l)(\text{range}(l)=R\ ,\ l_i=l^{(i)} \text{ for } i \in \text{indexset}(R))\ . \qquad (1.11)$$

Independence

According to our informal characterization above, we postulate independence as a partial relation that is irreflexive and symmetric. Independence from l implies independence from its components; for composite locations, the converse also holds (whereas flexible locations might use some "hidden" parts to store information concerning the current alternative).

Thus:

$$\neg(l \text{ indep } l)\ ,\ l \text{ indep } l' \equiv l' \text{ indep } l\ . \qquad (1.12)$$

For composite l' :

$$l \text{ indep } l' \equiv l \text{ indep } l'_i \text{ for all } i \in \text{indexset}(\text{range}(l'))\ . \qquad (1.13)$$

For flexible l' :

$$l \text{ indep } l' \supset l \text{ indep } l'^{R}_i \text{ for all } i \in \text{indexset}(R)\ , \qquad (1.14)$$
$$R \text{ composite},\ R \in \text{alternatives}(\text{range}(l'))\ .$$

1.4. Storages

Assume we are given a set $L_o \subseteq \mathcal{L}$ of independent locations, and a partial function

$$f_o : L_o \overset{\sim}{\to} V$$

from L_o to the set of values which is range-respecting, i.e. satisfies

$$f_o(l)\ ,\ \text{if defined,} \in \text{range}(l)\ .$$

We can extend f_o to a function $f{:}\mathcal{L} \overset{\sim}{\to} V$ that coincides with f_o on L_o , i.e.,

$$f(l)=f_o(l) \quad \text{for } l \in L_o$$

(strong equality), and is consistently complete under the construction of component and super-locations:

$$f(l)=v \equiv f(l_i)=v_i \quad \text{for all } i \in \text{indexset}(\text{range}(l)), \text{ for composite } l \in L, \text{ composite } v \tag{1.15}$$

$$f(l)=v \supset f(l_i^R)=v_i \quad \text{for all } i \in \text{indexset}(\text{range}(l)), R=\text{curralt}(\text{range}(l),v), \text{ for flexible } l \in L, \text{ composite } v . \tag{1.16}$$

Thus, for flexible locations l, we use the contents $f(l)$ of l to determine the "currently active" component locations.

It follows from the independence of the elements of L_0 and from our uniqueness assumptions on composite values and composite locations that such an extension is indeed possible, provided we identify, for composite l, the case " $f(l)$ undefined" with the case " $f(l)$=the $v \in \text{range}(l)$ such that all components v_i undefined". For example, any composite $l \in L_0$ will "reappear", in the course of constructing f, as the super-location built from its components l_i ; but then $f(l)$ will be $f_0(l)$, because both are the unique $v \in \text{range}(l)$ with $v=f(l_i)$.

In particular, we can consider the function $f=\text{extend}(f_0)$ generated from f_0 under the above rules, i.e., the smallest consistently complete extension of f_0, where the partial function $f:L \tilde{\to} V$ is smaller than the partial function function $f':L' \tilde{\to} V$, if $L \subseteq L'$, $f(l)=f'(l)$ for $l \in L$.

We define now a storage as a pair

$$S=(L, f_0 : L_0 \tilde{\to} V) \tag{1.17}$$

where L is a set of locations as introduced above (fixed in the present model, but variable in the applications), and f_0 is a partial range-respecting function from an independent subset $L_0 \subseteq L$ to V. We write

$$L=\text{Locs}(S), \quad f_0=\text{level 1 contents}(S), \quad L_0=\text{level 1 locs}(S)$$

and call L the locations, f_0 the level-one contents-function, L_0 the level-one locations of S. Extending f_0 to the function $\text{extend}(f_0)=f:L \tilde{\to} V$, we write

$$f=\text{contents}(S), \quad L=\text{actlos}(S)$$

and call f the contents-function, L the active locations of S. For $l \in L$, we define

$$l(S)=f(l),$$

thus using l as a "selector" of S .

We call f_0 a base of f. Clearly f has many bases, e.g., we can replace a composite location by its components. In the definition of S, we could have abstracted from the particular base by using f instead of f_0. However, it seemed advantageous to retain f_0, because level-one locations reflect the way locations get and loose existence (through allocating and freeing, e.g., by crossing block boundaries), and because they have special properties in PL/I.

1.5. Allocation, Freeing, Assignment

We can now define the main operations on storages:

Allocation

For $S=(L,f_0:L_0 \tilde{\to} V)$ and $l \in L$, l indep l' for all $l' \in L_0$, we define

$$(\text{allocate } l)(S)= \text{ the storage } S'=(L,f':L_0 \cup \{l\} \tilde{\to} V) \quad (1.18)$$
$$\text{such that } l(S') \text{ undefined, } l'(S')=l'(S) \text{ for } l' \in L_0 ,$$

i.e., we add the independent location l to the set of level-one locations without initializing it. In a programming language, l is usually given by its range R, so we need a non-determinate function generate such that

$$(\text{generate } R)(S)=\underline{\text{some}} \ l \in L , \ l \text{ indep } l' \quad (1.19)$$
$$\text{for all } l' \in L_0 , \text{ range}(l)=R .$$

Allocation then is performed by

$$\text{allocate}((\text{generate } R)(S))(S) .$$

Note that the conditions l indep l' for all $l' \in L_0$ and l indep l' for all $l' \in L$ are equivalent.

Freeing

For $S=(L,f_0:L_0 \tilde{\to} V)$, $l \in L_0$:

$$(\text{free } l)(S)= \text{ the storage } S'=(L,f_0':L_0-\{l\} \tilde{\to} V) \text{ such that} \quad (1.20)$$
$$l'(S')=l'(S) \text{ for } l' \in L_0-\{l\} ,$$

i.e., we restrict f_0 to $L_0-\{l\}$.

Assignment

For $S=(L,f_0:L_0 \ V)$, $l \in L=\text{actlocs}(S)$, $v \in \text{range}(l)$:

$(l:=v)(S)=$ the storage $S'=(L,f'_0 : L_0 \to V)$ such that (1.21)

$l(S')=v$,

$l'(S')=l(S')$ for $l' \in L$, l' indep l ,

$l'(S') \in curralt(l', l'(S))$ for flexible $l' \in L$, $\neg(l'$ indep $l)$,

l' not a sub-location of l .

Thus, we leave unchanged the set L_0 of level-one locations and define a new function $f':L' \to V$ by prescribing its value for l and for locations independent from l . These conditions would be sufficient, except for flexible locations that have parts with l in common, without being completely contained in l ; for those locations, we must explicitly add the condition that the current alternative will not be changed by the assignment.

2. STORAGE PROPERTIES OF ALGOL 68

The storage-related properties of ALGOL 68 can easily be introduced in terms of the notions of our general model. Thus, structures and "fixed" arrays from composite ranges, "flexible" arrays and unions form flexible ranges. "Names" are locations, and the relation "to refer to" is the contents-function.

We note the following points in which our description method differs from the one used in the ALGOL 68 Report, Van Wijngaarden (Ed.), (1969). In fact, these points were the original motivation in setting up the general model.

Declarers denote value classes

We associate with each "declarer" a class of values, so that the role of declarers can be described in the following simple way:

an "identity declaration" $\delta id=v$, where δ is a declarer, id an identifier, v denotes a value, tests v for being in the class δ and makes id denote v ;
a "generator" (essentially given by a declarer δ) chooses a new name with range δ ;
an assignment statement tests the value of the right-hand side for being in the range of the name denoted by the left-hand side and replaces the contents of the name.

No linearization of arrays

In the ALGOL 68 Report, arrays ("multiple values") are introduced as linear sequences of their elements, plus some descriptive information, rather than as n-dimensional aggregates of their elements. This linearization turns out to be a purely descriptional feature (unlike to the situation in PL/I, where, e.g., overlay-defining forces particular assumptions on linearization). Restoring the usual notion results, among other things, in a simpler definition of "slicing" (i.e., subscripting, forming cross-sections).

Flexibility a property of names

In the ALGOL 68 Report, part of the descriptive information in a multiple value are the "states" which indicate, for each bound, whether the value can be replaced by one with differing bound. But this really is a property of the range of the name containing the value, i.e., a property of names, not of multiple values.

No "instances"

To distinguish between values in different locations, i.e., referred to by different names, one just has to remember the names--there is no need to introduce "instances" of values.

2.1. Values, Modes, Ranges, Sub-Modes

Values are organized in certain classes, called modes; thus, the set of reals of given length is a mode, and the set of n-dimensional arrays (with arbitrary bounds) of elements in a given mode is again a mode. Declarers can prescribe some or all of the bounds of arrays; therefore, we introduce finer classes which, together with the modes, form the possible ranges of names. By prescriptions on bounds of array names (in identity declarations), we obtain even finer classes which, together with the ranges, we call sub-modes.

There are certain basic modes, e.g., the set of reals mentioned before, and certain rules for constructing new modes from given modes, e.g., constructing the set of procedures ("routines") with given argument and result modes.

For the present purpose, we are interested in the following modes and ranges:

(a) Arrays

An n-dimensional array (or "multiple value") v is characterized by:

an n-tuple of integer pairs, $l_1:u_1,\ldots l_n:u_n$, the lower and upper bounds of v ;

its element mode M ;

its elements $v[i_1,\ldots,i_n]$ M , for $l_k \leq i_k \leq u_k$, $1 \leq k \leq n$.

(We have to include the element mode as part of the information characterizing an array, similarly the field modes for structures below. For an example concerning structures, see the beginning of section 1.1.) Clearly, v can be regarded as a composite value, with

$$\text{indexset}(v)=\{<i_1,\ldots,i_n> \mid l_k \leq i_k \leq u_k\} ,$$

$$\text{compval}(v,<i_1,\ldots i_n>)=v[i_1,\ldots i_n] .$$

Given a non-array range R and an n-tuple $ol\ :ou\ ,\dots ol_n:ou_n$ of pairs of "optional" bounds, i.e., each ol_i,ou_i is either an integer or "unspecified", we define the <u>array range</u>

$$ol\ :ou\ ,\dots ol_n:ou_n\ R = \text{the set of n-dimensional arrays with} \tag{2.1}$$

$$\text{bounds} \begin{cases} \text{as given, where specified} \\ \text{arbitrary, otherwise ,} \end{cases}$$

element mode $M = \text{mode } R$,

elements $\in R$,

(where the <u>mode of</u> a range, or more generally of a sub-mode below, is obtained by ignoring restrictions on bounds).

We call [...]R <u>fixed</u> or <u>flexible</u>, and correspondingly classify it as composite or flexible in the sense of section 1.2, depending upon whether all bounds are specified or not. Similarly, we say that [...]R is fixed or flexible <u>at</u> the i-th lower-upper bound.

(b) <u>Structures</u>

A <u>structure</u> (or "structured value") v is characterized by:

an n-tuple $(n\geq 1)$ of identifiers $id_1,\dots,id_n$, its <u>selectors</u>,

an n-tuple of modes $M_1,\dots,M_n$, its <u>field modes</u>,

its <u>fields</u> id_i of $v \in M_i$ $(1\leq i\leq n)$,

(thus the ordering of the selectors is relevant).

Again, a structure v can be considered as a component value, with $\text{indexset}(v) = \{id_1,\dots,id_n\}$, $\text{subval}(v,id_i) = id_i$ of v . We define the composite <u>structure range</u>

$$(id_1{:}R_1,\dots,id_n{:}R_n) = \text{the set of structures } v \text{ with} \tag{2.2}$$

selectors $id_1,\dots,id_n$,

element modes $M_i = \text{mode } R_i$,

elements id_i of $v \in R_i$,

where the R_i are arbitrary ranges; if the R_i are modes, then the resulting range is a <u>structure mode</u>.

(c) <u>Unions</u>

If the M_i are modes, $M = M_1 \dots M_n$ is again a mode, the <u>union</u> of the M_i . If we disregard the empty set, it is sufficient to assume $n\geq 2$ and the M_i all different and not again unions. (There is a further restriction that the M_i in such a decomposition are not "related", i.e., transferable into each other by certain automatic conversions.) Unions are classified as flexible ranges.

(d) Names

Names are locations in the sense of section 1.3, with the predicates, operations, and relations postulated there. Thus, composite or flexible names, i.e., names with composite or flexible range, have sub-locations, two names may be independent, etc.

The new thing here is that names are values, i.e., we include the set of names in the set of values. For each range R, we postulate a countable set of independent names with range R. We define

$$\text{ref } R = \text{the set of names with range } R \,. \qquad (2.3)$$

Even if R is a mode, ref R is not a mode or range, but only a "sub-mode". We get a name mode if we form the union $\bigcup$ ref R over all ranges R such that mode R is a given mode M; we call this mode ref M (slightly ambiguously: ref has a different meaning whether we expect it to produce a mode or a sub-mode).

From given sub-modes T which are name sets, we can form others by the following two operations, starting with T's of the form ref R :

$[ol_1 os_1 : ou_1 ot_1, \ldots, ol_n os_n : ou_n ot_n]_{lhs} T$ = the set of n-dimensional array names (2.4)

which are fixed or flexible at the i-th lower-upper bound, where so restricted by os_i/ot_i,

which have bounds as given, where they are fixed and a bound is specified,

which have element mode M,

which have element names in T,

where the os_i, ot_i are optional states, i.e., each is "fix", "flex", or unspecified, the ol_i, ou_i are optional bounds, and M is determined by mode T=ref M ;

$(id\,:T\,, \ldots, id_n : T_n)_{lhs}$ = the set of structure names l with (2.5)

selectors $id_1, \ldots, id_n$,

field modes M_i,

id_i of $l \in T_i$,

where again mode T_i=ref M_i. Straightforward extension to certain notions like "fixed" or " id_i of l ", that have been introduced above for ranges or values, can be made for names.

Classification of ranges into elementary, composite, flexible

We have already classified arrays, structures, and unions. All remaining ranges, e.g., sets of names, are elementary. It follows that flexible ranges are indeed uniquely decomposable into disjoint non-flexible alternatives; for example, a flexible array range is decomposed into fixed array ranges; a union is decomposed into non-union alternatives, with those alternatives further decomposed if they are flexible arrays.

Denoting modes, ranges, sub-modes; declarers

Sub-modes (hence ranges, modes) are denoted by declarers; the distinction between modes, ranges, sub-modes, corresponds to the distinction between virtual, actual, formal declarers. We only give a few examples concerning arrays and array names; ε stands for "unspecified".

(a) virtual array declarer

[,]real denotes row^2(reals of length 1) .

(b) actual array declarer

[1:0]flex char denotes [1:ε]characters .

Thus a bound can, and in fact must, be specified in the flex case. This bound does not influence the range denoted by the declarer, but restricts the choice of a value at the automatic initialization coupled with allocation.

(c) formal array declarer in a name declarer

ref[1:flex,1:10either]char denotes

$[1\text{"fix"}:\varepsilon\text{"flex"},1\text{"fix"}:10\varepsilon]_{lhs}$(ref(characters)) .

Thus, in a state position of a formal declarer, "no state" means "fix", either means "unspecified".

2.2. Slicing, Selecting, Composing

We define briefly certain operations for getting parts of, or composing, arrays and structures; similarly for array and structure names.

Slicing

For an array v , and integers l_k, u_k, l'_k (resp. i_k) such that the interval $l_k:u_k$, resp. the integer i_k , is within the respective bounds of v :

$$v[s_1,\ldots,s_n]=\text{the m-dimensional array } w \text{ with} \tag{2.6}$$

$$\text{bounds } l'_{k1}:l'_{k1}+(u_{k1}-l_{k1}),\ldots,l'_{km}:l'_{km}+(u_{km}-l_{km}) \text{ ,}$$

$$\text{element mode } M=\text{element mode of } v \text{ ,}$$

$$w[l'_{k1}+j_{k1},\ldots,l'_{km}+j_{km}]=v[s'_1,\ldots,s'_n] \text{ for } 0\leqslant j_{ki}\leqslant u_{ki}-l_{ki}, 1\leqslant i\leqslant m \text{ ,}$$

where each s_k is either $l_k:u_k$ at l'_k or i_k and, correspondingly, s'_k is l_k+j_k or i_k ; $k_1,\ldots k_m$ are the positions (in ascending order) where an s of the first kind is specified. (This definition holds for the case $m\geqslant 1$; for $m=0$, $v[i_1,\ldots i_n]$ has already been defined.) Thus slicing takes a sub-aggregate (special case: an element) and possibly re-indexes it.

An analogous operation [l ...] is available for array names, yielding again a name.

Selecting

This is id_k of v , for structures v , which has already been defined; similarly id_k of l .

Composing

Depending on context, more precisely on a mode m provided by context, $(v_1,\ldots,v_m)$ denotes either an array or a structure:

(a) $M=row^{n+1}M'$

M' a non-array mode, $n\geqslant 0$: if there is a range $R=[l_1:u_1,\ldots l_n:u_n]R'$ such that all $v_i\in R$:

$$(v_1,\ldots,v_m)=\text{the } (n+1)\text{-dimensional array with} \tag{2.7}$$

$$\text{bounds } 1:m \text{ , } l_1:u_1,\ldots,l_n:u_n \text{ ,}$$

$$\text{element mode } M'=\text{mode } R' \text{ ,}$$

$$v[i,i_1,\ldots,i_n]=v_i[i_1,\ldots,i_n] \text{ , } (1\leqslant i\leqslant m) \text{ .}$$

(This includes the case $n=0$, if we ignore subscript and bound-pair lists of length 0 .)

(b) $M=(id_1:M_1,\ldots,id_m:M_m)$

For $v_i\in M_i$:

$$(v_1,\ldots,v_m)=\text{the structure } v \text{ with selectors } id_k \text{ ,} \tag{2.8}$$

$$\text{field modes } M_k \text{ , fields } v_k \text{ .}$$

"lhs"-composing

Besides slicing of names, only a very special case arises (in form of an automatic conversion known as rowing): for a name $l \in refrow^n M'$ (M' a non-array mode, $n \geq 0$) :

$$(l)_{lhs} = \text{the name } l' \in refrow^{n+1} M' \text{ defined analogously to } (v_1) \text{ in case (a) above.} \qquad (2.9)$$

2.3. Identity Declarations, Generators, Assignment

We can now use the association of declarers with value classes to describe the affect of identity declarations (which are concerned with storage properties only to the extent that the range-test performed by them includes a test on bounds and states of names), of generators, and of assignment.

There is one case, both with identity declarations and generators, in which our interpretation differs from that in the ALGOL 68 Report, namely the case that a declarer prescribes a bound but admits a corresponding flexible state.

Identity declarations

Identity declarations have the form

$$\tau id = E ,$$

where τ is a formal declarer, id an identifier, E an expression. They test the value v of E for being in the class T denoted by τ and make id denote v . Though identity declarations introduce "constants", they include as special case ALGOL 60's variable declarations (by choosing a name declarer τ and a generator E); they are also used to express the different kinds of parameter passing.

Generators

Generators are actual declarers. Execution of a generator ρ denoting a range R is defined as

$$(allocate_{A68} R)(S) = let\ l = (generate\ R)(S) \qquad (2.10)$$
$$(l := v)(allocate\ l(S)) ,$$

where v is some value in R . Thus allocation as defined in the general model is followed by non-determinate initialization.

Assignment

Assignment is assignment of the general model, preceded by a range test:

$$(l:=_{A68}v)(S)=\underline{if}\ \ v\in \text{range}(l)\ \ \underline{then}\ \ (l:=v)(S) \tag{2.11}$$

2.4. Some Further Points

Scopes

Scopes, i.e., the life-time of names and other "dynamic" values, are outside the subject of this paper. We remark only that the scope of a name can be influenced by writing loc or heap in front of a generator; a further test on assignment secures that a value is not assigned to a name with bigger scope (i.e., possibly, transported outside its scope).

Sub-names of flexible names

Sub-names of flexible names have a life-time even shorter than that of local names: they can die through re-assignment to the flexible name. A further test on several occasions (identity declaration, assignment, composing, rowing) secures that no access, other than via the flexible name itself through slicing, is established to a proper sub-name of a flexible name.

Nil

There is one special name, nil (serving as a null-pointer in chained structures), which receives its mode through context. In the ALGOL 68 Report, different "instances" of nil can have different modes. We can meet the situation by introducing different values $\underline{nil}_M$, one for each mode ref M .

3. STORAGE PROPERTIES OF PL/I

For presenting the storage properties of PL/I, we start with the general storage model of section 1 and proceed by giving it more special properties. The PL/I features related to these properties are: based and defined variables, areas, pointers, and offsets.

After a brief informal discussion of variables in PL/I, we present the ranges of values in PL/I, including area ranges, which are of particular interest. After introducing points and offsets, we are in a position to describe the special storage mapping properties of PL/I. Consequences of the definitions are shown in a few examples.

The resulting PL/I storage model differs in various respects from the one used in the complete formal description of PL/I (Walk et al. (1969), Lucas, Walk (1969)). There, storages were introduced as a set of entities characterized by axioms. Storage access gave a "value representation" which, via data attributes, could be partially interpreted as values. This approach comes nearer to an implementation (value representations may be thought of as bit patterns in a real machine), the relationship between this axiomatic model and an actual implementation was investigated in Henhapl (1969). The present more explicit model lends itself better to a common description of ALGOL 68 and PL/I.

3.1. Variables in PL/I

Each variable is associated by its declaration with a data attribute classifying it as array, structure, or scalar variable. The evaluation of the data attribute gives the range of the variable.

We distinguish proper, defined, and based variables, and parameters in PL/I.

By a reference to a non-based variable or a parameter, we mean a specification of the (unique) identifier of the variable and a list of indices (integers and/or identifiers). A reference to a based variable in addition specifies an expression whose evaluation gives a pointer. The evaluation of a valid reference gives a location, which in turn gives access to the current value in storage.

The way in which a variable becomes associated with a location depends upon its type (proper, defined, based, or parameter). The way in which a sub-location of this location is determined by the indices specified in a reference is common to all types.

By allocation of a proper variable, we mean the association of a properly selected new location with the (unique) identifier of the variable, and the allocation of that location in storage. The range of the location to be selected is equal to the range of the variable. At what point during the interpretation of a program a proper variable is allocated, and how long the resulting association between identifier and location is maintained, depends upon the declared storage class (STATIC, AUTOMATIC, CONTROLLED) of the variable and is of no concern for our present investigation.

Defined variables do not own locations. By its declaration, a defined variable is rather associated with a reference to a proper variable. The location associated with this reference is evaluated when a reference to the defined variable is evaluated. From this location, by appropriate steps of deriving component and super-locations, a location is constructed which is used as the current location of the defined variable at the point of reference. Thus, referring to a defined variable always means referring to storage owned by a proper variable.

A based variable serves two purposes. First, it can be used to allocate new locations, with the range of the based variable, either in main storage, or in an area. These locations do not become associated with the based variable, but are identified by the contents of pointer or offset variables assigned when the locations are allocated. The contents of pointer variables are called pointers. A pointer represents a piece of information derived from a location (it is not a location itself). Intuitively, a pointer identifies a point in storage, but does not necessarily contain information about a range of values. An offset has the same significance for an area, as a pointer has with respect to main storage.

The second use of a based variable is the reconstruction of a location from a pointer value. Like defined variables, based variables do not own locations, but locations are constructed at the point of reference. From the pointer evaluated from the reference to a based variable and the range of the based variable, a location is constructed which is used as the current location of the based variable at the point of reference. This construction does not necessarily give an allocated location; if it does not, the reference to the based variable is undefined. The rules governing the construction of locations are implied by the properties of storage mapping discussed in section 3.4.

Parameters own locations like proper variables. For value parameters a new location is allocated before the call of the corresponding procedure. For non-value parameters, the location of the argument (a reference) is associated with the parameter, so that argument and parameter share the same location.

3.2. Ranges of Values in PL/I

There is a set V_P of values which is the union of all possible ranges of PL/I variables. This set will be partially characterized in the following.

There is a set L_P of PL/I locations. PL/I locations have array, structure, or scalar range. In the sense of section 1.2, array and structure ranges are composite (there are no flexible arrays in PL/I), scalar ranges with the exception of area ranges are elementary, and area ranges are flexible ranges.

(a) Examples for elementary ranges are arithmetic, string, label, entry, pointer, and offset ranges. The significance of pointers and offsets is explained in the next section. The properties of the other elementary values are of no concern for our present purpose.

(b) an array range is characterized by

a pair of integers $l:u$, the bound pair (3.1)
a range R , the component range.

The index-set of an array range is the set of integers

$$\{i \mid l \leq i \leq u\} .$$

Note that in PL/I, we can treat ranges of multi-dimensional arrays as ranges of one-dimensional arrays with array components (this was not possible in ALGOL 68, since the property of some dimension to have flexible bounds makes a range of multi-dimensional

arrays flexible). We also do not need any further characterization of array or structure values, since values are always processed in scalar units.
A structure range is characterized by an n-tuple of ranges

$$R_1, R_2, \ldots, R_n \ , \qquad (3.2)$$

the component ranges. The index-set of a structure range is the set of integers

$$\{1,2,\ldots,n\} \ .$$

Note: Syntactically, the indices of structure components are identifiers. It is not necessary, however, to distinguish between ranges that differ only in identifiers of structure components.

The ordering of the index-set of array and structure ranges is significant. It gives special properties to the function which maps composite locations into component locations, which in turn are significant for the use of based and defined variables (see section 3.).

(c) Area ranges, though counting as scalar with respect to expression evaluation, are flexible ranges with composite alternative ranges.

Area variables serve the purpose of identifying storage to be used for the allocation of based variables. An area range, therefore, is a set of storages, i.e., we include a set of storages in the set of values V_P . Since the notion of storage has already been introduced, it will be possible to explain the handling of areas using the general storage model of section 1.

An area is a composite value. It components are the values of the level-one locations that have been allocated in the area. Let an area a be the storage

$$a=(M, f:M_o \rightarrow V_P) \ .$$

Then the index-set of a is the set of level-one locations M_o in a , and the component values are

$$m(a) \ , \text{ for } m \in M_o \ .$$

The set of "potential" locations $M \subseteq L_P$ of an area is determined by the declared size characterizing the area range. Let the declared size be the integer value s ; then the corresponding area range A_s is

$$A_s=\{a \mid locs(a)=M_s\} \ , \qquad (3.3)$$

where M_s is the set of locations determined by s . The relationship between size and set of locations is not fixed by the PL/I language. A PL/I implementation is free to establish this relationship, observing, however, the condition

$$s_1<s_2 \supset M_{s_1} \subseteq M_{s_2} . \qquad (3.4)$$

We now can define the functions alternatives, curralt, indexset, and comprange, for area ranges. The alternative of an area range A are those maximal subsets of A whose members have the same level-one locations:

alternatives(A)=the set of equivalence classes of members of A with respect to their level-one locations. (3.5)

The current alternative of A determined by a member $a \in A$:

$$\text{curralt}(A,a)=\{v|v\in A \ \& \ \text{level 1 locs}(v)=\text{level 1 locs}(a)\} . \qquad (3.6)$$

Let A^M be an alternative of A ; then

indexset(A^M)=the set of level-one locations of the members of A^M ; (3.7)

comprange(A^M,m)=range(m) .

Finally, we explain the conversion of areas. Before an area a is assigned to an area variable with size s , a is converted to an area with size s . This conversion is possible if M_s , the set of locations determined by s , contains the active locations of a :

$$\text{actlocs}(a)\subseteq M_s .$$

The result of the conversion is the area a' such that

$$\text{locs}(a')=M_s ,$$

level 1 locs(a')=level 1 locs(a) ,

level 1 contents(a')=level 1 contents(a) .

3.3. Pointers and Offsets

The set of pointers P and the set of offsets O are sets of elementary values in PL/I. Pointers and offsets are derived from locations and are used, in turn, for the construction of locations.

We first have to introduce the notion of "connected locations". As an auxiliary notion, we use "segment" of a location. Since the index-set of a composite range is ordered, we can determine for any composite location l the ordered list of its scalar (i.e. elementary or area) sub-locations. Let

$$l_1, l_2, \dots, l_n$$

be this list; then we call any list of locations

$$l_i, l_{i+1}, \dots, l_j \quad , \quad (1 \leq i \leq j \leq n) \ ,$$

a <u>segment</u> of l.

A location is connected if it is one of the following:

(1) a level-one location, (3.9)

(2) a location whose list of scalar sub-locations forms a segment of a connected location,

(3) a constructed location (see below).

The function addr is a mapping from connected locations to pointers and offsets:

$$addr : L_{conn} \rightarrow P \cup O \ . \qquad (3.10)$$

$L_{conn} \subset L_P$ is the set of connected locations in main storage and in areas. If l is a main storage location, then

$$addr(l) \in P \ .$$

If it is the location of an area, then

$$addr(l) \in O \ .$$

For a pointer (or offset) p and a range R , there is exactly one connected location $l \in L_P$

$$l = construct(p,R) \ \text{ such that} \qquad (3.11)$$
$$addr(l)=p \ ,$$
$$range(l)=R \ .$$

The function construct is used in the evaluation of references to based variables. If a reference combines a pointer which was derived from a location l, with a based variable whose range is equal to range(l) , then the evaluation of the based reference gives the location l. If only the above relation (3.11) between locations, pointers, and ranges is known, we only know how to reconstruct those allocated locations by based references of which the pointer was previously derived. There is, however, more freedom in PL/I for the combination of pointers and ranges of based variables, which derives from special properties of the mapping from locations to component locations discussed in the next section.

3.4. Special properties of Storage Mapping

Locations are mapped into component locations by the functions comploc and compflexloc introduced in section 1.3. For PL/I, these functions are given special properties in addition to those imposed already by the general model.

3.4.1. The mapping of connected array and structure locations

For connected array and structure locations, the ordering of the index-set is significant. In the previous section, we introduced the notion of a segment of a location. Analogously, we can determine for each range the ordered list of its scalar sub-ranges.

We require that the function comploc(l,i) for connected, composite l can be reduced to another function compconnloc :

$$\text{comploc}(l,i)=\text{compconnloc}(\text{addr}(l),\text{r-list}_i,r_i) \quad \text{where} \tag{3.12}$$

r-list_i = the list of scalar sub-ranges of range(l) up to, but excluding, the sub-ranges of the i-th component range,

r_i = the list of scalar sub-ranges of the i-th component range of range(l) .

This property is called structure-independent mapping. Furthermore, we require a "linear" property of the mapping function, which establishes a well-defined relationship between sub-locations of connected locations having the same pointer and the same list of scalar sub-ranges.

Let $\text{r-list}_1 \cap r_1$ be an initial segment of range(l) , and $\text{r-list}_2 \cap r_2$ an initial segment of r_1 (see the figure below). Then

$$\text{compconnloc}(\text{addr}(\text{compconnloc}(\text{addr}(l),\text{r-list}_1,r_1)),\text{r-list}_2,r_2)= \tag{3.13}$$
$$\text{compconnloc}(\text{addr}(l),\text{r-list}_1 \cap \text{r-list}_2,r_2) \; .$$

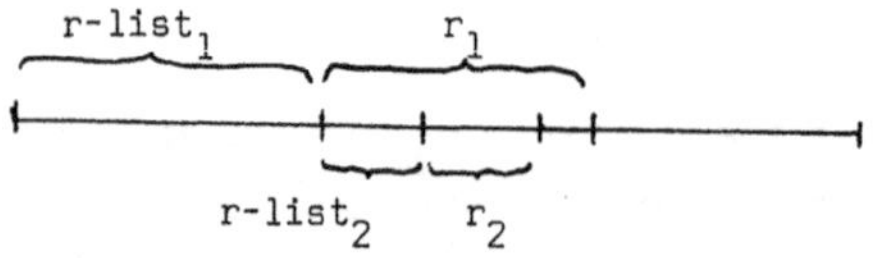

3.4.2. The mapping of area locations

The function compflexloc(l,A_c,m) , for l being an area location, A_c its current range, and $m \in$ indexset(A_c) , reduces to an operation between two arguments:

$$\text{compflexloc}(l,A_c,m)=m^{\circ}l \ . \qquad (3.14)$$

The operation $m^{\circ}l$ is called composition of locations. It is easily verified by the properties of compflexloc that

$$m^{\circ}l(S)=m(l(S)) \ ,$$

which explains the notation of functional composition for the operation, and that

$$\text{range}(m^{\circ}l)=\text{range}(m) \ .$$

There is a corresponding operation between pointers and offsets: Let l be an area location and m a connected location of the area; then

$$\text{addr}(l) \oplus \text{addr}(m)=\text{addr}(m^{\circ}l) \ . \qquad (3.15)$$

The reverse operation is introduced by

$$(p \oplus O) \ominus O=p \ . \qquad (3.16)$$

The operations $\oplus$ and $\ominus$ are called <u>conversion between pointers and offsets</u>. They give the possibility of identifying locations in different areas by the same means, namely offsets, and converting these offsets to pointers (and hence locations) via the pointers of the different area locations. In order to use this technique, we have to know, however, under which circumstances locations in two different areas have the same offset. These follow from properties of allocation in areas.

If a based variable with range R is to be allocated in an area a , a location of the area is selected by the function

newloc(level 1 locs(a),R) .

This function gives a location m such that

range(m)=R , and (3.17)

m is independent of all locations in level 1 locs(a) .

The new location, therefore, is determined independently of the size of the area.

Consequently, if the "history" of two areas is such that they have the same level-one locations, then a new allocation with the same based variable in both areas will identify the same location m . The actual allocation, however, is possible in a only if

$$m \in locs(a) ,$$

i.e., if the size of the area allows the allocation.

Some consequences of the above storage mapping properties are shown in section 3.6.

3.5. Reference, Allocation, Assignment

The process of referring to a variable after the evaluation of subscripts, identifiers of structure components, and possibly pointer expressions (in references to based variables) follows from the previous section. It should be noted, however, that this general mechanism gives more freedom than is given syntactically in PL/I. The reader is referred to PL/I Language Specifications (1966) or to the formal description Walk et al. (1969) on that subject.

The central part of allocation of variables is as described in section 1.5 for the general model.

Similarly, assignment of a value to a variable is taken over from section 1.5. The assignment function (1.21) is to be understood as being performed after the evaluation of the left-hand side and the right-hand side of an assignment statements, and after the conversion of the right-hand side value to the characteristics of the left-hand side location.

3.6. Some Consequences of the Storage Mapping Properties

A few examples will show the use of the mapping functions. This section presupposes some familiarity with PL/I notation.

(a) We consider the following program fragment:

```
DECLARE 1 R AUTOMATIC,
            2 A FIXED,
            2 B,
               3 C CHAR(5),
               3 D BIT(5),
            2 E FLOAT,
        1 T BASED,
            2 U FIXED,
            2 V CHAR(5),
            2 W BIT(5),
            2 X FIXED,
        P POINTER;
        P=ADDR(R);
        R.B.D='10110'B;
        ....P → T.W....
```

The automatic structure variable R is allocated at declaration time. Let l_R be the location of R ,

$$P_R = addr(l_R) \;;$$

P_R is assigned to the pointer variable P . The location associated with R.B according to (3.12) is

$$l_B = compconnloc(p, \langle sr_A \rangle, \langle sr_C, sr_D \rangle) \;,$$

where sr_A, sr_C, sr_D are the scalar (fixed point arithmetic, character string, and bit string) ranges associated with the scalar components R.A,R.B.C,and R.B.D , respectively.

The location associated with R.B.D. is

$$l_D = compconnloc(addr(l_B), \langle sr_C \rangle, \langle sr_D \rangle) \;,$$

which according to (3.13) is equal to

$$l_D = compconnloc(p, \langle sr_A, sr_C \rangle, \langle sr_D \rangle) \;.$$

l_D becomes associated with the bit string value '10110'B through the assignment statement. Let S be the current storage:

$$l_D(S) = \text{'10110'B} \;.$$

We now ask for the evaluation of the based reference P → T.W . A location l_T is constructed from the pointer p and the range R_T of T :

$$l_T = \text{construct}(p, R_T) \ .$$

The location associated with T.W is

$$l_W = \text{compconnloc}(p, \langle sr_U, sr_V\rangle, \langle sr_W\rangle) .$$

Since $\langle sr_U, sr_V\rangle = \langle sr_A, sr_C\rangle$ and $\langle sr_W\rangle = \langle sr_D\rangle$ according to the declaration, we have

$$l_W = l_D \ .$$

The reference P → T.W , therefore, is well-defined and gives the value

$$l_W(S) = \text{'10110'B} \ .$$

(b) We now show the use of offsets for identifying locations in areas. Let us again consider a program fragment:

```
DECLARE A1 AREA(50), A2 AREA(100),
        O OFFSET,
        B BASED;
        ALLOCATE B SET (O) IN (A1);
        A2=A1;
        ....POINTER (O,A2) → B....
        ALLOCATE B SET (O) IN A1;
        ALLOCATE B SET (O) IN A2;
```

Let the locations associated with the area variables be l_{A1} and l_{A2} and its initial values a_1 and a_2 (we denote successive storages by S,S',S",...) :

$$l_{A1}(S) = a_1$$
$$l_{A2}(S) = a_2$$

Initially, there are no active locations in the areas

$$\text{actlocs}(a_1) = \{ \ \}$$
$$\text{actlocs}(a_2) = \{ \ \} \ .$$

The allocation of B in A1 adds a new location m_1 to the level-one locations of a_1 . This location according to (3.17) is given by

$$m_1=\text{newloc}(\{\ \},R_B) \ ,$$

where R_B is the range of B . The offset o_1 derived from m_1 ,

$$o_1=\text{addr}(m_1) \ ,$$

is assigned to the offset variable O . With S' the current storage, we now have

$$l_{A1}(S')=a_1'$$

$$l_{A2}(S')=a_2$$

$$\text{level 1 locs}(a_1')=\{m\} \ .$$

Now comes the assignment of a_1' to A2 . a_1' is converted to the size of A2 giving a_2'' :

$$\text{level 1 locs}(a_2'')=\{m_1\}$$

$$\text{contents}(a_2'')=\text{contents}(a_1')$$

$$\text{locs}(a_2'')=\text{locs}(a_2)$$

and assigned to A_2 :

$$l_{A2}(S'')=a_2'' \ .$$

l_{A2} now has one component location $m^o l_{A2}$.

We now ask for the meaning of the reference POINTER(O,A2) → B . The builtin-in function POINTER performs the conversion of the offset value o of O and the pointer of the location l_{A2} to a pointer P_1 (see (3.15)):

$$P_1=\text{addr}(l_{A2}) \oplus o \ .$$

This pointer, together with the range R_B of B , is used to construct a location

$$l_1=\text{construct}(p_1,R_B) \ .$$

Using (3.15) and (3.14), we can show for the sub-location of l_{A2} that

$$addr(m_1 \, {}^{o}l_{A2})=p_1 \quad \text{and}$$

$$range(m_1 \, {}^{o}l_{A2})=R_B \, ,$$

which by (3.11) means that l_1 is precisely the sub-location of l_{A2} . POINTER(0,A2) → B , therefore, refers to this sub-location whose value is identical with the value of POINTER(0,A1) → B . A single offset value thus can be used for identifying locations in different areas. Finally, a new location is allocated in both of the areas. This new location is

$$m_2=newloc(\{m_1\},R_B)$$

identically for both areas, despite their different size. These new locations, therefore, can again be identified by the same offset.

(c) The last example shows the working of defined variables. We consider a declaration and an assignment.

```
DECLARE B(2,3),D(2,2) DEFINED B;
        D(1,1)=0;
```

The defined variable D is a two-dimensional array variable defined on the two-dimensional array variable B . Let the location of B be l_B , its component locations l_1 and l_2 , and its scalar sub-locations $l_{11},l_{12},l_{13},l_{21},l_{22},l_{23}$. For B we construct a super-location l_D with the range of B from the locations $l_{11},l_{12},l_{21},l_{22}$ such that

$$comploc(comploc(l_D,1),1)=l_{11}$$

$$comploc(comploc(l_D,1),2)=l_{12}$$

$$comploc(comploc(l_D,2),1)=l_{21}$$

$$comploc(comploc(l_D,2),2)=l_{22} \, .$$

An assignment to l_{11} via D(1,1) will clearly also define the value of B(1,1) . Note that the list of scalar sub-locations of l_D does not form a segment of l_B . l_D , therefore, is not a connected location; $addr(l_D)$ and hence ADDR(D) would be undefined.

CONCLUDING REMARKS

Storage properties of ALGOL 68 and PL/I have been presented using the same general storage model as the common basis. This allows a thorough comparison of the two languages with respect to storage handling, which is independent of the syntactic appearance of the two languages. Only a few remarks are made in the following.

There is obviously no counterpart of flexible arrays in PL/I, and no counterpart of areas in ALGOL 68. (Somewhat surprisingly, both these features can be modelled using the concept of flexible locations).

With respect to the building up of more general data structures like lists, rings, etc., the corresponding tools in ALGOL 68 and PL/I are names and pointers. Both serve the purpose of identifying locations in storage, which themselves are processable data. Name variables, however, are restricted with respect to the types of data their values may refer to. This allows compile time checking of the validity of references. PL/I pointer variables are not restricted in the types of data to which their values may point. Pointers also do not necessarily contain range information which makes even run-time checking a problem. Getting defined references in PL/I is the responsibility of the programmer, who has to take into account a number of special properties of storage mapping he need not know for ALGOL 68. On the other hand, PL/I pointers are certainly the most efficient way to realise identification of data. ALGOL 68 and PL/I differ with respect to the balance between economy and security in programming.

REFERENCES

Elgot, C. C. and Robinson, A. (1964). "Random-Access, Stored Program Machines, An Approach to Programming Languages", Journal ACM 11, pp. 365-399.

Henhapl, W. (1969). "A Storage Model Derived from Axioms", IBM Lab. Vienna, Tech. Report TR 25.100.

Lucas, P. and Walk, K. (1969). "On the Formal Description of PL/I", Annual Review in Automatic Programming, Vol. 6, Part 3, Pergamon Press.

PL/I Language Specifications (1966). IBM Systems Reference Library, Form No. C 28-6571-4.

Strachey, C. (1966). "Towards a Formal Semantics", Formal Language Description Languages (Steel, ed.), North-Holland.

Van Wijngaarden, A. (ed.), Mailloux, B. J., Peck, J. E. L., and Koster, C. H. A. (1969). Report on the Algorithmic Language ALGOL 68, Mathematisch Centrum, Amsterdam (second printing).

Walk, K. et al (1969). "Abstract Syntax and Interpretation of PL/I", IBM Lab. Vienna, Tech. Report TR 25.098.

ON THE FORMAL DEFINITION OF PROGRAMMING LANGUAGES

H. Bekic
IBM Laboratory Vienna
November 1970

ABSTRACT

The method underlying the Vienna formal PL/I definition is outlined; current developments in the direction of reduction and simplification are indicated.

(Manuscript for publication in the Proceedings of the International Computing Symposium, Bonn 1970)

1. INTRODUCTION

In the last ten years, formal methods have been applied to the description of the syntax and semantics of programming languages. We have succeeded in obtaining complete formal definitions of big languages; at the same time, the growing number of definition methods with their mass of intricate technical detail indicates that we have to look anew for simplicity and essential contents.

The original motivation for formal definition was to provide the basis for a mathematical theory of programs and programming languages. Such a theory would enable one to formulate and prove program properties and thus, as McCarthy /17/ has emphasized, to replace program debugging by correctness proofs. Formal definition may contribute to the analysis and clarification of language concepts and language structure, as is particularly evident in the work of Landin /11,12/. Finally, the size and complexity of present-day languages makes informal descriptions hopelessly inadequate, if only for the purposes of compiler building and of maintenance. This is obvious in the case of PL/I, and also the prose parts of the Algol 68 report have been compared to the description in ancient Greek mathematics of the algorithm for solving the quadratic equation.

What is formal definition? The answer to this question may depend on one's view on foundational questions. According to our point of view, we have to provide a model (consisting of mathematical objects, e.g., in the case of programming languages: "states", state-transformations, "computations",) and to interpret the expressions of the language in the model, i.e. define a correspondence between expressions and objects of the model. Both the correspondence and its two ends have to be described "formally", i.e. by mathematical means.

Thus our notion of "formal" is wider than the usual one in "formal system", i.e. first-order formalisation. While the latter notion is useful for problems of implementation and mechanical proofs, we think that e.g. free use of function variables or of implicit definition is convenient and therefore the question of mechanisation should be studied separately. In particular, we do not restrict our methods to purely combinatorial text manipulation. (Such restrictions have led to errors in early descriptions of systems of logic and of Algol 60).

The Vienna formal definition project. Using experience gained by the design and description of an Algol compiler /2/, and building on methods developed by Elgot /7/, McCarthy, and Landin, a first version of a formal definition of PL/I was completed at the IBM Laboratory Vienna by end of 1966. The latest version /19/ covers complete PL/I and is being used as a basis for controlling further development of the language. An introduction into the definition method is given in /15/; the method has also been applied to the definition of Algol 60 /14/.

In the main part of the present paper, we give an outline of the Vienna definition method. Our emphasis lies on showing how the method developed and on motivating choices that have been made. A quick look at a few other methods follows. Finally, occasional remarks concerning simplification of the underlying machine-state will be resumed when we advocate the idea of "mathematical" semantics as proposed by Scott /18/.

2. THE VIENNA DEFINITION METHOD

The basic notions of abstract syntax and abstract interpreting machine were taken over from existing work, the latter with the important refinement of allowing a non-determinate transition rule. The problem of dealing systematically with large amounts of information was solved by developing a general theory of structured objects and their transformations. A language for "programming" the abstract machine, i.e. notational conventions for defining state transformations, had to be provided.

2.1. Abstract Syntax

In defining the abstract syntax of a language - a notion that was already present in formal logic, e.g. in the work of Tarski, and was rediscovered for programming by McCarthy /16/ - we are interested in the structural properties of texts, not in particularities of their written representation. Since our problem is interpretation, we want to ask, for example, whether a particular expression is a sum, and if so, what are its first and second operand; we do not care whether sums are represented as x+y or xy+ or (PLUS X Y).

According to the original notion, to define an abstract syntax meant to specify a system of predicates (characterising programs and their parts), selectors (for getting the immediate components of an expression) and constructors (for composing an expression from its components), together with certain relations between them. This system could be thought of as characterising the essential properties of any concrete representation. Alternatively, we can interpret the system as defining a class of trees or abstract texts, which constitute a kind of normal form of their concrete representations. Thus, abstract sums may be defined as trees like the following:

Classes of such trees can conveniently be defined by the technique for structured object definition outlined below.

It would be sensible to consider the abstract normal form as the definition of the syntax of the language, for which then concrete representations could be defined. (To a very limited extent this has been done in Algol 68, where the representation of basic symbols is left open, though a particular one is suggested.) If, on the other hand, the concrete syntax is already given, e.g. by BNF rules, then we need a translator from concrete texts to abstract texts.

Among the features abstracted from the transition from concrete to abstract syntax are the following: precedence of operators, use of parentheses; the order of declarations in a block (as opposed to the order of statements, which is relevant for interpretation). In /12/, most of Algol 60 is treated as "syntactic sugar" of a simple class of expressions; in /13/, labels and goto are considered as syntactic sugar for writing graphs.

2.2. Abstract Interpreting Machine

The meaning of a program may be described by its effect on the state of an underlying (abstract) interpreting machine. In the simplest case, the machine state may be the pairing of the program variables with their current values; this state will be changed e.g. by the execution of assignment statements. Abstract machines have been introduced by Elgot /7/ and McCarthy /16/ for the interpretation of flowchart-type languages; Landin /12/ describes a machine for interpreting complete Algol 60.

We assume that the abstract program together with the initial data on which it is to operate determines an initial state ξ_0; this initial state is transformed into other states by iterated application of the state-transition function Λ, until an end-state is reached; from this end-state we can extract the result data. Taking into account also the translator, we get the following picture: [1)]

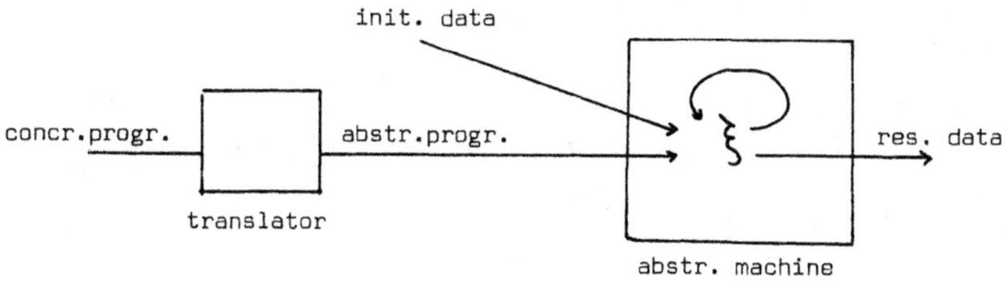

We tolerate the following possibilities: the state-transition function Λ (called language function in /19/) may be

1) In /19/, the situation is complicated by a prepass between translator and proper interpretation; this prepass deals e.g. with STATIC and EXTERNAL variables.

1. non-determinate: $\Lambda(\xi)$ may yield, for a given state ξ, a set of successor states, rather than a single successor state. This situation arises e.g. because the operands of an expression (with side-effects) may be evaluated in any order.

2. partial: $\Lambda(\xi)$ may not be defined at all, i.e. an erroneous program (containing errors that are not discovered syntactically) may lead into a state ξ which, although not an end-state, has no successor.

3. incompletely specified: $\Lambda(\xi)$ may not be fully defined, and an implementation of the language may have to provide additional information. This situation arises e.g. with the axioms describing storage properties of PL/I.

A computation is a (finite or infinite) sequence of states

$$\xi_0, \xi_1, \xi_2, \ldots$$

such that $\xi_{i+1} \varepsilon \Lambda (\xi_i)$ and the sequence terminates if and when an end-state is reached.

We note, that the program, in some form or another, is part of the state (see also section 2.4 and 5). We consider computations because we are interested in the algorithm performed by the program, not only in the gross-transformation from input to outputs. (For a reason to consider computations of subprograms even if one is only interested in the outcome of the whole program, see section 5).

2.3. A Theory of Objects

Both abstract programs and machine-states are finite structured objects (trees). The theory outlined below arose from the need to define such objects and their transformation in a systematic way.

Let a set EO of elementary objects and a set S_0 of simple selectors be given. ("Elementary" and "simple" in the sense that we are not interested in any further structure of the elements of these sets). An object is

(1) either elementary, i.e. an element of EO,

(2) or else composite and characterised by a finite set of pairs $<s_i:o_i>$, where the s_i are different elements of S and the o_i are again objects. Write $\mu_0(<s_1:o_1>,\ldots,<s_n:o_n>)$ for that object.

We understand composite objects to be different from elementary objects in EO (whatever internal structure the latter may have), and the set o of objects (over EO and S) to be the smallest set containing EO and closed under the operation (2). Objects can be pictured as trees with labelled branches,

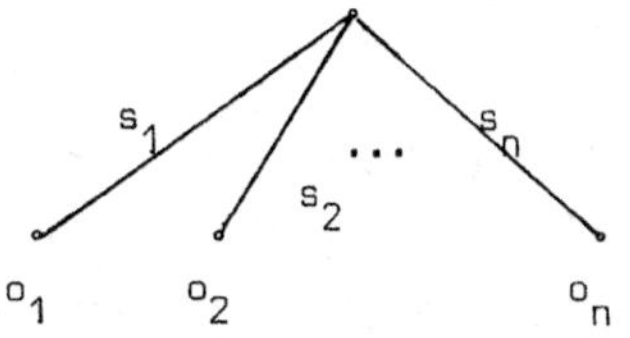

in particular elementary objects as trees consisting of a single labelled node:

We call the o_i <u>immediate components</u> of the object $\mu_0(<s_1:o_1>,\ldots,<s_n:o_n>)$. If an o_i is again composite, we can again take components, and so on. Thus define the set S of selectors as the set of finite sequences $s_1 \circ s_2 \circ \ldots$, where the s_i are in S_0 (i.e. as the free monoid generated from S_0, with a <u>composition</u> denoted by $\circ$).

Define selector <u>application</u> by

$$
\begin{aligned}
s(o) &= o_i && \text{for } o = \mu_0(\ldots,<s_i:o_i>,\ldots), \quad s=s_i\\
s(o) &= \Omega && \text{otherwise}\\
\sigma'\circ\sigma(o) &= \sigma'(\sigma(o))\\
I(o) &= o
\end{aligned}
$$

where $s \in S_0$, σ and $\sigma' \in S$, Ω is the <u>null object</u> $\mu_0()$ with no immediate components, I is the <u>identity selector</u>, i.e. the null sequence of simple selectors. (Thus simple selectors select immediate components, I corresponds to the identity function, and $\circ$ to functional composition.)

<u>Creating/updating</u>. For $o, o_1 \in O$, $\sigma \in S$ define

$\mu(o;<\sigma:o_1>)$ = the object o' such that
$\sigma(o') = o_1$, $\tau(o') = \tau(o)$ for τ independent from σ

where two selectors are independent if there is no x such that one is $x\circ$ the other (i.e. in the tree representation, where selectors correspond to paths from the root, none is an initial segment of the other). Thus, use of μ with a composite σ, like e.g. in

$\mu(sum;<multiplicand\circ augend:3>)$

provides a shorthand for nested uses of μ, but μ can also be used to add components not previously there, e.g. in

μ(list;<elem(n+1):'END'>)

We can extend the use of μ by defining $\mu(o;<\sigma_1:o_1>,\ldots,<\sigma_n:o_n>)$ as iterative substitution from left to right, and $\mu(o;\{<\sigma:o> \mid p(\sigma)\})$ as parallel substitution (provided $\{\sigma \mid p(\sigma)\}$ is an independent set of selectors). Finally we define

$$\mu_o(\ -\ ) = \mu(\Omega;\ -\ )$$

(in accordance with our use of μ_o above), and the delete-function

$$\sigma(o;\ \text{set of } \sigma\text{'s}) = \mu(o;\ \text{set of } <\sigma:\Omega>\text{'s})$$

Note: We would represent o by its characteristic set $\{<\sigma:eo> \mid \sigma(o) = eo \in EO\}$ (thus in particular eo by $\{<I:eo>\}$, Ω by $\{\}$), and define selector application and μ as operations on characteristic sets. (Set-theoretic model for objects used in /19/.)

Predicates. Given different simple selectors $s_1,\ldots,s_n$, and predicates (object-classes) $p_1,\ldots,p_n$, we can define a new predicate

$$p = (\ s_1:p_1\ ,\ldots,\ s_n:p_n\ )$$

as the class of all $x = \mu_o(<s_1:x_1>,\ldots,<s_n:x_n>)$ such that $p_i(x_i)$. Together with the use of $\vee$ for predicates ($(p_1 \vee p_2)(x) = p_1(x) \vee p_2(x)$) this gives us the main tool for defining abstract syntax; for example:

```
is-expr = is-binary-expr v ...
is-binary-expr = (<s-opd1:is-expr>,<s-opd2:is-expr>,
                  <s-opr:is-operator>)
is-operator = is-ADD v is-SUBTR v is-MULT v is-DIV
```

(where is-ADD characterises a certain elementary object ADD, etc.) There are certain more elaborate forms of predicate definitions provided in /19/.

Discussion. We note the following points:

1. We have systematised the characterisation of structured objects by predicates, selectors and constructors mentioned earlier; thus the constructor is derivable from the selectors (by use of μ), and the predicate from component predicates and selectors.

2. μ can add, delete and replace at any level of depth. Note that μ could be defined by composition from add/initialise/reset/remove immediate components (after giving

suitable meanings to $\mu(eo; -)$ and $\mu(- ;<I: - >)$; note that $\mu(eo; -)$ is responsible for the failing of identities like $o = \mu(o;<\sigma:\sigma(o)>))$. The totalness as function of σ (hence: versatility) of our μ results from

a. the totalness of simple selector application. Thus we lose the distinction between "not present" and "present, but not initialised" (both being modelled by "initialised to Ω"), and hence the possibility of a μ that refuses to set non-existing components.

b. the absence of range-restrictions on positions. Thus we lose another possibility of implicit error-check on resetting.

Examples where dropping a. and/or b. might be useful are: modelling of storage; out-of-range check for computed indices.

3. We have no infinite-depth trees. Thus in modelling self-referentially defined objects (e.g. recursive procedures, Algol 68 infinite modes) we have to use pointers.

2.4. Programming the Abstract Machine

The main bulk of the definition in /19/ is a series of instruction definitions, like int-program(...), etc. In this section we discuss how to write and interpret such instruction definitions; in particular, we will have to consider the control-part of the abstract machine and to be more specific about the language function Λ.

Instruction definitions:syntax. An instruction definition has the form

$$\underline{in}(x_1,\dots,x_n) = \varepsilon$$

where in is the name of the instruction, the x_i are variables, and ε is

either basic and has the form

$$PASS:E_o,\ sc_1:E_1,\dots,sc_m:E_m$$

where the sc_i are simple selectors identifying state-components;

or self-replacing, i.e. is a control-representation $\mathcal{C}$

where $\mathcal{C}$ is

either $\underline{in}'(E_1,\dots,E_m)\ \mathcal{S}$

$\underline{in}'(E_1,\dots,W_m)$;

where the set-expression $\mathcal{S}$ is composed of element-expressions of the form $\mathcal{C}'$ or $a:\mathcal{C}'$ or $x(a):\mathcal{C}'$ where a is a variable and x is a selector-expression;

or is $p_1 \to \varepsilon_1, \ldots, p_m \to \varepsilon_m$,

where the p_i are propositional expressions.

(The E_i are conventional expressions; to complete the definition, we would have to add conventions for proper grouping, like use of parentheses or indentation.) Examples for instruction definitions are

update-env(id,v) =

PASS:v ,

s-e:μ(E;<id:v>)

(assuming a state-component E = s-e(ξ), the "environment"), or

int-expr(t) =

is-binary-expr(t) → bin-op(v_1,v_2,s-opr(t));
{v_1:int-expr(s-opd1(t)),
v_2:int-expr(s-opd2(t))}

...

The control-part, control-trees. We assume the existence of a state-component C = s-c(ξ), the control of the abstract machine. C is either empty, or is a control-tree:

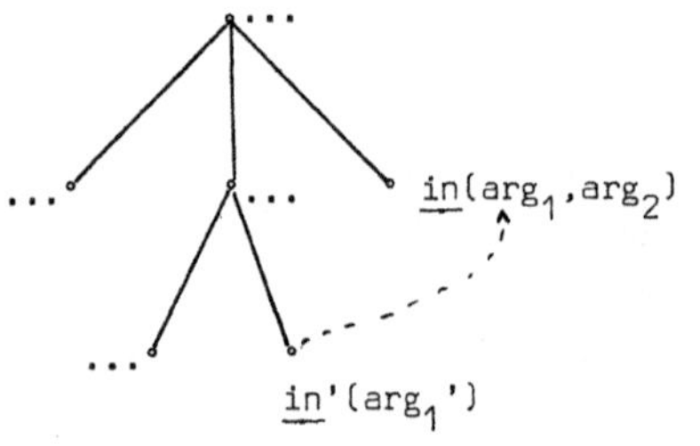

Control-trees have node labels that are instruction-calls with evaluated arguments (objects, including Ω); additional arrows may lead from nodes to previous argument positions or sub-positions. Obviously control-trees can be formalised as objects, and we will indicate below such a formalisation. Also, control-representations $\mathcal{C}$, as introduced above, can be interpreted to denote control-trees, hence objects; we will write $\ulcorner\mathcal{C}\urcorner$ for (a conventional expression denoting) this object. (Essentially, the object $\ulcorner\mathcal{C}\urcorner$ is a representation of the expression $\mathcal{C}$ - not its value ! - with the values of the free variables plugged in.)

Instruction definitions: interpretation; the language function Λ. The mentioned non-determinacy of Λ is brought about by the convention that the instruction to be obeyed next may be chosen arbitrarily from any of the terminal nodes of the control $\underline{C}$. Thus

$$\Lambda(\xi) = \{\psi(\xi,\tau) \mid \tau \in tn\circ s\text{-}c(\xi)\}$$

where $tn(\underline{C})$ denotes the set of terminal nodes of $\underline{C}$. (The computation stops when an end-state is reached; it is convenient to characterise end-states by $\Lambda(\xi) = \{\}$, hence by an empty $\underline{C}$.) The function ψ looks at the instruction-call at node $(\underline{C})$; it destroys that call from the state but remembers the information:

$$\psi(\xi,\tau) = \phi_{\underline{in}}(al, \delta(\xi;\tau \circ s\text{-}c), \tau, ri)$$

where $\underline{in}$, al, ri =
instruction name, arg-list, return information at $(\underline{C})$.

The definition of the function $\phi_{\underline{in}}$ is obtained from the instruction definition for $\underline{in}$. If the latter is $\underline{in}(a_1,\ldots,x_n) = \varepsilon$ then we have

$$\phi_{\underline{in}}(x_1,\ldots,x_n,\xi,\tau,ri) = \varepsilon^*$$

where ε^* is obtained as follows: first, replace complete (i.e. not-nested-within-other) control-representations $\mathcal{C}$ in ε by $\ulcorner\mathcal{C}\urcorner$; now:

1. if ε is PASS : $E_0, sc_1:E_1,\ldots,sc_m:E_m$, ε^* is
$\mu(\mu(\xi;\{<(\tau+\alpha)\circ s\text{-}c:E_0> \mid \alpha \in ri\});$
$<sc_1:E_1>,\ldots,<sc_m:E_m>)$;

2. if ε is $\ulcorner\mathcal{C}\urcorner$, ε^* is $\mu(\xi;<\tau\circ s\text{-}c:\mu(\ulcorner\mathcal{C}\urcorner;<s\text{-}ri:ri>)>)$;

3. if ε is $p_1 \to \varepsilon_1,\ldots,p_m \to \varepsilon_m$, ε^* is $p_1 \to \varepsilon_1^*,\ldots,p_m \to \varepsilon_m^*$.

Thus, in case 1 the components sc_i are reset, but first the result E_0 is inserted at previous control positions (ri is a possibly empty set of backwards arcs α; for $\tau+\alpha$, see below). Case 2 is instruction expansion; in toto, i.e. taking the definition of ψ, the return-in-formation at $(\underline{C})$ is left unchanged (for s-ri, see below). Case 3 is instruction definition by cases.

Formalising control trees as objects. To define the object $\ulcorner\mathcal{C}\urcorner$, where $\mathcal{C}$ is a control-representation, use a set SUCC of simple selectors for labelling the branches of control-trees; use additional simple selectors s-in, s-al, s-ri for modelling the instruction calls at control-tree nodes as subobjects. (Thus selectors s_i from SUCC provide the gross structure, and selectors s-in, s-al, s-ri, plus standard selectors $elem_i$ for selecting list elements, plus selectors x within arguments the fine structure of $\ulcorner\mathcal{C}\urcorner$). The use of dummy names "a" in argument-positions and instruction-prefixes "a:" or "x(a)" (see syntax of instruction definitions) suggests how to construct backwards arcs α leading from control-tree nodes to argument (sub-) positions of preceding nodes. If α leads from $\sigma\circ\tau'$ to $x'\circ\tau'$:

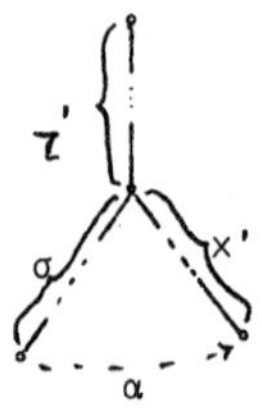

$(\sigma = s_1\circ s_2 \ldots, x' = x\circ elem_i\circ s\text{-}al)$, represent it by the pair $<\sigma,x'>$; define the operation $\tau+\alpha$ used by $\sigma\circ\tau'+<\sigma,x'> = x'\circ\tau'$. Now it is easy to define $\ulcorner\mathcal{C}\urcorner$, e.g.

$$\underline{in}(a_1,\ldots,a_n) = \mu_0(<s\text{-}in:\underline{in}>,<s\text{-}al:<a_1,\ldots,a_n>>),$$

$$\underline{in}(a);\{x(a):\mathcal{C}\,|\,p(x)\} = \mu_0(<s\text{-}in:\underline{in}>,<s\text{-}al:<\Omega>>, \{<s_x:\mu(\ulcorner\mathcal{C}\urcorner;<s\text{-}ri:\{<s_x,x'>\}>)>|\,p(x)\})$$

(if $\mathcal{C}$ does not again contain "a" in a prefix), similarly in more complicated cases. (Here the s_x are different elements of SUCC, and x' is $x\circ elem_1\circ s\text{-}al$.)

Discussion. We want to note the following points:

1. The main difference to Landin's SECD-machine (see section 4) is that we need non-determinate expression evaluation, hence a tree, not a stack, of intermediate results. This suggested that the stack be abandoned altogether and intermediate results be kept in the (tree-like) control itself.

2. The language of instruction definitions is usable quite generally for describing state-transformations. A particular feature is that the control (i.e. more or less, the "program") is part of the state to be transformed. There are two respects in which the language may be too general:

a. As a consequence of the previous remark, the control is explicitly resettable (we may use the selector s-c as one of the sc_i in the basic instruction format). Use of this feature is likely to confuse the structure of the definition (just as uncontrolled use of goto is likely to confuse the structure of a program).

b. The state can be copied (we can use "ξ" on the right-hand side of the instruction definitions). Again this is too general, both from the point of view of implementation, and of the programming languages to be modelled.

3. On the other hand, the language would allow obvious (and useful) generalisations. Thus one might want to write instruction-calls directly as arguments of other instructions or functions; again, one might want a general mechanism of auxiliary definitions (where-clauses), instead of the rather restricted "a:"-notation. In fact it is possible to embed our language in a general language of imperative applicative expressions (in the sense of Landin, see section 4), with suitable primitives and a non-determinate evaluation rule.

3. MODELLING PARTICULAR LANGUAGE CONCEPTS: STRUCTURE OF THE MACHINE STATE

The PL/I-machine in /19/ has 23 (immediate) state-components, ranging from the parallel action part PA over the file union directory FU to the attention directory AN. Continuing our outline of the Vienna definition method, we consider in this section a few central concepts present in most high-level languages, and the state-components they give rise to. We have already introduced the control C.

Block structure. The declarations of a block create a new local environment, i.e. set of <id,den> (identifier-denotation) pairs, under which the rest of the block is interpreted. It is convenient (in the case of recursive procedures, see below, and for uniformity otherwise) to introduce as an intermediate link unique names n; we then have a (block-local) state-component E, the environment, consisting of <id,n> pairs, and a (global) state-component DN, the denotation directory, consisting of <n,den> pairs. Unique names are provided by the unique name counter UN. [1]

On entering a block, a new level of block-local components has to be opended; the old level (like E, C, D) is dumped in the dump D. Then E and DN are updated by new id-n-den entries according to the local declarations. On exit from the block, the old components can then be re-installed from D.

(The reason fro having D is that certain block-local information, like E, is part of the state; if instead such information were organized as additional parameters of the interpreting functions, see section 5, then D could be dispensed with. A particular reason for D in the case of PL/I is that execution of procedure calls may not be merged with execution of other operands of the containing expression.)

---

1) In the latest version /19/, unique names are directly substituted into (dynamic copies of) program text, and no E is used.

Variables. In the case of a variable-identifier id, we have the following picture:

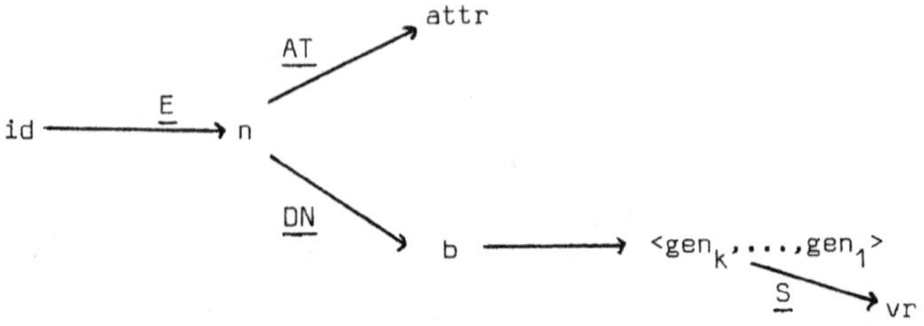

A *generation* gen (known in other languages as "variable", "left-hand value", "location", "name") is, in the case of PL/I, a pair <p,eda> where p is a *pointer* (more generally, in the case of cross-sections of arrays, we may have a pointer-list), and eda are *evaluated data attributes*. The *storage* S associates pointers with *value-representations* vr; the association, as well as pointers themselves and the relation between mathematical values and their representations, are to a large extent implementation-dependent and hence not completely defined; they are characterized by a set of axioms.

In the simplest case, the denotation of a variable-identifier could be a generation. However, CONTROLLED variables denote stacks of generations that can be augmented/decreased by ALLOCATE/FREE statements; hence the additional link b (another unique name) and the *aggregate directory* AG. In the picture, we have also shown the *attribute directory* AT which pairs n's with unevaluated attributes (which are needed for the interpretation of some kinds of identifiers).

We can now have different patterns of *sharing*. For example, two n's may lead to the same gen (this arises when a parameter is called "by reference"); again, two n's may lead to the same b (in the case of CONTROLLED parameters, i.e. "call by stack", or two declarations of the same EXTERNAL CONTROLLED identifier).

Procedures. In the case of a procedure-identifier we have:

$$n \xrightarrow{\underline{DN}} \langle \text{text, env} \rangle$$

i.e. a procedure is characterized by a piece of text (the body and the formal parameters) *plus* an environment under which the body is to be interpreted. In particular, env may contain the pair <id,n> where id is the identifier under which the procedure was declared (due to "recursive" i.e. self-referential, procedure declarations) - hence the use of an intermediate link n.

A call of the procedure will open a new block-level, with "text" (essentially) as the new C and env as the new E; parameters will lead to new E/DN entries f-n-a where f is the formal, a the value of the actual. Regarding modes of parameter-passing, we may distinguish call by reference, where a gen is passed, call by value, where a new gen is created and initialized with the value of the actual, and call by denotation, where a den is passed (e.g. passing a procedure, or the call by stack mentioned above).

Labels. Labels can be thought of as positions in the (dynamic) program. Given that the state is organized in block levels, we choose therefore in case of a label-identifier:

$$n \xrightarrow{DN} \langle \text{dynamic position, static position} \rangle$$

where the dynamic position identifies a block activation and the static position a position within the block. We can take for the dynamic position the depth of the dump, or e.g. introduce unique block activation names; the latter are necessary when the possibility arises that the block we want to go to is no longer active and a corresponding check must be made, e.g. when unrestricted assignment to label variables is allowed. The static position is an index-list.

A goto then undumps successive levels until the target block level is reached and afterwards uses the index-list to reset C and CI (the control-information, another block-local component). In the simplest case, C will be (an instruction interpreting) a compound statement, and CI a single index serving as statement counter; more complicated cases arise through labels in nested compounds, conditionals and for-statements.

Under certain restrictions, one might avoid "positions" and represent labels more directly as pairs <block-rest, dump>; again, one might have organized auxiliary information in such a way that the state can be restored at once from the target block, rather than by piece-meal closing of the intermediate block levels (which involves actions like e.g. freeing local AUTOMATIC variables).

Evaluation in unspecified order. The tree-structure of the control C can be used directly to model expression evaluation in unspecified order, i.e. the arbitrary merging of the sequences of transition steps that make up the evaluations of the single operands of the expression. A particular mechanism has been used to model PL/I tasking, although in principle again the tree-structure of C could have been used; only merging of the - well-defined! - elementary actions of the machine, not true parallelism, is shown.

4. A LOOK AT OTHER METHODS

Many other definition methods, of varying degree of formality, have been proposed (see de Bakker /1/). We mention in particular the following, because they seem important in their own right, and also because they illustrate points we want to emphasize in the next section. Thus the translation to IAEs (although not the way their interpretation is described) exhibits a clear homomorphic structure; one of the declared aims of the axiomatic method is to avoid all book-keeping details; again, the definition of the semantics of ALGOL 68 exhibits a clear recursive structure.

Landin's imperative applicative expressions. Church /6/ had introduced a calculus for formalizing the notion of computable function (of natural numbers). The relevance of this lambda-calculus for programming was particularly exploited by Landin, who considers in /11/ a class of applicative expressions (AEs) and shows how various notations, e.g. "where"-clauses (auxiliary definitions), conditionals, recursive definitions, can be viewed as "syntactically sugared" AEs.

An AE is either an identifier, or a combination consisting of two AEs, its operator and its operand, or a λ-expression, consisting of an identifier, its bound variable, and an AE, its body. The value of a combination MN is the result of applying the value of M (a function) to the value of N; the value of a λ-expression $\lambda x.M$ is the function which the value of M is the value of x. Thus AEs feature functional application and functional abstraction. A machine is specified, whose state consists of four components, a stack for holding intermediate results, an environment, a control, and a dump (the latter three components very much like those discussed earlier, except that the control is a list, not a tree). The transition rule for this SECD-machine is such that sufficiently many iterations of it have the effect

$$\langle S, E, X:C, D\rangle \rightarrow \langle valEX:S, E, C, D\rangle$$

(if the value valEX of the expression X under the environment E exists at all), i.e. the top expression will have been taken from the control and its value loaded on top of the stack. The transition rule is determinate because suitable conventions on sequencing are made, e.g. that an operand is evaluated before its operator and both are evaluated before application. One reason for considering such a machine is that its transition rule is explicit and mechanisable, whereas the definition of valEX is highly implicit.

In /12/ it is shown that all of ALGOL 60 can be modelled as AEs except assignment and goto. A second reason for introducing the machine is that its state and transition rule can be elaborated to deal with these two "imperative" features. Two new operators, essentially differing from any previous ones in that they have "side-effects", are introduced; the resulting enlarged class of expressions is called imperative applicative expressions (IAEs). The state of the machine is elaborated by introducing an equivalence relation, called sharing, between state-positions. The transition rule must also specify now in each case how the sharing-relation changes (this specification is left informal in /12/). Instead of the values of identifiers, their positions are loaded onto the stack. Assignment can now operate on a position and a value; it resets the occupants of all positions in the equivalence class. Labels and goto are dealt with by the second operator: J operating on a closure (i.e. a text-environment pair arising as value of a λ-expression, cf. the treatment of procedures in the previous section) adds the current dump to it to produce a program-point; on going to, i.e. executing, the program point, the dump can then be installed.

Translation to IAEs, no matter how one formalizes the interpretation of the latter, is a highly economic, structure transparent approach that necessitates a good deal of analysis. It is of course easier to add a new state component whenever the need for one comes to mind.

The axiomatic method. One of the objectives of this method, which has been proposed in particular by Hoare /8/, is to consider only essential program properties, instead of getting involved in particular evaluation mechanisms. A second objective is to obtain a system in which formal proofs of program properties can be carried out. The method consists in setting up a set of axioms and rules of inference to characterize the meaning of the programming language to be described. So far, the method has been applied to a small number of language concepts; the application to a bigger language (a considerable part of ALGOL 60) in Burstall /4/ is in fact highly algorithmic, reintroducing much organisational detail.

Keeping organisational information small is a valuable objective. If we separate questions of definition as such from questions of proof theory, we may ask whether that objective is not served better by choosing the state small and giving explicit definitions where they come most natural. (The reverse situation also arises: in a mainly algorithmic approach, characterization through axioms may come more naturally sometimes; we have already mentioned the storage axioms in /19/).

The definition of ALGOL 68. In the official description of ALGOL 68 /20/ a computational model, consisting of (linguistic) "objects", "values", and certain relations between them, is used. For example, the relation "to possess" (as used for identifiers) is essentially our state-component DN, and the relation "to refer to" corresponds to our S (see section 3).

The meaning of programs, i.e. the association between programs and "actions" transforming the model, is defined in informal, though very precise language. This definition has a clear recursive structure in that the action associated with a composite expression is defined in terms of the actions associated with the parts of the expression. (On the other hand, a certain preoccupation with texts and textual substitution, already visible in the two-level syntax system, seems to be less fortunate. It leads to difficulties with "infinite" productions to unnecessary lengths in the treatment of the union-mode, and to a restriction on procedures, according to which definitions like, using λ-notation, $f(x) = \lambda y.x + y$ cannot directly be modelled).

5. MATHEMATICAL SEMANTICS

Most of the methods we have been considering so far are, in the main, "constructive" (or "algorithmic", or "operational") in the sense that they consist in describing a process for "evaluating" or "executing" expressions of the language. This may be contrasted to the situation in descriptive languages, e.g. first-order function-predicate-calculus (cf. model-theoretic treatments of logic, e.g. Kreisel /10/), where we have the following:

(1) There is a function, call it "meaning", or "denotation", or "value", from expressions to values.

(2) The value of a composite expression depends only on the values of its parts.

Values are certain mathematical objects, like numbers, truth-values, etc. Thus, given an environment which maps identifiers into numbers, the value of the expression $x + y$ will be a number, and the value of the expression $E_1 + E_2$ will be a certain function of the values of E_1 and E_2, namely their sum. We can express (2) also by saying that the function "value of" is a homomorphism from expressions to values; i.e. there is a certain structure on expressions, a corresponding structure on values, and the function preserves the structure (see e.g. Burstall-Landin /5/).

Can this "mathematical" approach to semantics be carried over to imperative languages? Yes it can, as is shown by recent work of D. Scott (see /18/). Of course, the objects arising as values of expressions will be more complicated - we prefer to call them now denotations, to distinguish them from the values of the old kind, which will also be around. Thus, consider an assignment statement like a := a + 1. A suitable environment would now be one that pairs identifiers with locations. Let a state be a function from locations to numbers. Then a := a + 1 denotes a certain function from states to states, i.e. an element of the set (states → states).

Observe that (in this all-to-simple example) 1. the program, i.e. here the statement a := a + 1, is not part of the state; 2. also the environment is not part of the state, but is an auxiliary parameter to the denotation function.

Again, consider compound statements, like s_1; s_2 or

l:s_1; if p then goto l else s_2;s_3

We can define the state-transformation denoted by the latter statement if we know the state-transformations denoted by the s_i and the predicate (on states) denoted by p.

There is the following motivation (additional to the motivation for formal definition in general) for pursuing this mathematical approach:

1. The approach corresponds closely to the intuitive understanding of programs: one composes programs by composing meanings! In particular, validation of any more constructive definition (or implementation) needs a basis which is both precise and close to the intuitive understanding.
2. By choosing the state "small" we can hope to get a notion of essential meaning, and hence useful notions of equivalence of programs in the same or different languages.
3. The inductive nature of the definition will ease inductive proofs.

So far, the approach has been applied (in unpublished work by Scott-Strachey) to simple languages containing flowcharts, expressions (with determinate, say left-to-right, evaluation), procedures. We conclude this section by listing some immediate problems:

Labels/goto: To deal with the general goto (outside procedure boundaries, as opposed to the simple case in the example above) we may introduce something like dynamic program positions l and say that a statement operating on a state ξ produces either a state ξ' or a pair (ξ',l) (compare the action "to appoint a successor" in ALGOL 68). Question: Can we avoid program positions in favour of more explicit label denotations and yet keep the homomorphic character of the definition?

Procedures: In ALGOL 60, a procedure with a procedure parameter can be applied to itself (this is true even for "purely functional" procedures, i.e. procedures without side-effects). The notion of self-applicable or self-returning function does not square with the usual notion of function as set of ordered pairs $\langle a,b \rangle$, where the a and b are taken from previously given sets A and B. We may compare the situation with "definitions" like

$$l = \langle a,l,b \rangle$$

There is no finite-depth list l satisfying this equation, but there is an infinite-depth list which we may think of as arising by "infinite" substitution for l. (If we model lists as functions, then l gets a non-founded set of pairs.) In the computer, such lists are all-familiar: we represent l by an address under which a word is stored that contains as one of its parts this address.

The same technique of infinite substitution may be applied to deal with self-referentially defined, self-applicable, self-returning procedures. Whether the model we expect to get that way will be the same as Scott's model for the λ-calculus (which also uses a concept of infinite completion) remains to be seen.

Side-effects in unspecified order: So far, it was sufficient to model statements as state-transforming functions. Now there may be reasons to consider, given an initial state, a particular way in which the result state is computed, i.e. a derivation of the result state, rather than just this result state itself; for example, we may want to consider the efficiency of a program, etc. But non-determinate order of expression evaluation forces us to consider derivations, even if we are interested only in the result of the whole program. Namely, to merge the evaluations of two subexpressions, it is not sufficient to know the transformations corresponding to these subexpressions; we must know the particular decomposition of those transformations into elementary transformations.

Not only successive states but also intermediate results of expressions will have to appear in the derivation, i.e. we will have to consider "polyadic" derivations; more precisely, we need something that has the same relation to polyadic derivations as lists of unary functions have to "monadic" derivations.

6. CONCLUSIONS

We have emphasized the need for formal language definition and outlined the method underlying the Vienna PL/I definition. This formalization has lead to the clarification of language concepts, e.g. the result that AUTOMATIC variables cannot be explained as CONTROLLED variables with implied ALLOCATE/FREE at block entrance/exit; it has been applied to the comparison of language concepts, e.g. in Bekić-Walk /3/, and to the problem of proving correct certain implementation techniques, e.g. in Jones-Lucas /9/.

We have also tried to indicate the direction of reduction and simplification in which we think future work should go. For example, we may have a better basis for judging particularities of PL/I's ON-inheritance rules after having tried to explain ON-units in terms of procedures. Only after such reduction, problems like proving equivalence of (big) programs or correctness of (complete) implementations should be attacked.

Acknowledgements. The methods leading to the formal definition of PL/I have been developed jointly by the members of the IBM Laboratory Vienna, in particular by P. Lucas and K. Walk. More or less vague ideas of this author on a "mathematical" treatment of semantics have gained clarity through the contact with work of D. Scott.

REFERENCES

/1/ J.W.de Bakker: Semantics of Programming Languages.- Mathematisch Centrum Amsterdam, 1968 (unpublished).

/2/ H. Bekić: Mechanical Transformation Rules for the Reduction of Algol to a Primitive Language *M* and their Use in Defining the Compiler Function.- IBM Laboratory Vienna, Techn. Rep. TR 25.051, 1965.

/3/ H. Bekić, K. Walk: Formalisation of Storage Properties.- To be published in: E. Engeler (Ed.): Symposium on the Semantics of Algorithmic Languages, Springer Lecture Notes.

/4/ R.M. Burstall: Formal Description of Program Structure and Semantics in First Order Logic.- In: B. Meltzer, D. Michie (Eds.): Machine Intelligence 5, pp. 79-98, Edinburgh 1969.

/5/ R.M. Burstall, P.J. Landin: Programs and their Proofs: an Algebraic Approach.- In: B. Meltzer, D. Michie (Eds.): Machine Intelligence 4, pp.17-43, Edinburgh 1968.

/6/ A. Church: The Calculi of Lambda-Conversion.- Princeton University Press, 1941.

/7/ C.C. Elgot, A. Robinson: Random-Access Stored-Program Machines. An Approach to Programming Languages.- J. ACM 11 (1964), No.4, pp. 365-399.

/8/ C.A.R. Hoare: An Axiomatic Basis for Computer Programs.- Comm. ACM 12 (1969), No.10, pp.576-580.

/9/ C.B. Jones, P. Lucas: Proving Correctness of Implementation Techniques.- To be published in: E. Engeler (Ed.): Symposium on the Semantics of Algorithmic Languages, Springer Lecture Notes.-

/10/ G. Kreisel, J.L. Krivine: Elements of Mathematical Logic (Model Theory).- North-Holland, Amsterdam 1967.

/11/ P.J. Landin: The Mechanical Evaluation of Expressions.- Comp. J. 6 (1964), No.4, pp. 308-320.

/12/ P.J. Landin: A Correspondence between ALGOL 60 and Church's Lambda-Notation.- Comm. ACM 8 (1965), No.2, pp. 89-101 and No.3, pp. 158-165.

/13/ P.J. Landin: A Program Machine Symmetric Automata Theory.- In. B. Meltzer, D. Michie (Eds.): Machine Intelligence 5, pp. 99-120, Edinburgh 1969.

/14/ P. Lauer: Formal Definition of ALGOL 60.- IBM Laboratory Vienna, Techn. Rep. TR 25.088, 1968.

/15/ P. Lucas, K. Walk: On the Formal Description of PL/I.- Annual Review in Automatic Programming 6 (1969), Part 3, pp. 105-152, Pergamon Press.

/16/ J. McCarthy: Towards a Mathematical Science of Computation.- In: C.M. Popplewell (Ed.): Information Processing 1962, pp.21-28, North Holland, Amsterdam 1963.

/17/ J. McCarthy: Problems in the Theory of Computation.- In: W.A. Kalenich (Ed.): Information Processing 1965, pp. 219-222, Spartan Books, Washington 1965.

/18/ D. Scott: Outline of a Mathematical Theory of Computation.-
In: Proceedings of the Fourth Annual Princeton Conference on Information Sciences and Systesm, 1970.

/19/ K. Walk et al.: Abstract Syntax and Interpretation of PL/I.-
IBM Laboratory Vienna, Techn. Rep. TR 25.098, 1969.

/20/ A.van Wijngaarden (Ed.), B.J. Mailloux, J.E.L. Peck, C.H.A. Koster:
Report on the Algorithmic Language ALGOL 68.-
Mathematisch Centrum Amsterdam, MR 101, 1969.

IBM LABORATORY VIENNA, Austria

A FORMAL DEFINITION OF A PL/I SUBSET

by

H. Bekić

D. Bjørner

W. Henhapl

C. B. Jones

P. Lucas

ABSTRACT

This report provides a formal definition of large portions of the ECMA/ANSI proposed Standard PL/I language. The metalanguage used is described in the style of the "Mathematical Semantics". That is, the definition of PL/I is given by generating a function from a source program. A commentary is also provided to cover the less clear parts of the chosen model. For the convenience of the reader who wishes to have the commentary side by side with the formulae, the report is divided into two parts: Part I contains the description of the notation, the commentary and a cross-reference; Part II contains all the formulae.

NOTE

This document is not an official PL/I language specification. The language defined is based on the working documents (BASIS/1-9 to BASIS/1-11 [1]) of the joint ECMA/ANSI working group. It has not, however, been offered to them for review and has in no way been approved. Furthermore the subset chosen is not an indication of any IBM product plan.

TR 25.139

20 December 1974

A FORMAL DEFINITION OF A PL/I SUBSET

CONTENTS

PART I

PART II

Introduction

The aim of this report is to illustrate ideas about language definition on a "real" programming language. The language chosen is a subset of PL/I as defined in [1]. The main language features excluded are

CONTROLLED	storage
AREA	data
BY NAME	assignment
DEFINED	variables (other than overlay)
ALIGNED	attribute
REPEAT	option on DO
some Built in functions	
PICTURE	attribute
ENTRY	statement

The (limited) parts of Input/Output have been written up separately and will be made available later. Certain detailed restrictions are given below in lines marked "BASIS-11".

The current definition differs in a number of respects from the earlier ones (e.g. [2]) written in the Vienna Laboratory. The need for change was largely observed in the attempts to base implementation proofs on "VDL" definitions (see [3]).

The removal of some of the shortcomings which had been noticed was attempted in [4]. The period since 1969 has also seen the development of "Mathematical Semantics" as proposed by D. Scott and C. Strachey ([5]). The definition given below follows this style by defining PL/I programs via a mapping to the functions they denote. Although, not fully described in the same style, the extension of these concepts to parallel computation has been the particular interest of one of the authors (see [6]). This report should be seen as summarising "work in progress" in the area of applying formal definition to compiler development.

The report is divided into two major parts: Chapter N of Part I describes the metalanguage used in the definition; Chapter C of Part I contains a commentary on the more difficult parts of the model; the model is contained in Part II. A cross-reference of all the formulae is included as Chapter X of Part I.

Acknowledgements

The authors are grateful to the following for their contributions

H. Izbicki — collected from the BASIS document all of the "static checks" which are defined in D1.2;

V. Kudielka — produced an early draft of F5 and co-ordinated the commentaries section;

F. Schwarzenberger and
M. Stadler controlled the updates to the documents;
F. Mayrhofer,
E. Moser and reviewed F3;
W. Plöchl
W. Pachl provided frequent and very thorough reviews of the consistency of the formulae, he also wrote the cross-reference program;
K. Walk reviewed D2.2;
F. Weissenböck co-operated in the production of the commentary for F5.

Last, but by no means least, the accurate data entry of the formulae from our somewhat varied handwritings was performed by Mrs. H. Neiss.

References

[1] ECMA.TC10/ANSI.X3J1
PL/I BASIS/1-11
European Computer Manufacturers Association
Feb. 1974, 346 p.

[2] K. Walk, K. Alber, M. Fleck, H. Goldmann, P. Lauer, E. Moser, P. Oliva, H. Stigleitner, G. Zeisel
Abstract Syntax and Interpretation of PL/I (ULD Version III)
Techn. Report TR 25.098, IBM Lab. Vienna,
Apr. 1969.

[3] P. Lucas
On Program Correctness and the Stepwise Development of Implementations
Proceedings of the Congress on Theoretical Informatics, Pisa,
March 1973, pp.219-251.

[4] C. D. Allen, D. N. Chapman, C. B. Jones
A Formal Definition of ALGOL 60
Techn. Report TR 12.105, IBM UK Labs Ltd.,
Aug. 1972, 197 p.

[5] D. Scott, C. Strachey
Toward a Mathematical Semantics for Computer Languages
Techn. Monograph PRG-6, Oxford Univ. Computing Lab.
Aug. 1971, 42 p.

[6] H. Bekić
Semantics of Parallel Programs
Techn. Report, IBM Lab. Vienna (forthcoming)

[7] P. J. Landin
The Mechanical Evaluation of Expressions
The Computer Journal, Vol.6 (1964) No.4; pp.308-320.

[8] H. Bekić, K. Walk
Formalization of Storage Properties
Symposium on Semantics of Algorithmic Languages
Springer Lecture Notes in Mathematics, No. 188 (1970), p.28-61.

Notation

Introduction

The purpose of this Part is to document the intended meaning of the metalanguage used in Part II to define PL/I: the list of "non-objectives" is rather longer!

Firstly, it should be made clear that the description given below is not intended to be tutorial. It has been written for an audience which is assumed to have been already exposed to Formal Definition ideas. In particular no attempt is made to introduce those parts of the notation which are in common use. (One of the authors hopes to produce a more tutorial guide in the future).

Secondly, it cannot be claimed that the metalanguage is the final word of the authors: even in the PL/I definition the construct used to express arbitrary ordering is not defined in a completely satisfactory manner. Moreover, although application to new problems has been considered, it is likely that other constructs would be proposed for a more general specification language.

A related, but perhaps less credible, restriction to our aims is that there is no wish to fix a notation. The approach to the definition and its use in justifying implementations has lead us to certain concepts. It has, of course, been necessary to agree a notation to employ these concepts.

That brings us to the subject of how the definition is written. The definitions written in "VDL" (Vienna Definition Language, cf. [2]) notation were abstract interpreters. The interpreting machine was made rather powerful because of the inclusion of a Control Component which could be explicitly manipulated. Subsequent work aimed at proving implementations correct (see [3]) showed that not only the control, but a number of other concepts were inconvenient: in nearly all cases the need was to make the definitions even more abstract by giving only properties required by the language. Ideas already existed for removing the need for explicit changes to the control as a model for GOTO (cf. [4]). Furthermore, the whole field of Mathematical Semantics style definitions of languages had been developed (cf. [5]).

PL/I is defined here by showing how to map any (abstract) program to a "transformation", that is, a function from states to states.

Classes of objects (including programs) can be described by Abstract Syntax Descriptions: such descriptions are discussed in Section 2. Section 1 describes the other classes of objects used, for instance, to describe states.

The functions which define the generation of transformations, and the transformations themselves are defined by means of a notation which is defined in terms of the lambda calculus in sections 3 and 4. The arbitrary order parts of the meta-language are discussed in 4.4.

The created transformations are defined by recursive equations with the intention that their value is the minimal fixed point. A constructive way of obtaining this is discussed in section 5.

The Appendix defines the concrete syntax of the metalanguage.

(Ed: Sections 1-3 omitted)

4. Transformations

In this section we introduce ways of expressing transformations, i.e. functions of type $\Sigma \to \Sigma$ or (value-returning transformations) $\Sigma \to \Sigma\ R$, where Σ is the set of states. A state is a mapping from a set of references to other objects. References are elementary objects. We write REF for the set of all references, ref v for the set of references whose "contents", in any state σ, are restricted to values in v:

$$(\forall r \in \underline{D}\sigma)\ (r \in \underline{\text{ref}}V \supset \sigma(r) \in V)$$

As an abbreviation in type clauses, we use:

$$\Rightarrow R \ \sim\ \Sigma \to \Sigma\ R, \qquad D \Rightarrow R \ \sim\ D \to (\Sigma \to \Sigma\ R)$$

(similarly if R is omitted). Thus transformations become =>, value-returning transformations become =>R, and functions from D to transformations (like the int/eval functions, see also section 5) become D=> or D=>R.

4.1. Declaration, Contents, Assignment

Programming languages provide a "variable-free" notation for state-transformations, i.e. a way of writing state-transformations without explicit reference to the state σ, and this is very much what the "combinators" introduced in this and the following subsections achieve. We assume types:

$$s: \Rightarrow, \qquad e: \Rightarrow R \text{ (for various R)}$$

(s for "statement", e for "expression"), similarly for s_1, s_2, s(i), e_1, e_2, e(i).

Declaration extends the state:

$$\begin{array}{lcl} (\underline{\text{dcl}}\ r := v; & \sim & \lambda\sigma.(\underline{\text{let}}\ r\ \underline{\text{be}}\ \underline{\text{s.t.}}\ \neg(r \in \underline{D}\sigma); \\ \ f(r) \qquad) : \Rightarrow & & \quad \underline{\text{let}}\ \sigma' = f(r)\ (\sigma \cup [r \mapsto v])\ ; \\ & & \quad \sigma' \backslash \{r\}) \end{array}$$

(for f(r): =>, similarly f(r): =>R).

Contents takes the value of σ at a given reference $r \in \underline{D}\sigma$:

$$\underline{c}r: \Rightarrow V \qquad \sim \qquad \lambda\sigma.\langle\sigma,\sigma(r)\rangle$$

(this has been made of type =>V - returning the unchanged σ - rather than Σ->V in order to be usable by the other combinators).

Assignment changes the contents of a reference $r \in \underline{D}\sigma$:

$$(r := v): \Rightarrow \qquad \sim \qquad \lambda\sigma.\ \sigma + [r \mapsto v]$$

Derived references. Given a reference r to a mapping $m{:}I \to V$, we sometimes use $i \circ r$ (for $i \in I$) as a "derived reference" to m(i):

$$\underline{c}(i \circ r) \sim (\underline{c}r)\ (i), \qquad (i \circ r := v) \sim r := \underline{c}r + [i \mapsto v]$$

(see 4.5 for the use of $\underline{c}r$ in a position where its result m is intended).

4.2. Sequencing

First we introduce a variant of let (distinguished by the use of ":" instead of "=") which permits side-effects:

For e: =>V, f:V=>, we have:

$$\begin{array}{lcl} (\underline{let}\ v\!: e; & \sim & \lambda\sigma.(\underline{let}\langle\sigma',v\rangle = e(\sigma); \\ \ f(v) \quad): \Rightarrow & & \qquad f(v)\ (\sigma')) \end{array}$$

(similarly for f:V=>R).

The return statement raises a value $v \in V$ to a transformation:

$$(\underline{return}\ v): \Rightarrow V \qquad \sim \qquad \lambda\sigma.\langle\sigma,v\rangle$$

The following all are transformations of type =>.

$\underline{I}$ is identity on states:

$$\underline{I} \qquad \sim \qquad \lambda\sigma.\sigma$$

Semicolon is sequential execution:

$$s_1;s_2 \qquad \sim \qquad \lambda\sigma.s_2(s_1(\sigma))$$

(similarly s;e).

The conditional

if b then s_1 else s_2

(for b:B), similarly if b then e_1 else e_2, and its variants are as described for expressions in general (see 3.2.). We also allow:

if b then s ∿ if b then s else I

and

if e then s_1 else s_2 ∿ let b: e;
if b then s_1 else s_2

(for e: =>B - a special case of the convention described in 4.5.).

Iterative statements and expressions are

for i = m to n do s(i) ∿ s(m); ...;s(n)

<e(i) | for i = m to n> ∿ let v(m): e(m);
...
let v(n): e(n);
return <v(i) | m≤i≤n>

(for m,n:intg), and:

while e do s ∿ let w = (let b: e;
if b then s;w else I);
w

(for e: =>B). See 4.4. for the for all statement.

4.3. Exit

The exit mechanism described in this section deals with the situation that execution of a (sub-) phrase has to be terminated "abnormally", i.e. abandoned; it also permits specification of the action that has to be performed on abnormal termination. This mechanism has been used to model the PL/I GO TO (cf. CF3) and RETURN statements, it can also be used to deal with error situations.

Formally, we can explain abnormal termination by slightly complicating our transformations, i.e. re-interpret =>:

D=> ∿ D ->(Σ -> Σ (nil | abn ABN))
D=>R ∿ D ->(Σ -> Σ (res R | abn ABN)) (similarly with D omitted): the flags res and abn are used to make normally and abnormally returned values disjoint. Transformations not involving sequencing combinators (like cr, r:=v, I, return v) can be re-interpreted immediately:

```
s                                  ∿   λσ.<s (σ),nil>

e                                  ∿   λσ.(let <σ',v> = e(σ);
                                            <σ,<res,v>>)
```

The exit statement returns a value abnormally:

```
exit(abn)                          ∿   λσ.<σ,<abn,abn>>
```

The trap exit becomes:

```
(trap exit(abn) with f(abn);       ∿   let r: s;
 s              ): =>                  cases r:
                                       (nil -> I, <abn,abn> -> f(abn))
```

(f(abn): =>), similarly with e instead of s:

```
(trap exit(abn) with f(abn)        ∿   let r: e;
 e              ): =>R                 cases r:
                                       (<res,v> -> return(v),<abn,abn> ->f(abn))
```

(f(abn): =>R).

A variant like trap exit(go,abn') with f(abn') causes a test on the arguments passed to exit, the f(abn') being executed only when the constants match; several trap exit's can be specified for one block as long as the argument ranges do not overlap.

Also semicolon (similarly: let:) have to be slightly more complicated:

```
s1;s2                              ∿   let r: s1;
                                       cases r:
                                       (nil -> s2, <abn,abn> -> exit(abn))
```

The error handling is defined by:

```
error: =>                          ∿   exit(ERROR)
```

where no trap exit for ERROR is provided.

See next section for exit from a parallel phrase.

4.4. Arbitrary Order

The comma between two transformations denotes quasi-parallel execution of them: the "elementary" steps of the two transformations are merged in arbitrary order, preserving only the two orderings within the given transformations. Which steps are considered elementary is left open, a sensible choice would be to take the "terminal" operations of the metalanguage (like c, :=) as elementary. Thus:

(s_1,s_2): =>	∿	elementary steps merged in arbitrary order

For e_1: =>V_1, e_2: =>V_2 :

<e_1,e_2>: =>V_1V_2	∿	same, with pair <v_1,v_2> of returned values as returned value

(similar for several e(i)).

The context where this is most used are parallel let's:

let v_1: e_1, v_2: e_2; f(v_1,v_2)	∿	let <v_1,v_2> : <e_1,e_2>; f(v_1,v_2)

Sometimes the s(i) or e(i) are not enumerated explicitly:

for all i∈ I do s(i)	∿	execute s (i) in parallel

For e(i): =>V (for each i∈ I) :

par{e(i) | i∈ I}: =>V-set	∿	execute the e(i) in parallel; return the map [i → v(i) | i∈ I] where v(i) is returned by e(i)

(The operator par is only used implicitly, see next section).

Arbitrary order and exit. If in (s_1,s_2) (similarly: <e_1,e_2>) one of the two transformations, say s_1, terminates abnormally with value abn, then an (implied) exit (abn) is executed in s_2, which will cause execution of the relevant trap exit's in s_2.

If this eventually terminates s_2 abnormally with the same value abn, the whole transformation (s_1,s_2) terminates abnormally with abn. (If the implied exit leads to normal termination of s_2, or to abnormal termination with a different value abn', then (s_1,s_2) terminates with error; no such, error producing, use of exit in parallel transformations has been made in the PL/I-Definition).

Non-determinism and recursion. The arbitrary choice operator let v be s.t. p(v) (see 3.2.) introduces an element of non-determinism and thus, strictly speaking, forces transformations to be functions from states to sets of states, rather than from states to states. The quasi-parallel merging operator, which also introduces non-determinism, additionally complicates transformations because now we have to consider their component steps, rather than the functional product of those steps. A particular problem arises with recursive definitions and non-determinism: The ordering relation ("v is less defined than v' ") on which the familiar way of solving recursive equations is based does not immediately carry over from elements to sets. One way to solve this problem is to evaluate the expressions of the metalanguage under an additional hidden parameter serving as a "choice tape" (e.g. an infinite sequence of truth values); evaluation under a given choice tape is deterministic, the set of all solutions is obtained by considering all choice tapes (cf.[6]).

4.5. Value-Returning Transformations in Value Positions

Often it is convenient to write a value-returning transformation in a place where a value is required, with the understanding that the transformation is executed as a side-effect. Thus:

For f:V->R, e: =>V, we have:

```
f(e): =>R                      ~    let v: e;
                                    return(f(v))
```

This makes f(e) a transformation (of type =>R) whereas the context requires a value (of type R), and so we can apply the same rule to this context, say g(f(e)). Eventually we will come to a context which is intended to produce a transformation (e.g. g(v) might be return (v)); this is covered by the analoguous rule:

For g:V=>R, e: =>R, we have:

```
g(e): =>R                      ~    let v: e;
                                    g(v)
```

For f or g with several arguments we get a parallel transformation as the right hand side of the let).

Where the e(i) are given implicitly, par is implied:

For e(i): =>V (for each $i \in I$):

{e(i) | i∈ I}: =>V-set	∿	let m: par{e(i) | i∈ I}; return Rm
<e(i) | i∈ I>: =>V*	∿	let m: par{e(i) | i∈ I}; return <m(i) | i∈ I>

(where I is an interval {m:n} - this really only re-explains <e(m),...,e(n)>).

[i → e(i) | i∈ I]: =>(I->V)	∿	let m: par{e(i) | i∈ I}; return m

5. Constructive Interpretation of the Metalanguage

5.1. Macro-Expansion

The int/eval functions of the PL/I Definition are correspondences from text-classes θ (and auxiliary parameters) to transformations:

int-θ: θ ENV ... -> (Σ -> Σ)

eval-θ: θ ENV ... -> (Σ -> Σ V)

The aim of this section is to outline a method to constructively interpret the highly recursive definitions of these correspondences. The idea is to (1) macro-expand, for given t∈ θ, env, ..., the call int-θ(t,env,...), i.e. replace it by its definition, similarly for nested calls of int/eval functions; this will eventually lead to a description of the corresponding transformation which no longer refers to any int/eval functions, whereupon (2) application of this transformation (description) to a given state can be left to a conventional call-by-value interpreter.

5.2. "Unfounded" Uses of int-θ

Usually, int-θ(t,...) is defined by structural induction on the text t, i.e. in terms of int-θi(ti,..) where the ti are the (immediate) components of t, so that the expansion process will get to ever smaller components and eventually stop. There are, however, a few cases where int-θ(t,..) itself recurs in its definition.

Example 1 (while-statement) (cf F3; this and the following examples are somewhat simplified extracts from corresponding examples in the F Chapters):

```
int-wh-st(<e,st>,env) =
   let b: eval-expr(e,env);
   if b then (int-st(st,env); int-wh-st(<e,st>,env)) else I
```

We can formally avoid the recurring use of int-wh-st by a (recursive!) let:

```
int-wh-st(<e,st>,env) =
   let f = (let b: eval-expr(e,env);
            if b then (int-st(st,env); f) else I;
   f
```

Example 2 (compound-statement, omitting env, cf. F3):

```
int-cpd-st(t) = cue-int-cpd-st(t,lab1)

cue-int-cpd-st(t,lab) =
   trap exit(abn) with if ... then cue-int-cpd-st(t,abn) else exit(abn);
   int-st(t[lab]);
   if ... then cue-int-cpd-st(t,lab+1) else I
```

(lab1 = label of first statement, lab+1 = label of next statement), which becomes

```
int-cpd-st(t) =
   let f(lab) = (trap exit(abn) with if ... then f(abn) else exit(abn);
                 int-st(t[lab]);
                 if ... then f(lab+1) else I);
   f(lab1)
```

(Of course the let f style could be used directly. In Example 1, the re-use of int-wh-st has actually been avoided by using the while-construction of the metalanguage).

5.3. Recursive "let:" - clauses

Whereas the rewriting just discussed was only necessary to get a closed expression for the resulting transformation ("to stop the expansion") but did not make any difference for an interpreter, the case

```
let v: f(v)
```

of a transformation defined in terms of the value (to be) returned by its execution is more serious:

Example 3 (blocks, cf. F1):

```
int-bl(<dcls,procs,st>,env) =
   let lenv: [id → eval-dcl(dcls(id),env) | id∈ Ddcls]
             [id → eval-proc(procs(id),env+lenv) | id∈ Dprocs];
   int-st(st,env+lenv)
```

(assuming dcls is a map from id to dcl, similarly for procs).

```
eval-dcl(dd,env) =
   let edd: ...dd...;
   alloc(edd)

eval-proc(<idl,st>,env) =
   λlocl.(let penv = [idl[i] → locl[i] | 1≤i≤lidl];
          int-st(st,env+penv))
```

Observe that call-by-value would immediately run into a loop with int-bl: to compute lenv, we would first have to compute lenv in order to pass it to the eval-proc calls. Expanding we get:

```
int-bl(<dcls,procs,st>,env) =
   let lenv: [id → (let edd: ...dcls(id)...; alloc(edd)) | id ∈ Ddcls] ∪
             [id → λlocl.(let penv = [s-idl(procs(id))[i] → locl[i] | ...];
                          int-st(s-st(procs(id)),env+lenv+penv))
                   | id ∈ Dprocs];
   int-st(st,env+lenv)
```

(note that side effects in eval-dcl, e.g. alloc(edd), are to be executed at let lenv - time), and we see that the use of lenv within the definition is now "shielded" by occuring within the scope of λlocl. This can be dealt with by a call-by-value interpreter (provided a λ-expression is not evaluated before it gets applied). (It is easy to see that this is the only kind of unshielded use in the PL/I-Definition - the only recursive definitions in PL/I are procedure declarations).

5.4. Distinction between Static and Dynamic Properties

We started this section by asking for a constructive interpretation of the very implicit definitions, but the process of expansion we have described is of interest also in other respects. It gives a (more) closed description of the transformation denoted by given t under given env,... . It exploits, and makes visible, the distinction between static and dynamic case distinctions, i.e. between decisions that are made to arrive at the transformation, and decisions that are part of the transformation. Obviously, this distinction is important for deriving a compiler from the language definition, but it is also relevant for showing which "steps" make up the resulting transformation (see 4.2.). One could go further in the expansion (and sharpen the distinction), e.g. expand the let-clause for the local environment lenv into several let-clauses, one per local identifier, arriving at a description which does not use env at all. All the uses made of the for all and (implied) par operator (cf. 4.4.) are such that they can be statically expanded into $(s_1,\ldots,s_n)$ resp. $(e_1,\ldots,e_n)$.

Commentary

C0. Overview

The purpose of the commentary part of the report is to provide a description of some of the less obvious aspects of the model given in the formal part. Given a knowledge of the meta-language the reader is assumed to be able to interpret the formulae as such, and no translation into words is attempted. (If at any place there should be some contradiction, it is the formulae rather than the text which define the model.)

One aid to reading provided by the commentary is the elucidation of the abbreviations used. The set given at the end of this section apply uniformly to function names and names of abstract syntax classes. The use of names for locally defined objects has been less consistent: these are defined at the point of uniform usage (e.g. section, sub-section or formula).

The structure of the commentary is the same as that of the formal part. The major division is between the objects which are manipulated by, and the defining functions themselves. The first of these ("Domains") separates abstract programs from the other objects. A set satisfying is-prog is first defined by abstract syntax rules. A large number of static properties can be described for valid programs. Assuming that these properties are fulfilled makes it possible to write the defining functions in a clearer way. (It is also a way of making the language properties clearer than if they were mixed with the dynamic tests). The class of programs to be used as the domain of int-prog, is, then, defined as a subset of is-prog whose members also satisfy the given context conditions. The "States" portion of the Domains section describes the other objects manipulated. Principal among these is "Storage" which models PL/I variables. The reasons for choosing an implicit definition for this are discussed below.

The "Functions" section is divided into six parts, in this way formulae relating to a particular language concept are grouped together. The section on input/output is only a place holder for the required functions. (The actual formulae will be the subject of a separate report).

The functions themselves are sometimes supported by pre and post conditions and assertions. When given the function is only defined over a restriction of the domain given in the type clause: those elements satisfying pre. That the function is only used over this restricted domain results from other constraints. Post conditions and assertions provide an insight into the formula by stating relations the authors were trying to preserve.

Abbreviations

aa	activation identifiers
abs	absolute
act	action
addr	address
ag	aggregate
aid	activation identifier
alloc	allocate
approx	approximate
arg	argument
arith	arithmetic
ass	assign, assignment
atm	atomic
augm	augment[ed]
auto	automatic
bi	builtin
bif	builtin function
bin	binary
bl[s]	block[s]
bool	boolean
boe	block cn-establishment
bp	bound-pair
bpl	bound-pair list
bs	base
c	cond-pref-set,context
cat	concatenate
cbif	condition built-in function
ccn	comp-cond-nm
c-nm	non-io-cond-nm or io-cond
ceil	ceiling
char	character
cl	class
clng	closing
cmp	composite
cn	cond-nm
comp	computational, component (the latter used more often!)
compar	compare
cond	condition
conn	connected
const	constant
constr	construct

cont	content
conv	conversion, convert
cprefs	cond-pref-set
cpv	cond-pv
ctl	control
ctld	controlled
cur	current
dcl	declaration
dcls	declaration set
dd	data-description
dec	decimal
def	defined
der	derived
descr[s]	descriptor[s]
dft	default
digitl	digit list
dim	dimension
distr[ib]	distributive
div	divide
dsgn	designator
dtp	data-type
ebp	evaluated bound-pair
edd	evaluated data description
el	element, elementary
elem	element
enab	enabled
env	environment
eq	equal
eu	executable-unit
evd	evaluated
eval	evaluate
eval-l	eval-to-left-value
ex-unit	executable-unit
expr	expression
ext	external
fact	factor
fct	function
f	field
fix	fixed
flt	float
fofl	fixed overflow

ge	greater or equal
gen	generate
grp	group
gt	greater
hbound	high bound
id[s]	identifier[s]
im	immediate
impl	implementation
indep	independent
indices	set of index lists
indl	list of indices
inf	infix, information
init	initial, initialize
init-wh-do	DO statement with init and while
int	internal
int	interpret(in fn names)
intg	integer
io	input-output
ioc	io-cond
iter	iteractive, iteration
l	list
l-	location
lab	label
lb	lower bound
lbound	low bound
le	less than or equal
len	length
loc[s]	location[s]
locr	locator
loe[r]	local on-establishment [by reference]
lt	less than
l-to-r	left to right
max	maximum
maxl	maximum length
min	minimum
mod	modulo
mult	multiply
ne	not equal
nm[s]	name[s]
nmd	named
nod	number-of-digits
num	number,numeric

obs	objects
ofl	overflow
onsource	onsource location
op	operator
opng	opening
opt[s]	option[s]
ou	on-unit
parm[s]	parameter[s]
pdd	parameter data descriptor
pos	position
pos-cond-nm	positive-condition-name
prec	precision
pref[s]	prefix[s]
proc	procedure
prog	program
prom	promote
prop	proper
ps	proper statement
ptr	pointer
pv	pseudo variable
qual	qualifier
r	right
rec	recursive
recity	recursivity
ref	reference
rel	relevant
rep	representation
res	result
ret	return
ret-descr	returns-descriptor
rev	revert
sc	scalar
sdd	statically determined data description
scomp-	static computational-
sdtp	static data description
sect	section
sels	selector set
sentry	static entry data description
sig	signal
snap	SNAP or nil
snms	statement names
snom-comp-	static non-computational-

source	onsource-char-str-val
spec	specification
st[s]	statement[s]
step-do	DO statement with TO
stg	storage
str	string
strg	string range
struct	structure
strz	stringsize
subjs	subjects
subr	subroutine
subrg	subscript range
subscr	subscript
substr	substring
subt	subtract
t	text
targ	target
term	terminal
tp	type
truth	truth (truth value)
ub	upper bound
udf	undefined
ufl	underflow
uid	unique identifier
unal	un-aligned
v-	value
val	value
var	variable
varity	variability
vary	variability
vr	value reference
wh	while
zdiv	zerodivide
1-loc	level-one location

CD1.1 Abstract Programs

The explicit selectors are those used in chapters D2 through F5; selectors used in D1.2 are explicit when given, otherwise implicit.

The reader should note the choice of defining symbol (: : or =, cf. N2) used in the various rules. The construction has been rather cautious in that elements of unions (unless themselves unions) have usually been given constructors, even if one could have shown this not to be necessary to ensure disjointness.

In a number of places (e.g. dcl-set) it is now thought that rather than use a set, a mapping (in this case id -> dcl-tp) would provide a shorter definition.

ad 31 entry: Deviating from BASIS-11, we distinguish between: no requirements on parameters, and empty parameter list required. In concrete syntax: ENTRY vs. ENTRY().

CD1.2 Context Conditions and Functions

CD1.2.1 Static Data Descriptions

Static data descriptions are used to capture the declarative information available in the program text. Thus, it is not, in general, possible to know more than the dimensionality of an array: the bounds may be computed only in relation to a particular storage. (Some benefit could be gained by combining the definitions of dd, sdd, pdd, and edd).

CD1.2.2 Rule-by-Rule Conditions and Functions

Within the class of objects satisfying is-prog there are some which can be considered "statically wrong" programs (e.g. using variables which are not declared). It would be possible to build checks for such errors into the defining function. It was felt by the current authors that it was better to show such properties statically. The predicates of this section define a subclass of is-prog, as follows: for each phrase class θ defined in terms of $\theta_1, \theta_2, \ldots, \theta_n$ there is a rule which is either provided explicitly or by default is:

$$\text{is-wf-}\theta(\text{o},\text{env}) = \text{is-wf-}\theta_1(\text{s-e1}(\text{e}),\text{env}) \wedge \ldots \wedge \text{is-wf-}\theta_n(\text{s-e}_n(\text{e}),\text{env})$$

The env component contains the declaration or procedure for each known identifier. This, together with the function el-sdd (see below) provides the way of checking those context conditions governing types.

Another important class of context conditions is those which simply express a context-free subset of the abstract syntax (e.g. is-no-refers) : these are expressed as predicates of c-comp-θ, although they could have been handled by duplicating rules. Those context conditions prohibiting duplication of names are defined using the predicate is-unique-ids. Certain consistency checks are made (e.g. locator qualifiers must be available by default if not explicit). There are also "geometrical" (e.g. is-refer-geom) and value (e.g. EXTERNAL dd's must evaluate to same edd) constraints.

The numbers used for the functions are those of the abstract syntax.

ad 1 is-wf-prog: to simplify notation, quantifiers over contained objects (here: p1, p2) have been omitted throughout this section.

ad 39 is-wf-bl: notice that passing the old environment minus local names (nenv'), prevents for example automatic declarations relying on block local quantities.

CD1.2.3 Auxiliary Functions

The function el-sdd yields the sdd of an expression. That is, it determines the descriptions of its atomic elements and applies rules for combining operand types with particular operators. In the uses of this function outside D1, the second argument (textual environment env, which can always be determined statically) has been omitted. For a discussion of the distribution mechanism see CF5.

CD2. States, Auxiliary Parameters

Programs denote functions from states to states, and this Section defines the notion of (PL/I)state. As explained in N4, a state is a map from references ("variables") to other objects (the "contents" of the variable). The five major state components are treated in the first three sub-sections: AA and PA (dealing with activation identifiers) in 2.1, storage in 2.2, external storage and file state (dealing with input/output) in 2.3.

The int/eval functions establishing the correspondence between texts and state-transformations need auxiliary parameters. These are defined in the remaining sub-sections, namely the environment in 2.4, the on-establishment (dealing with on-conditions) in 2.5, and the cbif-part (dealing with condition builtin functions) in 2.6.

Abbreviations for this Section:

Σ	set of states
σ	a state
S	[ref to] storage
ES	[ref to] external storage
FS	[ref to] file state
AA	[ref to] active aid's
PA	[ref to] previous aid's
aid	activation identifier

1 Σ:

See N4. The present definition is more specific in that it enumerates the object classes over which the contents of a state component can range. The first four alternatives are due to the major (global) state components (AID arising twice); OE (cf 2.5) and the "other" objects arise as the contents of local state components.

2 (major state components):

By systematic ambiguity, these five names are used both as references (e.g. when appearing on the left of :=, cr as argument of c) and as names for the sets over which the references range (e.g. in syntax rules).

CD2.1 Activation Identifiers

An activation identifier (aid) serves to uniquely identify the activation of a block or procedure; it is needed to make the denotation of a label unique, and also for discovering uses of "dead" label- and entry values. PA records all aid's used so far (it is never decreased), AA the currently active ones.

CD2.2 Values, Locations, and Storage

The storage model used here is a version of the general model described in [8], specialised to the needs of PL/I. The basic idea behind the model is quite simple: Storage is, essentially, a function f from locations to values:

f: L -> V

thus associating with each location l in L a value v = f(l), the "contents" of the location, with the following two properties:

1. f is range-respecting: each location has associated with it a certain range, i.e. subset of V, and can contain values from this subset only.

2. f is structure-preserving: a location may have components, and then the contents of the component location is the "corresponding" component of the contents of the whole location.

The present model is more explicit than the general model. For example, composite locations (and values) are defined explicitly as lists or maps. Also, the only instance of "flexible" locations (i.e. ones whose active components depend on the current contents) is provided by VARYING strings. (A price to pay for this explicitness is that "width zero" locations, e.g. string locations of length 0, now seem to be over-specified, at least in connection with pointers, see CD2.2.3). Still, many notions are characterised implicitly, by axioms. For example, there is no need to say what an elementary location "is"; also, PL/I pointers are so implementation-defined that they are best described by (incomplete) axioms.

u-edd	unit-edd (of an array-edd)
ebpl	evaluated bound pair list
tp	string-type
vy	variability
v	value
vl	value list
vals	values
l	location
m, mm'	map
-l	-list

CD2.2.1 Evaluated Data Descriptions

Evaluated data descriptions (edd's) arise from dd's by evaluating expressions for array bounds and string lengths (and dropping initial and REFER elements); they serve, among other things, to represent the range of a location, see values(edd) below.

Indices are used to select components from locations or values, see CD2.2.2 and CD2.2.3 below. (The functions given here are purely auxiliary).

19 width:
counts characters, bits, and non-string scalars.

20 is-all-str:
tests whether edd consists of NONVARYING characters or bits only (tp = CHAR or BIT).

CD2.2.2 Values

An array value is a map from a multi-dimensional rectangle of integers (the subscripts) to values of a given type. A structure value is the list of its field values. Note that, by use of ::, the empty character string value and the empty bit string value are different. An entry value is a function (cf. CF1) together with an identifier (needed for entry comparison) and an aid (needed for checking against "dead" entries).

28 mk-STR-VAL:
needed where not statically known whether to use mk-CHAR-STR-VAL OR mk_BIT-STR-VAL.

39 udf-val,
40 is-defined-val:

Undefined values are needed to discover uses of uninitialised variables. One value ? is used for single elements of NONVARYING strings, and for the other scalars (note that the undefined VARYING string is *one ?* - nothing about the current length of the string is known!); composite undefined values are composed of ?'s; a value is *defined* if it contains no ?.

41 values:

Connects edd's with "ranges", i.e. value sets. Note that the preceding rules for VAL etc. did not list ? with STR-VAL or the alternatives of ELEM-VAL, so it has to be added to the ranges here.

43 v-augm-indices,
44 v-indices:

The indices returned by v-indices(v) are integer-lists selecting the elements of an array, integers selecting the (immediate) fields of a structure, and pairs <i,i> selecting the one-element substrings of a string; v-augm-indices also includes * for arrays (for forming cross-sections) and <i,j> for strings, it is only used in the pre of comp-val.

CD2.3 Locations

LOC is the set of *all* (potential) locations, not only the currently allocated ones. The definitions are analogous to those for VAL; *atomic* locations(elementary, i.e. non-string scalar locs, and single character and bit locs) are left unanalyzed - except that elementary locs have an edd extracted by the function l-edd. Note that CHAR-LOC and BIT-LOC are not subsets of LOC- they cannot be denoted in PL/I.

Due to distribution over all its arguments, the SUBSTR pseudo-variable (see F2) can generate "inhomogenous" array locations violating the constraint given for ARRAY-LOC. The use of this constraint in the definition of l-edd could be avoided by associating with array locations a map from indices to edd's, rather than the present array-edd (which would arise as the special case of a constant map).

53 CHAR-STR-LOC,
54 BIT-STR-LOC:

The corresponding constructors mk-CHAR-STR-LOC and mk-BIT-STR-LOC must be assumed as non-unique in the case of (at least the VARYING) empty string, see "Independence" below.

The function comp-loc is completely analoguous to comp-val.

66 sub-loc:

m' is an array-loc, except that the elements may be arrays again; this is rectified by the function array-loc.

68 ordered-sc-locs,

69 sc-locs:

give list/set of scalar sub-locations.

70 ordered-atm-locs,

71 atm-locs:

similar for atomic locations, with an irregularity for VARYING strings explained presently.

73 1-LOC:

The set 1-LOC of level-one locations is used as a pool from which to allocate storage for PL/I level-one variables. The dissection into AUTO and BASED locations is used for a test on freeing, see F2.

74 is-indep:

Two locations are independent if they have no parts in common. (The reason for including length-zero VARYING string locations in atm-locs above is that they have no atoms yet need to be distinguishable: they have two possible contents, namely the empty string and ?. The latter does not hold in the NONVARYING case). Different level-one locations, and different components of the same given location, are postulated to be independent.

77 is-conn,

79 is-l-to-r-loc:

A location is connected if it is a contiguous part of a level-one location. Left-to-right equivalence is defined, contrary to BASIS/1-11, down to arbitrarily nested structure levels.

80 PROP-PTR-VAL,

81 addr,

82 constr-loc:

A connected location has an address which is a (non-null) pointer. Intuitively, the address may be regarded as location "minus" edd, hence the loc should be reconstructable from its address and its edd (axiom 83). Independent locations have different addr (axiom 84, postulated only for locations not of width 0, in view of the difficulties with the latter; for locs with the same edd, this axiom follows from the previous one). Left-to-right equivalent locations have the same addr (axiom 85), and an all-CHAR or all-BIT location has the same addr as its first atomic location (axiom 86; these last two axioms are compatible with the view that addr is the "starting point" of a location).

CD2.2.4 Storage

L_o currently active level-one locations

f_o storage, viewed as a map over L_o

L all locations derivable from L_o

f storage, viewed as a function over L

87 S:

For finite representation, storage is viewed as a map from (active) level-one locations only. The two properties of storage required in the introduction to CD2 above are ensured, then, first by the constraint to this formula, and second by the way in which the map is extended to L:

91 extend:

The "parts" of a location go down to characters and bits, but not inside VARYING strings; the "current parts" also take into account components of the latter within the current length. The extended set L consists of all locations whose parts are among the current parts of locations in L_o. The given map over L_o uniquely generates a function over L which satisfies the required properties, i.e. is range-respecting and structure-preserving. (The set of active locations actually expressible in PL/I is a finite subset of L. It seemed better, however, to give a simple extension rule than to enumerate cases).

CD2.2.5 Allocate, Free, Contents, Assignment

Allocation uses env-cond (the "environment" for condition raising, see F4), because the STG condition has to be raised on storage overflow. Only level-one locations can be freed. Contents checks for non-initialised locations.

96 assign:

f_o' the updated (level-one) storage

f' the updated extended storage

The updated storage must ascribe contents v to location l, and leave unchanged the contents of locations independent from l. This alone does not ensure that a VARYING string location (dependent from l but) not contained in l has its current length unchanged, which therefore has to be postulated explicitly.

CD2.3 External Storage, File State

DS	data set
REC	record
K-[R]	keyed [record]
uid	unique identifier

107 c-uid,

108 file-id:

The function c-uid is used in F1 to associate different uid's with different occurrences of file constant declarations, except that external declarations of the same identifier are commoned; the id is retrieved and represented as character string by the function file-id.

CD2.4 Environment

The environment pairs identifiers with denotations: locations for proper variables and parameters (cf F1 and F2), values for named constants (cf. F1), and certain functions or pairs of functions for DEFINED and BASED variables (cf. F2).

For BL-ENV (block environment, used for STATIC and EXTERNAL identifiers) and the function bl-env(pb), see CF1.

CD2.5 On-Establishment

On-establishments are named: oe, oe-0, oe-1, boe(block-), loe(local-) and loer (ref to local). oe's are passed (by value) to the int-bl function 'inside' which the passed oe is named boe. The loe is passed by reference to all functions which can update this loe, these functions then name the passed oe loer; otherwise the loe is passed by value (by taking c of loer) and 'keeps' the name loe (except for the case of int-bl).

on-ENTRY-VAL is a set of functions -- with many similarities between these and the functions of ENTRY-VAL.

CD2.6 Cbif-Part

Instances of CBIF are named cbif, $cbif_{o}$, cbif-1. They are all maps. Specifically a cbif is a map from (a finite set of) cond-bif-nm's to either LOCations, NUMber-VALues or CHARacter-STRing-VALues depending on the cond-bif-nm. Cond-bif-nm ONSOURCE maps into a LOC whose type (i.e. edd) is CHAR-STR-VAL.

CF1 Block Structure

This section deals with program, block, and procedure interpretation. It covers both procedure declaration, which associates with the procedure identifier the function denoted by the procedure, and procedure activation, which applies that function to the evaluated arguments.

Abbreviations for this Section

acty[s]	ref to activity flag[s] (for non-RECURSIVE procedures)
en-f	entry function (denoted by a proc id)
major	"this is the major proc activation" (truth value)
st-env	static environment
nenv	new environment
abn	value returned on abnormal termination

CF1.1 Programs

1 int-prog

main-id	id of main proc
pb-sels	selectors to contained procs and blocks
	similarly: non-RECURSIVE procs, STATIC EXTERNAL dcls
st-ext-ids	STATIC EXTERNAL identifiers
st-int-ids	similarly, indexed by declaring proc or block
st-ext-locs	locations for st-ext-ids, indexed by id
st-int-locs	also indexed by sel to declaring proc or block
env-1	pairs EXTERNAL proc ids with their denotations
prog'	prog with dens for STATIC and EXTERNAL ids inserted
main-en-f	entry function denoted by main proc

Syntactically, prog is a set of procedures. Semantically, it behaves very much like a block whose declarations are these (EXTERNAL) procs, and whose body is a call to one of them, identified by main-id (hence the "pre:"). Other declarations which in a sense belong to this artificial outermost block are those of STATIC variables and those of file and EXTERNAL entry constants.

After a few "pure" auxiliary definitions, the first action is initialisation of the state. Like for genuine block activations, an id (aid-0) uniquely characterising the activation is generated. Next, storage for STATIC variables is allocated; the difference between EXTERNAL and INTERNAL is that in the former case declarations of the same id are commoned.

Since prog' has inserted into it, amongst other things, the denotations of the EXTERNAL procedures, the definitions of env-1 and prog' are mutually recursive (cf. N5.3). The third argument of eval-proc-dcl distinguishes the outermost use of the main proc from any other: it is true only for the former. (This is used in the interpretation of the

RETURN statement, see below). - The function bl-env'(spb) collects into a bl-env (block-environment) the denotations to be inserted into a given (occurrence of a) block; the actual insertion is done by postulating a context function bl-env(pb) which retrieves the inserted bl-env (cf D2.4). For procedures not declared RECURSIVE, the activity flag (initialised to INACTIVE) is used for testing that they are indeed used non-recursively; this flag is also made part of bl-env.

After all the preparatory actions, the function denoted by the main proc is called, with dummy arguments except that condition names are paired (in oe-1) with their system actions. Finally, STATIC storage is freed and the activation closed.

CF1.2 Blocks

2 int-bl:

Immediately calls int-bl-1, the common part of block and procedure interpretation. By context conditions, it can be assumed that st-env and lenv (in int-bl-1) have disjoint domains.

3 int-bl-1:

lenv	local environment
loer	reference to local oe

Again the new environment nenv is defined recursively, due to recursive procedures (see again N5.3 for a constructive reading). Note that parameters are not dealt with here, but in eval-proc-dcl. The loer is initialised to the passed oe but can be reset by ON and REVERT statements. The block epilogue is performed both on normal and abnormal termination.

CF1.3 Procedures

5 eval-proc-dcl:

This is a pure function - it returns a function with side effects, en-f, which is (the main part of, see int-bl-1) the denotation of the procedure identifier. Besides a list of locations (the "arguments" in the PL/I sense), en-f has additional arguments, passed to it from the calling block: oe and cbif, whose passing as arguments reflects the dynamic inheritance rules for PL/I on-units, and the statically determinable entry attribute of the entry reference; the latter is checked against the parameter and RETURNS attributes of the actually called procedure, which may be determinable only dynamically.

The function en-f tests and sets the activity flag for non-RECURSIVE procedures, checks the argument attributes against the parameter declarations and the RETURNS descriptor against the result attribute prescribed by the caller, and then sets up the new environment env' to be passed to int-bl-1; again, by context conditions, parameters and STATIC variables are disjoint. Since the RETURN statement terminates intermediate blocks, it is modelled by using the exit mechanism, with ret used to flag the returned value; therefore, this call of int-bl-1 always terminates abnormally (with ret or go), and the epilogue need not be written after it.

7 int-call-st:

Both the en-ref (an expression of type ENTRY) and the argument list are evaluated (see next function), and the value of the former, a function en-f, applied to the value of the latter (and to auxiliary arguments). Dummy locations allocated during argument evaluation have to be freed on termination.

8 eval-proc-ref:

The activation identifier (aid) is used to discover use of a "dead" entry value, i.e. one whose declaring block activation has been terminated. The (syntactic) case distinction in computing the elements of loc-l is made to see whether the argument matches the parameter descriptor without conversion.

11 int-ret-st:

If an expression is specified in the RETURN statement (which, by context conditions, is the case if the terminated procedure is a function procedure, i.e. has an rdd), the expression value is converted to the completed rdd (RETURNS descriptor). The passing down of "major" from eval-proc-dcl has not been shown explicitly; it is necessary in order to ensure that the FINISH condition is raised (and the relevant on-units are executed) before termination of intermediate blocks.

(Ed. remainder of "Commentary" omitted)

Abstract Programs

Contents:

1.1 Rules

1.1.1 Programs

1	prog	= proc-set
2	proc	:: id s-parms:id* s-ret-descr:[pdd] s-dcls:dcl-set proc-set s-cprefs:cond-pref-set s-recity:[REC] ex-unit*

1.1.2 Data

1.1.2.1 Declarations

3	dcl	:: s-id:id s-dcl-tp:(prop-var | parm | based | def | BI | nmd-const)
4	prop-var	:: s-dd:dd s-stg-cl:(AUTO | static-cl)
5	static-cl	:: scope
6	parm	:: s-dd:dd
7	based	:: s-dd:dd s-dft-qual:[val-ref]
8	def	:: s-dd:dd s-base-item:var-ref s-pos:expr
9	nmd-const	= file-const | ext-entry | LAB
10	ext-entry	:: entry
11	scope	= INT | EXT

1.1.2.2 Descriptions

12	dd	= array-dd | struct-dd | sc-dd
13	array-dd	:: s-unit-dd:(sc-dd | struct-dd) s-bpl:(bp | *)+
14	struct-dd	:: (s-f-nm:id s-f-dd:dd)+
15	bp	:: s-lb:extent s-ub:extent
16	extent	:: expr s-refer-opt:[id+]
17	sc-dd	:: dtp s-init:[init-elem+]
18	init-elem	= simple-init | * | iterated-init
19	simple-init	:: expr
20	iterated-init	:: s-iter-fact:expr init-elem+

1.1.2.3 Types

```
21   dtp            = comp-tp | non-comp-tp
22   comp-tp        = arith | str
23   non-comp-tp    = entry | LAB | PTR | FILE
24   arith          :: base scale prec
25   base           = BIN | DEC
26   scale          = FIX | FLT
27   prec           :: s-nod:intg s-scale-fact:[signed-intg]
28   str            :: str-tp s-maxl:(extent | *) varity
29   str-tp         = CHAR | BIT
30   varity         = VARYING | NONVARYING
31   entry          :: s-parm-descrs:[pdd*]s-ret-descr:[pdd]
                       s-opts:[/*impl.def.*/]
32   pdd            = array-pdd | struct-pdd | sc-pdd
33   array-pdd      :: s-unit-dd:unit-pdd s-bpl:(bp|*)+
34   unit-pdd       = sc-pdd | struct-pdd
35   struct-pdd     :: pdd+
36   sc-pdd         :: dtp
```

1.1.3 Statements

```
37   ex-unit        :: s-cprefs:cond-pref-set s-st-nms:id-set prop-st
38   prop-st        = bl | iter-grp | non-iter-grp | on-st | if-st |
                      call-st | goto-st | NULL | ret-st | rev-st | sig-st |
                      io-st | ass-st | alloc-st| free-st
39   bl             :: s-dcls:dcl-set proc-set ex-unit*
40   iter-grp       = ctld-grp | wh-only-grp
41   ctld-grp       :: targ-ref
                       (expr [s-by-opt:expr s-to-opt:[expr]] s-wh-opt:[expr])+
                       ex-unit*
42   wh-only-grp    :: s-wh-opt:expr ex-unit*
43   non-iter-grp   :: ex-unit*
44   on-st          :: [SNAP] cond-nm+ (proc | SYSTEM)
45   if-st          :: expr s-then-unit:ex-unit s-else-unit:[ex-unit]
46   call-st        :: proc-ref
47   proc-ref       :: val-ref arg*
48   goto-st        :: val-ref
49   ret-st         :: [expr]
50   rev-st         :: cond-nm+
51   sig-st         :: cond-nm
52   ass-st         :: targ-ref+ expr
53   alloc-st       :: (id s-set-opt:[var-ref])+
```

```
54     free-st              :: (s-locr-qual:[val-ref] id)+
```

1.1.4 Names

```
55     cond-nm              =  non-io-cond-nm | nmd-io-cond
56     non-io-cond-nm       =  comp-cond-nm | ERROR | FINISH | STG
57     cond-pref            :: comp-cond-nm (ENABLED | DISABLED)
58     comp-cond-nm         =  CONV | FOFL | OFL | SIZE | STRG | STRZ | SUBRG | UFL |
                               ZDIV
```

1.1.5 Expressions

```
59     expr                 =  inf-expr | pref-expr | val-ref | const
60     inf-expr             :: expr inf-op expr
61     inf-op               =  OR | AND | GT | GE | EQ | LE | LT |
                               NE | CAT | ADD | SUBT | MULT | DIV
62     pref-expr            :: pref-op expr
63     pref-op              =  NOT | PLUS | MINUS
64     val-ref              =  var-ref | proc-fct-ref | bif-ref | nmd-const-ref
65     var-ref              :: s-locr-qual:[val-ref] s-main-id:id s-qual-ids:id* subscr*
66     subscr               =  expr | *
67     proc-fct-ref         :: val-ref arg*
68     arg                  =  expr | by-ref-var
69     by-ref-var           :: var-ref
70     bif-ref              =  cond-bif-nm | distr-bif-ref | non-distr-bif-ref
71     cond-bif-nm          :: ONCHAR | ONCODE | ONCOUNT | ONFILE | ONSOURCE | ONKEY
72     distr-bif-ref        :: distr-bif-nm arg+
73     non-distr-bif-ref    :: non-distr-bif-nm arg*
74     distr-bif-nm         =  ABS | BIN | BIT | BOOL | CEIL | CHAR | DEC | FIX | FLT |
                               FLOOR | INDEX | LENGTH | MAX | MIN | MOD | PREC |
                               SIGN | SUBSTR | TRANSLATE | VERIFY
75     non-distr-bif-nm     =  ADDR | COLLATE | DATE | DIM | HBOUND | LBOUND |
                               NULL | STR | TIME
76     nmd-const-ref        =  lab-ref | entry-ref | file-ref
77     lab-ref              :: id
78     entry-ref            :: id
79     targ-ref             =  var-ref | pv-ref
80     stg-pv-ref           :: stg-pv-nm arg*
81     stg-pv-nm            =  STR | SUBSTR
82     pv-ref               =  cond-pv | stg-pv-ref
83     cond-pv              =  ONCHAR | ONSOURCE
84     const                :: scomp-tp symbol+
```

1.1.6 Input/Output

```
85    io-st           =  file-ctl-st | record-st | stream-st
86    file-ctl-st     =  open-st | close-st
87    record-st       =  read-st | write-st | rewrite-st | delete-st | locate-st
88    stream-st       =  get-st | put-st

89    open-st         :: opng+
90    opng            :: val-ref s-title:[expr] file-descr layout-inf
91    layout-inf      :: s-lsz:[expr] s-psz:[expr] s-tabs:[expr+]
92    close-st        :: clng+
93    clng            :: val-ref [environment]
94    file-descr      :: s-org:[STR|REC] s-mode:[IN|OUT|UPD] s-order:[SEQ|DIR]
                         s-pr:[PR] s-keyed:[KEYED] [environment]

95    read-st         :: val-ref s-data-part:(into-inf|ptr-set-inf|ignore-inf)
                                 s-key-part:[key-inf|keyto-inf]
96    write-st        :: val-ref s-from:var-ref [key-inf]
97    rewrite-st      :: val-ref s-from:[var-ref] [key-inf]
98    delete-st       :: val-ref [key-inf]
99    locate-st       :: val-ref s-based:id [ptr-set-inf] [key-inf]

100   get-st          :: val-ref s-skip:[expr] s-data-list:targ-ref+
101   put-st          :: val-ref s-skip:[expr] s-page:[PAGE] s-data-list:expr*

102   into-inf        :: var-ref
103   ptr-set-inf     :: var-ref
104   ignore-inf      :: expr
105   key-inf         :: expr
106   keyto-inf       :: targ-ref

107   environment     =                        /* implementation defined */

108   nmd-io-cond     :: io-cond val-ref
109   io-cond         =  ENDFILE | ENDPAGE | KEY | RECORD | TRANSMIT | UNDEFINEDFILE
110   file-ref        :: id
111   file-const      :: file-descr scope
```

1.1.7 Elementary Domains

```
intg
signed-intg
id
symbol
```

1.2 Context Conditions and Functions

1.2.1 Static Data Descriptions

```
112   sdd              =  array-sdd | struct-sdd | sc-sdd
113   array-sdd        :: s-unit-dd:(sc-sdd | struct-sdd) s-bpl:*+
114   struct-sdd       :: sdd+
115   sc-sdd           :: sdtp
116   sdtp             =  scomp-tp | snon-comp-tp
117   scomp-tp         =  arith | str-sdd
118   snon-comp-tp     =  sentry | LAB | PTR | FILE
119   sentry           :: s-parm-descrs:[sdd*] s-ret-descr:[sdd]
120   str-sdd          :: str-tp s-maxl:*

121   ENV-t            =  ID -> (dcl|proc)
```

1.2.2 Rule-by-Rule Conditions

```
1  is-wf-prog(procs) =
      p1,p2∈procs ∧ s-id(p1)=s-id(p2) ⊃ p1=p2  ∧
      (let main-pr = (ιp∈procs) (s-id(p)=main-id);
         /*main-id given s.t. (∃p∈procs) (s-id(p)=main-id)*/
       s-parms(main-pr) = < >  ∧
       s-ret-descr(main-pr) = nil) ∧
      /* dcls of ENTRY EXT "match" p∈procs */
      (let ext-dcls = {dcl∈comp-dcls(procs) | is-prop-var(s-dcl-tp(dcl)) ∧
                                         s-stg-cl(s-dcl-tp(dcl)) = EXT};
       d1,d2∈ext-dcls ∧ e1∈comp-exprs(d1) ∧ e2∈comp-exprs(d2) ⊃
               eval-restr-expr(e1) = eval-restr-expr(e2))  ∧
      (let env = [s-id(p) → p | p∈procs];
       p∈procs ⊃ is-wf-proc(p,env))
```

```
2  is-wf-proc(<nm,parm-l,rdd,dcls,procs,cprefs, recity,eu-l>,env) =
      is-unique-ids(parm-l) ∧
      id∈Rparm-l ⊃ (∃dcl∈dcls) (dcl=mk-dcl (id,mk-parm() ) ∧
      is-unique-cprefs(cprefs)  ∧
      is-wf-bl(mk-bl(dcls,procs,eu-l),env)
      (let rets = ret-sts(eu-l);
       rdd=nil ∧ rs∈rets ⊃ rs=nil   ∧
       rdd≠nil ∧ rs∈rets ⊃ rs≠nil  ∧ is-prom-conv(rdd,el-sdd(s-expr(rs),env)))  ∧
      /* last stmt (executed) must be RETURN */

3  is-wf-dcl(<id,dcl-tp>,env,r-env) =
      /* any contained iterated-init in dcl-tp is contained in an array-dd */
      (cases dcl-tp:
       mk-prop-var( ,AUTO) -> is-wf-prop-var(dcl-tp,r-env)
       mk-prop-var( ,)     -> is-wf-prop-var(dcl-tp,[])
       mk-parm( )          -> is-wf-parm(dcl-tp,r-env)
       mk-based( )         -> is-wf-based(dcl-tp,env)
       mk-def( )           -> is-wf-def(dcl-tp,r-env)
       BI                  -> id∈(distr-bif-nm ∪ non-distr-bif-nm))

4  is-wf-prop-var(<dd,stg-cl>,env) =
      is-starless(dd)  ∧
      conts-no-refers(dd)    ∧
      is-static-cl(stg-cl) ⊃ conts-restr-exprs(dd)  ∧
      is-static-cl(stg-cl) ∧ sc-sdd∈comp-sc-dds(dd) ∧ s-dtp(sc-dd) ∈ {LAB} ∪ entry ⊃
               s-init(sc-dd)=nil

6  is-wf-parm(<dd>,env) =
      conts-no-refers(dd)  ∧
      conts-no-inits(dd)  ∧
      conts-restr-exprs(dd)

7  is-wf-based(<dd,dft-qual>,env) =
      is-starless(dd) ∧
      dft-qual=nil v el-sdd(dft-qual,env)=mk-sc-sdd(PTR)  ∧
      is-refer-geom(dd) ∧
      mk-extent(e,nil)∈comp-extents(dd) ⊃ is-const(e)

BASIS-11:     does not constrain non-refer bounds.
```

```
8  is-wf-def(<dd,base,pos>,env) =
      is-starless(dd)    ∧
      conts-no-refers(dd)  ∧
      conts-no-inits(dd)  ∧
      is-scomp-tp(s-sdtp(el-sdd(pos,env)))  ∧
      /* relation twixt base desc. and dd */ ∧
      (let <lq,id,id-l,ssc-l> = base;
       s-dcl-tp(env(id)) ∈ (prop-var∪parm)  ∧
       (∃tp) (is-all-str(tp,s-dd(s-dcl-tp(env(id))))))

14 is-wf-struct-dd(<f-l>,env) =
      is-unique-ids(<s-f-nm(f-l[i]) | 1≤i≤lf-l>)

16 is-wf-extent(<ex,ref-opt>,env) =
      is-scomp-tp(s-sdtp(el-sdd(ex,env)))  ∧
      is-id-list(ref-opt)  ⊃
         (let ref-obj-sdd = el-sdd(mk-var-ref(nil,hidl,tidl,<>), env);
          ref-obj-sdd = intg-tp() )

   BASIS-11: only restricts to is-scomp-tp(ref-obj-sdd)

17 is-wf-sc-dd(<dtp,init>,env) =
      e∈comp-simple-inits(init) ⊃ /* el-sdd(e,env) "matches" dtp */

19 is-wf-simple-init(<e>,env) = is-sc-sdd(el-sdd(e,env))

20 is-wf-iterated-init(<ifct, >,env) =
      is-scomp-tp(s-sdtp(el-sdd(ifct,env)))

31 is-wf-entry(<pdd-l,rdd, >,env) =
      dtp∈comp-entries(pdd-l) ⊃ dtp=entry0()

32 is-wf-pdd(pdd,env) =
      conts-restr-exprs(pdd) ∧
      conts-no-refers(pdd)

37 is-wf-ex-unit(<prefs,  , >,env) =
      is-unique-cprefs(cprefs)
```

```
39 is-wf-bl(<dcls,procs,eu-l>,env) =
      dp1,dp2∈(dcls∪procs) ∧ s-id(dp1)=s-id(dp2) ⊃ dp1=dp2  ∧
      (let labl = labels(eu-l);
       is-unique-ids(labl) ∧
       id∈Rlabl ⊃ (∃dcl∈dcls) (dcl=mk-dcl(id,LAB))) ∧
      (let r-env' = env\{s-id(pd)|pd∈(dcls∪procs)};
       let env'   = r-env' ∪ [s-id(pd) → pd | pd ∈ (dcls∪procs)];
       dcl∈dcls ⊃ is-wf-dcl(dcl,env',r-env') ∧
       proc∈procs ⊃ is-wf-proc(proc,env') ∧
       is-wf-ex-unit-list(eu-l,env'))
```

(Ed: remainder of D1.2.2 omitted)

Block Structure

Contents

1.1 Programs

```
1  int-prog(prog,main-id) =
      let pb-sels = comp-proc-sels(prog) ∪ comp-bl-sels(prog),
          nonrec-sels = {spb ∈ comp-proc-sels(prog) | s-recity(spb(prog)) = nil},
          st-ext-sels = {sdcl ∈ comp-dcl-sels(prog) |
                         sdcl(prog) = mk-dcl(id,mk-prop-var(,mk-static-cl(EXT)))};
      let st-ext-ids = {id | (∃sdcl ∈ st-ext-sels) (s-id(sdcl(prog)) = id)},
          st-int-ids(pb) =
            {id | mk-dcl(id,mk-prop-var(,mk-static-cl(INT))) ∈ s-dcls(pb)};
      initialise-state();
      let aid-0: extend-AA();
      let st-ext-locs: [id → (let sdcl' ∈ st-ext-sels be s.t. s-id(sdcl'(prog))=id;
                              eval-static-dcl-tp(s-dd(sdcl'(prog)),<[],[],[]>)) |
                         id ∈ st-ext-ids],
      let st-int-locs:
            [spb → [id → (let dcl ∈ s-dcls(spb(prog)) be s.t. s-id(dcl) = id;
                          eval-static-dcl-tp(s-dd(dcl),<[],[],[]>)) |
                    id ∈ st-int-ids(spb(prog))] | spb ∈ pb-sels];
      dcl actys := [spb → INACTIVE | spb ∈ nonrec-sels];
      let env-1 = [s-id(p)→<eval-proc-dcl(p,env-1,false),s-id(p),aid-0> | p∈prog'],
          prog' =
            (let bl-env'(spb) =
                  <(let dcls = s-dcls(spb(prog));
                    [id → st-ext-locs(id) |
                     mk-dcl(id,mk-prop-var(,mk-static-cl(EXT))) ∈ dcls]
                    ∪ st-int-locs(spb)
                    ∪ [id → c-uid(id) | mk-dcl(id,mk-file-const(,)) ∈ dcls]
                    ∪ [id → env-1(id) | mk-dcl(id,mk-ext-entry()) ∈ dcls]),
                   (spb ∈ nonrec-sels -> spb°actys, T → nil)>;
             /* prog modified by associating, for each spb ∈ pb-sels, a BL-ENV
                with spb(prog) so that bl-env(spb(prog)) = bl-env'(spb) */,
         main-en-f = eval-proc-dcl((ιp ∈ prog') (s-id(p) = main-id),env-1,true);
      let oe-1 = [cn → system-ou-entry-val(cn) |
                  cn ∈ non-io-cond-nm ∪ rel-evd-io-cond-nms(prog) ];
      main-en-f(entry0(),oe-1,[]);
      for all id ∈ st-ext-ids do free (st-ext-locs(id)),
      for all spb ∈ pb-sels do
          for all id ∈ st-int-ids(spb(prog)) do free(st-int-locs(spb) (id));
      restrict-AA(aid-0)
```

```
    type: prog id =>
    pre: s-parms(main-proc) = < >, s-ret-descr(main-proc) = nil.
```

1.2 Blocks

```
2   int-bl(bl,<env,oe,cbif>) =
       let <dcls,procs,eu-l> = bl,
           <st-env,nil> = bl-env(bl) ;
       int-bl-1(dcls,procs,eu-l, env+st-env,oe,cbif>)

    type: bl (ENV OE CBIF) =>


3   int-bl-1(dcls,procs,eu-l,<env,oe,cbif>) =
       let aid: extend-AA();
       let nenv:
          (trap exit (abn) with error;
           let lenv:
                [id → eval-dcl(dtp,nenv,<env,oe,cbif>) |
                   mk-dcl(id,dtp) ∈ dcls ∧
                   (dtp ∈ (based∪def) ∨ is-prop-var(dtp) ∧ s-stg-cl(dtp=AUTO)] ∪
                [id → <id,aid> | mk-dcl(id,LAB) ∈ dcls] ∪
                [s-id(proc) → <eval-proc-dcl(proc,nenv,[false]),s-id(proc),aid> |
                   proc ∈ procs] /* false passed iff proc EXTERNAL */;
           return(env+lenv));
       dcl loer := oe;
       (trap exit(abn) with (bl-epilogue(dcls,nenv,aid); exit(abn));
        int-ex-unit-list(eu-l,<env,loer,oe,cbif,aid>)) ;
       bl-epilogue(dcls,nenv,aid)

    type: dcl-set proc-set ex-unit* (ENV OE CBIF) =>


4   bl-epilogue(dcls,nenv,aid) =
       for all mk-dcl(id,mk,prop-var(dd,AUTO)) ∈ dcls do free(nenv(id));
       restrict-AA(aid)

    type: dcl-set ENV AID =>
```

1.3 Procedures

1.3.1 Definition

```
5    eval-proc-dcl(proc,nenv,major) =
        let <id,parm-l,ret-dd,dcls,procs,cprefs,recy,eu-l> = proc;
        let en-f(dtp,loc-l,oe,cbif) =
             (let <st-env,acty> = bl-env(proc) ;
              if recy = nil          /* assert acty ≠ nil */
                 then if cacty = ACTIVE then error else acty := ACTIVE;
              let n = lparm-l;
              let parm-dcls = <(ιdcl∈dcls) (s-id(dcl) = parm-l[i]) | i ∈{1:n}>;
              if ¬entry-match(<s-dd(s-dcl-tp(parm-dcls[i])) | 1≤i≤n>,ret-dd,dtp)
                 then error;
              let env' = nenv + ([parm-l[i] → loc-l[i] | 1≤i≤n] ∪ st-env);
              trap exit(ctl,arg) with
                 (if recy = nil then acty := INACTIVE;
                  if ctl = ret
                    then if ret-dd≠nil then return (arg)
                    else exit(ctl,arg));
              int-bl-1(dcls \ {parm-dcls[i] | 1≤i≤n},procs,eu-l,<env',oe,cbif>));
     en-f

     type: proc ENV [B] -> (entry LOC* OE CBIF => [VAL])
     assert: call of int-bl-1 terminates abnormally (with go or ret).
```

```
6    entry-match(parm-dd-l,ret-dd,mk-entry(pdd-l,rdd, )) =
        (if rdd=nil then ret-dd=nil else ret-dd≠nil ∧ match(rdd,ret-dd)) ∧
        pdd-l≠nil ∧ lpdd-l=lparm-dd-l ∧ (∀i ∈ {1:lpdd-l}) (match(parm-dd-l[i],pdd-l[i])

     type: dd* [pdd] entry -> B
```

1.3.2 Call

```
7   int-call-st(mk-call-st(en-ref,arg-l),<env,loe,cbif>) =
       let <dtp,en-f,loc-l>: eval-proc-ref(en-ref,arg-l,<env,loe,cbif>);
       (trap exit (abn) with
         (free-dummy(arg-l,loc-l);
          exit(abn));
        en-f(dtp,loc-l,loe,cbif));
       free-dummy(arg-l,loc-l)

    type: call-st (ENV OE CBIF) =>



8   eval-proc-ref(en-ref,arg-l,env-ex) =
       let dtp = c-entry(en-ref);
       let <,loe,cbif> = env-ex;
       let <en-f,nm,aid>: eval-expr(en-ref,env-ex);
       if ¬(aid ∈ cAA) then error;
       let mk-entry(pdd-l, , ) = dtp;
       trap exit (abn) with error;
       let loc-l:
           <(if is-by-ref-var(arg-l[i])
              then eval-l-var-ref(arg-l[i],env-ex)
              else
               (let arg-v: eval-expr(arg-l[i],env-ex);
                let dummy-loc: alloc(complete-pdd(pdd-l[i],arg-v),AUTO,<loe,cbif>);
                prom-ass(dummy-loc,arg-v,<loe,cbif,cur-cond-prefs(arg-l) >);
                return(dummy-loc)))
           |  1 ≤ i ≤ larg-l>;
       return(<dtp,en-f,loc-l>)

    type: val-ref arg* (ENV OE CBIF) => entry (entry LOC* OE CBIF => [VAL]) LOC*
    BASIS-11: Assume any order allowed cf 6.3.6.1.1.
              Ban on goto fits with prologue, not yet resolved with ANS cf 6.3.7



9   complete-pdd(pdd,v) =
       /* returns an edd like the pdd but with *'s filled in from v,[1:1] if scalar*/

    type: pdd VAL -> edd
```

```
10  free-dummy(arg-l,loc-l) =
       for all i ∊ {1:larg-l} do if ¬is-by-ref-var(arg-l[i]) then free(loc-l[i])

    type: arg* LOC* =>
```

1.3.3 Return

```
11  int-ret-st(mk-ret-st(t),<env,loe,cbif>) =
       let proc = /* the (statically known) proc terminated by this mk-ret-st(t) */
       if is-expr(t)
          then (let rdd = s-ret-descr(proc);
                let v: eval-expr(t,<env,loe,cbif>);
                let cv:prom-conv(complete-pdd(rdd,v),v,<loe,cbif,cur-cond-prefs(t)>);
                exit (ret,cv))
          else (if /* proc is EXTERNAL, static property */
                   then (let major = /*switch passed down from eval-proc-dcl */;
                         if major then raise-cond(FINISH,true,<loe,cbif>));
                exit(ret,nil))

    type: ret-st (ENV OE CBIF) =>
```

MATHEMATICAL SEMANTICS
AND
COMPILER CORRECTNESS

define

- source language
- target machine
- relation of correctness

argue - or still better prove
that the relation holds

H. Bekić

IFIP WG 2.1
München, 25 Aug. 75

FORMAL SEMANTICS :

Interpreters (abstract machines) :

McCarthy

Landin's SECD machine

IBM Lab Vienna: (old) PL/I Def "ULD"

axiomatic method :

Floyd, Hoare, Manna

mathematical semantics :

Scott - Strachey

Vienna: (new) PL/I Def TR 25.139

in algebraic terminology :

Thatcher et al.

Reynolds

COMPILER PROOFS :

McCarthy - Painter: μ Algol

Lucas - Jones - Henhapl: block structure
("twin machine")

L. Morris: algebraic methods

Milne - Strachey: MS and implementation correctness

MS AND COMPILER CORRECTNESS :

$$J[\![text,env]\!] = tr: \delta \rightarrow \delta'$$

den's of free id's

$$M[\![text,\ell,dict]\!] = tr_t: \tau \rightarrow \tau'$$

machine opds for free ids

nesting depth

Correctness:

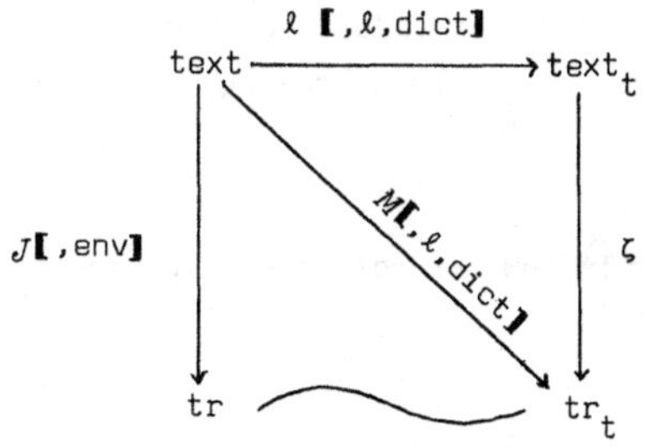

i.e.

$$\underline{if} \quad \delta \sim \tau$$

$$tr = J[\![text,env]\!] \quad \quad tr_t = M[\![text,\ell,dict]\!]$$

$$\underline{then} \quad \delta' \sim \tau'$$

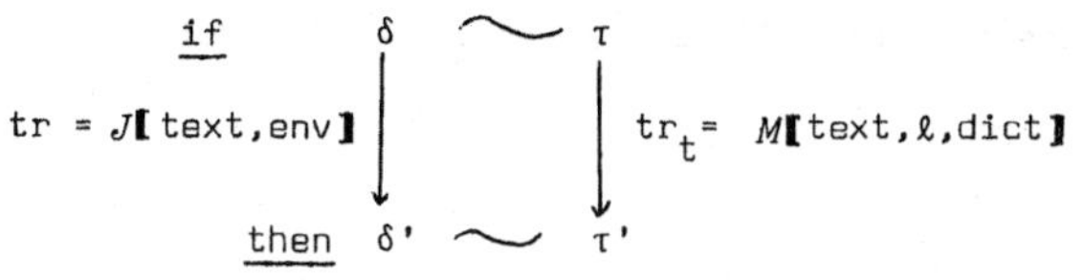

(assuming that meanings of free id's
are equivalent   )

Proof by induction on the structure of text.

ABSTRACT SYNTAX

programs =

set of objects freely generated from given terminals by given constructors.

generated : each object arises by applying the construction rules a finite number of times.

free : objects with different construction history are different.

NOTATION for composing, decomposing, and discriminating objects.

DEFINITION of functions/predicates on objects, and

PROOF of properties of objects, by structural induction.

DOMAINS

(of "semantical" objects)

Domain D = "inductive partial order" (i.p.o.) :

$\bot \in D$ with $\bot \sqsubseteq x$ for all $x \in D$ (minimal element)

$\sqsubseteq$ "less defined than"

$x_1 \sqsubseteq x_2 \sqsubseteq \ldots \in D \qquad x = \bigsqcup_{n=1}^{\infty} x_n \in D$ (l.u.b.'s for chains)

$f: D \rightarrow D'$ continuous : $f(\bigsqcup_n x_n) = \bigsqcup_n {}' f(x_n)$

The set $Fct = D \underset{c}{\rightarrow} D'$ of continuous functions from D to D' is again an i.p.o.

Least fix-point of a continuous function :

$F: D \underset{c}{\rightarrow} D \qquad x = F(x)$

$a = YF = \bigsqcup_{n=0}^{\infty} F^n(\bot)$ is the smallest solution of $x = F(x)$.

EXAMPLE : SYNTAX

Programs :

```
Prog   = Id Proc

Proc   = (Id(var|proc))*  Id-set  Id →m Proc   Stmt*
          \                \       \
           \                \       local procs
            formals          local vars

Struct = Id := Expr | call Id Id* | ...

Expr   = val Id | Expr Op Expr
```

Domains :

$S = Loc \underset{m}{\rightarrow} Val$

$Fct = (Loc|Fct)^* \underset{c}{\rightarrow} (S \nrightarrow S)$

$Env = Id \underset{m}{\rightarrow} Loc|Fct$

(Notation :

$A \underset{m}{\rightarrow} B$ = set of (finite) maps $m = <a_1:b_1, \ldots, a_n:b_n>$ $(a_i \neq a_j)$

with $a_i \in A$, $b_i \in B$; $\underline{D}m = \{a_1, \ldots, a_n\}$, $\underline{R}m = \{b_1, \ldots, b_n\}$

$A \nrightarrow B$ = set of partial functions from A to B,

with the ordering "more defined than")

EXAMPLE : SEMANTICS

$\mathcal{J}$[mk-prog (id,proc)] =

  <u>let</u> fct = $\mathcal{J}$[proc, <id:fct>];

  fct(<>)

$\mathcal{J}$[mk=proc (<<f_i,$spec_i$>|1≤i≤I>, V, <$proc_q$|1≤q≤Q>, <st_k|1≤k≤K>), env]

  <u>let</u> fct (<arg_i|1≤i≤I'>) =

    <u>let</u> args = <u>if</u> I = I' (∀i≤I.arg_iε$\mathcal{J}$[$spec_i$]) <u>then</u> <f_i:arg_i|i≤I>

      <u>else</u> <u>error</u> ;

    <u>let</u> locs : $//_{v\varepsilon V}$ create;

    <u>let</u> fcts = <$\mathcal{J}$[$proc_q$,env + (args∪locs∪fcts)] | q≤Q> ;

    $;_{k\leq K}$ $\mathcal{J}$[st_k, env + (args∪locs∪fcts)] ;

    $//_{v\varepsilon V}$ <u>destroy</u> locs(v) ;

  fct

$\mathcal{J}$[id<u>:=</u>e, env] = env(id) := $\mathcal{J}$[e, env]

$\mathcal{J}$[<u>call</u> id <id_i|i≤I>, env] = env(id) (<env(id_i) | i≤I>)

$\mathcal{J}$[<u>val</u> id, env] = <u>c</u> env

$\mathcal{J}$[<e1, op, e2>, env] = $\mathcal{J}$[op] ($\mathcal{J}$[e1, env], $\mathcal{J}$[e2, env])

$\mathcal{J}$[<u>var</u>] = Loc, $\mathcal{J}$[<u>proc</u>] = Fct

Notation :

tr;tr' = λσ.tr'(tr(σ))

(<u>let</u> v:tr; ...v...) = λσ.(<u>let</u> <v,σ'> = tr(σ) ; (...v...)(σ'))

<u>c</u> loc = λσ.σ(loc)

MACHINE

T = <p:Ptr, ep:Ptr, cp:Ptr, ra:Ptr, Br:Ptr, — 5 standard pointer registers

pms: (Ptr | <ep:Ptr, ca:Ptr>)*> — standard area for parameter passing

"env-ptr", "code-address" (for <u>proc</u> parms)

∪

(Ptr $\underset{m}{\rightarrow}$ <ep:Ptr, cp:Ptr, ra:Ptr, pms:..., vrs:Wrd*, tmps:Wrd*>)

(as above)

1 <u>d</u>ynamic <u>s</u>torage <u>a</u>rea per procedure activation

$\tau = env_t + \delta_t$

p - "pointer" (to current dsa)

(ep,cp,ra,pms,tmps)(dsa)

- tmps: "temporaries"
- pms: "parameters"
- ra: "return address
- cp: "call-ptr" (to calling dsa)
- ep: "env-ptr" (to declaring dsa)

more "static" state-components

ep,cp,ra,pms,br

vrs(dsa) — "variables"

br: "branch register"

more "dynamic" state components

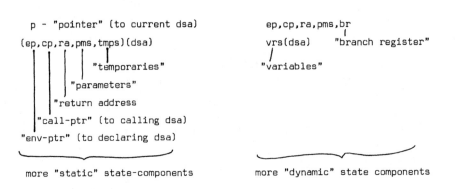

EXAMPLE : IMPLEMENTATION

```
M[mk-prog (id, proc)] =
    ep,p,pms := nil, nil, <>;
    call L;
    stop
 L: M[proc, 0, <id:mk-proc-id (0,L)]

M[mk-proc(<<f_i,spec_i>|i≤I , V, <proc_q|qεQ>, <st_k|k≤K>), ℓ, dict] =
    cp := c p ;
    p  := create Dsa (<M[spec_i]|i≤I>, |V|) ;
    if c pms ∉  Π   M[spec_i]  then error ;
               i≤I
    (ep,cp,ra,pms) (p) := c (ep,cp,ra,pms) ;

    ;  M[st_k, ℓ+1, dict + (<f_i:(ℓ+1,pms⊕_i) | i≤I> ∪ <ℓ+1, vars⊕_j | v_jεV> ∪
   k≤K
                              <(ℓ+1,L_q) | qεQ>)]  ;

    cp,ra := c (cp,ra) (p) ;
    destroy c p ;
    p := c cp ;
    return

<L_q: M[proc_q, ℓ+1, dict + ...] | qεQ>
```

[*M*, cont'd]

```
M[id:=e,ℓ,dict] =

     M[e,ℓ,dict] ;
     M[id,ℓ,dict] := pop

M[call<id id_i|iεI>,ℓ,dict] =
     pms:= <M[id_i,ℓ,dict] | iεI> ;
     ep,br:= M[id,ℓ,dict] ;
     call c br

                                  on tmps(p)
M[val id,ℓ,dict] =          push c M[id,ℓ,dict]
M[<e1,op,e2>,ℓ,dict] =      ...

M[v,ℓ,<...,v:mk-var(n,d),...>] = d(ep^(ℓ-n)(p))
M[f,ℓ,<...,f:mk-prm(n,d),...>] = c d(ep^(ℓ-n)(p))
M[q,ℓ,<...,q:mk-prc(n,L),...>] = <c ep^(ℓ-n)(p), L>

M[var] = Ptr,      M[proc] = <ep:Ptr, ca:Ptr>
```

EXAMPLE : CORRECTNESS

$val \sim wrd \quad = Df \quad \ldots$

$loc \overset{lc}{\sim} loc_t \quad = Df \quad lc: loc \rightarrow loc_t$

$\sigma \overset{lc,env_t}{\sim} \tau \quad = Df \quad \tau = env_t + \sigma_t \quad lc: \underline{D}\sigma \leftrightarrow \{(vrs \oplus j)(dsa) \mid dsa \in D\sigma_t \land$

$j \leq \underline{\ell}\ vrs(dsa(\sigma_t))\} \land \forall loc, loc_t \,.\, loc \sim loc_t \supset \sigma(loc) \sim \tau(loc_t)$

$tr \sim tr_t \quad = \forall \sigma, \tau \,.\, \sigma \sim \tau \supset tr(\sigma) \sim tr_t(\tau)$

$fct \overset{lc,env_t}{\sim} \langle dsa^{dcl}, L\rangle = Df \quad \forall al, a\ell_t \,.\, (\forall i. a\ell(i) \overset{lc^{call}, env_t^{call},}{\sim} a\ell_t(i)) \supset$

$fct(a\ell) \overset{lc^{call}, env_t^{call},}{\sim} (pms := a_t;$

$ep := dsa^{dcl};\ \underline{call}\ L)$

for all $lc^{call} \supseteq lc,\ env_t^{call} \supseteq env_t$

<u>Theorem.</u> If

$\underline{D}env = \underline{D}dict \land \forall id \in \underline{D}env. env(id) \sim \mathcal{M}[\![id, \ell, dict]\!](env_t)$

then

$\mathcal{J}[\![st, env]\!] \sim \mathcal{M}[\![st, \ell, dict]\!]$

$\mathcal{J}[\![expr, env]\!] \sim \mathcal{M}[\![expr, \ell, dict]\!]\ ;\ \underline{pop}$

$\mathcal{J}[\![proc, env]\!] \sim \langle(\underline{c}p)(env_t),\ L{:}\mathcal{M}[\![proc, \ell, dict]\!]\rangle$

<u>Proof.</u> Use induction on the structure of st|expr|proc; this is sufficient for (recursive) proc decl's also because of $\bot_{Fct} \sim \bot_{Fct_t}$ and continuity : $\underset{Fct}{\sim}$ is "directed complete".

IBM LABORATORY VIENNA, Austria

TOWARDS A MATHEMATICAL THEORY OF PROCESSES

H. BEKIĆ

ABSTRACT

A recent "mathematical" approach to the semantics of programming languages is extended to allow for quasi-parallel execution of processes. A notion of "action" is proposed as a formalization of the kind of process involved, and various ways of action composition are studied. The relevance of the approach for applications in the areas of language design, language description, and proof of program correctness is indicated.

TECHNICAL REPORT
TR 25.125
17 December 1971

C O N T E N T S

1. INTRODUCTION

A High Level Approach to Processes

Objectives of a mathematical theory of processes might be: to define processes as certain mathematical objects; to study ways of composing processes; to formulate and prove properties of processes (like: equivalence of two processes, correctness of a process with respect to given objectives, correctness of the implementation of one process in terms of another).

Compared to that, the aim of this report is rather limited: we will develop a certain notion of process (or, as we shall call it, "action"), and define certain composition operations on actions. (A crude approximation to the notion we have in mind would be: action = sequence of state transformations, and one might then define serial composition as concatenation of two sequences, and quasi-parallel composition as a non-determinate merging operation respecting the individual orderings.) We will define one or two notions of equivalence, and also indicate in examples why we think the chosen approach will be useful for attacking e.g. problems of correctness, but we will not formulate, let alone prove, any actual correctness properties.

Our plan to develop an algebra of processes may be viewed as a high-level apprcach: we are interested in how to compose complex processes from simpler (still arbitrarily complex) ones. This may be contrasted to the situation with machine languages, or e.g. the notion of Turing machine, where the finished program does not show any such structure (the only exception are subroutine calls in machine languages). A similar comment seems to apply to more recent explications of parallel processes, e.g. Petri nets /11/, where everything is built up "from below".

Mathematical Semantics

The term "high-level" is usually applied to languages, and indeed the starting point for the present study was the problem of a mathematical approach to the semantics of high-level programming languages. More precisely, the notion of "action" arose as an answer to the following question: what are the objects denoted by (the sensible parts of) programs, if we want these objects (1) to contain no unnecessary information of a merely "book-keeping" character, but (2) to contain enough information so that the object denoted by a composite program depends only on the objects denoted by its parts. (In other words: there is a set of programs with a certain structure, and a set of processes with a corresponding structure, and "to denote" is a correspondence from the one set to the other preserving the structure.) Now, unless one is concerned with the formalization of a particular given language, the really interesting part is, of course, the "right-hand" or "semantical" end of that correspondence, i.e. the algebra of processes referred to above. Of course, in order to talk about that algebra one will develop a suitable metalanguage, and this may well have an influence back on programming language design.

Following that line of development, we will first give, in the next chapter, an outline of Mathematical Semantics as developed by D. Scott /12/ - /15/. There, as in the original work of Scott, we will consider only the "extensional" meaning of programs i.e. programs as functions from inputs to outputs, disregarding any information of how the output is computed. Such functions are, of course, perfectly respectable mathematical objects, and that may be the reason why mathematical semantics has been concerned so far exclusively with the extensional meaning of programs. It is one of the theses of the present study that the approach need not cease to be mathematical by going to more "intensional" notions of meaning. There is enough reason for wanting more intensional meaning: in the first place, the extensional notion of gross-transformation hardly corresponds to any intuitive notion of "process" one may have. Second, and more technically, there is at least one way of program composition for which the extensional meaning violates the "homomorphism" postulate (2) above: to know the function(s) denoted by the quasi-parallel composition of two programs, we need to know not only the functions denoted by the two programs, but the particular decomposition of those functions into elementary steps.

Actions

In chapter 3, we introduce the notion of action to close the gap. (Some inspiration for its development was provided by the -informally described - notion of equal name in the Algol 68 Report.) Thus, a more modest title of the present report would have been: Mathematical semantics as extended to deal with quasi-parallel execution.
- We also deal with certain ways of combining actions, in particular with "recursive" definitions. The actions considered so far work on, and produce, "states". In the next chapter, we sketch a generalization which allows for "values" as additional arguments and results of actions thus catering for "expressions" (which deliver anonymous results) as opposed to "statements" on the one hand, and for (parameterful) procedures on the other. Again, we will define, together with these actions, certain ways of combining them; in particular, there arises the problem (to be briefly discussed in chapter 5) of self-applicable or self-returning procedures, which, together with the definition by recursion, plays a central role in Scott's work. We also indicate the need for further refinement: the notion proposed so far contains too much sequencing information.

Possible Uses of the Method

If anything of what we propose can be called a "method", it is certainly not the particular choice of "action", but the decision to explore the "essential" notions first, separating them both from aspects of representation (language) and implementation. Expected advantages of this method, which will be illustrated in chapter 6 by briefly sketching some possible applications, can be summarized under the following headings (see also 2.3):

a) A semantical approach to language design

In section 6.1 we present two examples where the semantical viewpoint gives an "obvious" choice between two alternatives; these examples are the "right" kind of recursion, and semantical rules for determining the scope, i.e. dynamic life time, of procedures.

b) More concise formal language definition

It is anticipated that the method will lead to shorter and better structured formalizations of (big) programming languages. This claim is illustrated, choosing the example of Algol 68, in section 6.2 which contains also a few comments on the treatment of language features not dealt with elsewhere in this report.

c) Easier equivalence, correctness, and proofs thereof

The omission of "unnecessary" details in the semantical notions will facilitate the formulation of properties of (programs or) processes, the inductive nature of the definition their proof. The example chosen in section 6.3 is the correctness of the implementation of the block concept.

d) Expressing other models

Again, the separation of essential from organizational features may lead to a framework in which to reformulate and compare various proposed models of computation. In section 6.4, we indicate such a reformulation of the model of parallel computation proposed by Karp and Miller.

e) Refined notions of computation

One "unnecessary" feature to abstract from is irrelevant ordering of computation steps. Ideally, the correctness criterion for a proposed transformation of programs into a more parallel form would be that the two programs "denote the same set of computations" (see section 4.3).

f) A philosophy for introducing language features

This is very much related to point a) above, but we want to stress here in particular the need to separate semantical aspects from aspects of implementation (not: to ignore the latter!). This is illustrated in section 6.5 by developing a proposal to treat the mutual exclusion problem.

2. MATHEMATICAL SEMANTICS

The present situation in Formal Language Definition is rather awkward (compare also Bekić /1/): The semantics of a language like PL/I or Algol 68 is defined by rather large and complex evaluation mechanisms. It is then difficult to ask for the "meaning" of a given (part of a) program. In the first place, there is not a sharp correspondence from program parts to semantical objects: everything takes part in the one evaluation algorithm. Second, and more important, there is too much information kept on the semantical side. For example, both in /16/ and /17/ the program itself is part of the state being transformed, hence of the computation. If one calls two programs (in the same or different languages) equivalent if they denote the same set of computations, then two different programs will never be equivalent on the basis of those definitions.

2.1 Descriptive Languages

The situation is much simpler in purely "descriptive" languages (like arithmetic expressions, or predicate calculus). There, we have a set of expressions with a certain structure (e.g. arithmetic expressions, where one of the operations is forming the sum of two expressions), a set of denotations with a corresponding structure (e.g. numbers, where one operation is addition), and a mapping from expressions to denotations preserving that structure. More precisely, meaning or denotation of, or value of, is a mapping

$$\text{expressions} \xrightarrow{\text{"meaning"}} \text{denotations}$$

such that

(a) each (sub)expression has a denotation

(b) the denotation of a composite expression depends only on the denotations of its parts.

(In other words, "meaning" is a homomorphism from the algebra of expressions to the algebra of numbers. Property (b) is often called "referential transparency"). For example, if our language uses Roman numerals and a Lisp-like notation for operators, two examples of the correspondence would be:

(expressions:)	(numbers:)
III	the number 3
(PLUS e_1 e_2)	$v_1 + v_2$

(where v_1, v_2 are the numbers denoted by the expressions e_1, e_2).

The environment. Usually, expressions contain free variables (or, as we shall say, identifiers). Thus, (PLUS X Y) contains freely the identifiers X, Y, and to know the number denoted by it we have to know an environment pairing those identifiers with numbers. Generally, our expressions denote numbers given such an environment. Thus, III denotes 3 under any environment E, but the number denoted by (PLUS e_1 e_2) under E is the sum of the numbers denoted by e_1 and e_2 under E.

Formally, we may define environments as functions from identifiers to numbers:

$$\text{envs} = \text{ids} \longrightarrow \text{numbers}$$

and complicate our denotations to functions from environments to numbers. Then our two examples become

	(envs numbers:)
III	the constancy function K3 i.e. K3E = 3
(PLUS e_1 e_2)	the function $\mathfrak{m}$ such that $E = \mathfrak{m}_1 E + \mathfrak{m}_2 E$

A more significant example, where we have to change the parameter E, is provided by functional abstraction (and hence by auxiliary definitions: "e_1 where $x = e_2$" may be rendered as "$(\lambda x.e_1)e_2$"): $\lambda x.e$ is "(the value of) e as function of (the value of) x", formally:

	(envs $\longrightarrow$ (numbers $\longrightarrow$ numbers):)
$\lambda x.e$	the function $\mathfrak{f}$ such that $\mathfrak{f} E a = \mathfrak{e} E^x_a$

i.e. $\lambda x.e$, under environment E, denotes the function f (called $\mathfrak{f}$E above) defined by fa = value of e under the environment E^x_a which is identical to E except that it pairs x with a.

In what follows we will take it for granted that expressions are evaluated under suitable environments and no longer show the latter explicitly in the formulas.

2.2 Imperative Languages

Can the semantical approach be carried over to "imperative" languages? The answer of Mathematical Semantics is: Yes, it can, if only we choose suitable denotations.

States. A state, or "contents-function", is a pairing of "locations" with "values":

$$\text{states} = \text{locations} \longrightarrow \text{values}$$

<u>Locations</u> ("addresses" in machine languages, "variables" in Algol 60) and <u>values</u> (e.g. numbers) are not further analyzed here. Given a state ξ and a location a, the value $f = \xi a$ may be viewed as "contents of location a in state ξ". (We ignore the question of partially defined states, i.e. the possibility that ξa is undefined; only in the simplest languages are locations in one-to-one correspondence with identifiers; we also ignore any further structure on locations; see also 6.2).

<u>State transformations</u>. "Statements" (as we will call the type of expressions of imperative languages we want to study now) denote state transformations, i.e. functions from states to states:

$$\text{dens} = \text{states} \longrightarrow \text{states} .$$

As a first example, consider a simple assignment statement:

(statements:)	(states $\longrightarrow$ states:)
1. a := a + 1	the function transforming into ξ', where $\xi'\alpha = \xi\alpha + 1$, $\xi'\beta = \xi\beta$ for $\beta \neq \alpha$

(assuming an environment that pairs a with location α). Next, consider two cases of a "compound statement":

2. s_1; s_2	$f_2 \circ f_1$, i.e. the function $f\xi = f_2(f_1\xi)$
3. l:s_1; <u>if</u> b <u>then</u> <u>goto</u> l;	the function $f\xi = \underline{\text{let}}\ \xi' = f_1\xi$ $p\xi' \longrightarrow f\xi'$ $T \longrightarrow f_2\xi'$

(assuming that the s_i denote functions f_i and b in the last example denotes a predicate on states p). <u>Notation</u>: We use the arrow " $\longrightarrow$" for conditional expressions; T is the truth-value "true". This is not to be confused with our other use of the arrow, as in $A \longrightarrow B$ which denotes the set of functions from A to B.

The last example needs some comment: Note that the f to be defined occurs on the right-hand side of the definition. A detailed account would require a study of the set of (partial) functions from states to states: it is by no means clear that equations like the one for f do have solutions, or which solution to choose if there are several. (We will return to the subject of "recursive" definitions in 3.3). Also, the "goto" requires a more sophisticated treatment in general (see 5.1).

In the above examples (as already in those of the preceding section) we could have replaced unanalyzed subexpressions (like a, s_i, b) by their semantical counterparts (α, f_i, p). This shows that we can immediately "read" the expressions, and in particular the operators involved, semantically: Thus, $\alpha := \alpha + 1$ is the transformation "augment the α-component of the state by 1" (and more generally, ":=" defines a transformation in terms of a given location and value: $\alpha := v$ replaces the α-component by v). Again, $f_1;f_2$ is the functional product i.e. ";" is functional composition from left to right. In example 3, the given functions f_1, f_2 and predicate p are combined to a new function for which a perhaps self-evident notation might be f_1; while p repeat $f_1;f_2$.

Our present choice of denotations is not adequate to deal with the following example:

4. s_1 // s_2 ?

where the intended meaning of "//" is quasi-parallel execution; this will be taken up in chapter 3.

2.3 Motivation

The foregoing examples should be sufficient to indicate that a semantical approach to programming languages is possible. Amplifying some of the remarks at the end of the introduction, we want to show why it is useful.

a) Semantical approach vs. evaluation mechanism

Languages "express" something, or, to say the same in other words, one composes programs by composing meanings. From this point of view, it is not sufficient to define the meaning of a program by giving just a mechanism that comes out with the correct answer. On the other hand, the point of view is precisely emphasized by the semantical approach, as we tried to indicate by giving the "semantical readings" in the previous section.

b) Small state

Compared to existing "mechanistic" (formal or informal) definitions, like /15/ and /16/, the approach is likely to lead to a "small" state ξ. Already in the simple cases considered so far, we see two examples for this: (1) The program (or some form of control) is not part of the state - it is on the "left-hand side" of the correspondence. We have already mentioned the advantage this may present for a definition of equivalence. (Even in a flowchart or machine language, the "program pointer" or "instruction counter" identifies, from a semantical point of view, the "computation yet to be done"; see also 5.1). (2) Also the environment E is not part of the state - rather, it may be viewed as an additional parameter to the interpreting function. We have seen that E arises already in descriptive languages where there is no notion of state; also, in examples like a := a + 1, the information which location is denoted by a is quite different from the state to be transformed. E cannot be changed by assignment, whereas ξ can; the separation into (read-only) association lists and store may be useful even for implementation, see 6.3. - A more elaborate example where we think the semantical treatment would reduce the state in comparison to /16/ is provided by PL/I's ON-conditions, which can be described in terms of procedures and procedure variables.

c) Essential semantics

The "small" state will contribute to a more economic description, but also to bringing out the essential semantical notions. This, in turn, may influence language design and will lead to easier formulation of interesting program properties, like equivalence of programs.

d) Inductive structure of the definition

The inductive nature of the definition, resulting from defining the meaning of the whole as function of the meanings of the parts, immediately invites the use of inductive proof methods.

2.4 Existing Work

The semantical approach to descriptive languages is known from formal logic, in particular from the work of Tarski. Although mathematical semantics for programming languages was initiated only by the work of Scott, there is some relevant previous work, in particular in connection with the extension to more intensional meanings to be treated in the next chapter.

Evaluation mechanisms. The work on the formalization of (big) languages, in particular /16/ (and preceding work of McCarthy and Landin) provides a large body of experience and hence a feeling of "what needs to be there" (in some form or another) in any treatment, and what difficulties are likely to be encountered. (Examples: the notion of environment; goto's terminating procedures; the need for some kind of "short representation" in implementing recursion).

Algol 68. The official definition /17/ of Algol 68, although to be classified as mechanistic, is particularly relevant for the following two reasons. First, a number of clear and simple semantical notions is introduced (albeit together with some others serving only alleged descriptive needs). For example, "names" are our locations, and "to possess" and "to refer to" are our E and ξ, respectively. Examples of simple semantical treatment are provided by the variable declaration (real x is expanded into ref real x = loc real, showing that x will denote a (newly created, local) name of type ref real, i.e. a location whose contents varies over reals), and by the parameter passing mechanism (which is reduced to declarations, i.e. auxiliary definitions, mirroring the known different "calling modes" as differences of the right-hand side, either actual or implied by the declarer on the left). - Second, programs denote "actions", and different ways of program composition correspond to different ways of action composition (this is partially blurred by the fact that "everything goes into the state").

The algebraic approach. The "meaning as a homorphism" approach comes from more recent work of Landin. In particular, Burstall and Landin /4/ deal with a language of simple expressions and correctness proof for its implementation, and Landin /8/ with a (generalized) flowchart-type language.

The work of Scott. When Scott started his mathematical treatment of semantics, a main difficulty to be solved was the problem of "recursive", i.e. self-referentially defined, functions, and the related (in fact, more general) problem of self-applicable or self-returning functions (see also sections 3.3 and 5.2, respectively). Thus /13/ introduces a class of "infinite" flowcharts, like the "infinitely periodic" flowchart shown below, and /14/ gives a model for the lambda-calculus (in which, like e.g. in Algol 60, a function may be applied to itself, which is in conflict with the usual mathematical notion of function as a mapping between two previously given sets). In both cases, lattices, i.e. certain partially ordered sets, of (partial) functions are used, where the ordering relation can be interpreted as "less defined than". (Also the flowcharts mentioned above form a lattice, and it is claimed that the idea of a lattice can also be used for non-functional data, e.g. for approximations to real numbers). Scott and Strachey /15/ apply the theory to deal with more language features.

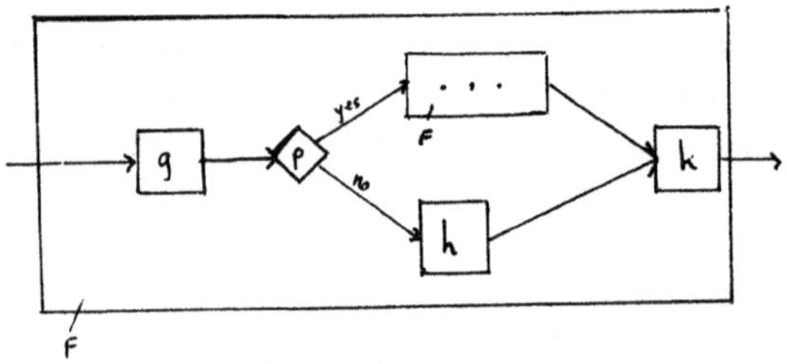

3. ACTIONS

In this chapter we propose a notion of "action" as the kind of thing denoted by a program. We define various kinds of action composition, e.g. serial composition and quasiparallel composition. We then consider "partially defined" actions and an ordering "less defined than", which allows us to deal with recursion. Finally, we define two kinds of equivalence: performing the same computations, and computing the same results. The actions are "monadic" in the sense that the elementary transformations they consist of are monadic functions from states to states. "Polyadic" actions will be considered in the next chapter.

3.1 (Monadic) Actions

Let X be the set of states. An action tells us, at each stage, either to stop or to perform the next "elementary" step $f:X \to X$. This information may depend, at each state, on the current state (i.e. there may be decisions in the program); also, the information may be non-determinate, i.e. several continuations may be possible (due to non-determinate programs).

Definition: A (monadic) action (over X) is a correspondence A,

$$A\xi = \begin{cases} \underline{\text{null}} \\ (f,A') \end{cases}$$

which gives, for each state $\xi \epsilon X$, non-determinately either null (a given constant object) or a pair consisting of the next step, a function $f:X \to X$, and of the rest-action A' which is again an action.

(Warning: Intuitively, the definition seems to be clear; formally, there is the following difficulty: A viewed as a correspondence from states to the set {null} $\cup$ set of pairs (f,A') contains (pairs containing) itself in its own range; hence this is not the usual notion of correspondence - or of function, if we view A as a function to sets of objects null or (f,A'). The subsequent remarks on representation and formalization should be sufficient to indicate the possibility of a reduction to conventional notions; see also the end of section 3.3 below).

Representation as infinite trees. We intend two actions to be equal if they give, at each state, the same f's for the same ξ's. We may therefore represent an action by an infinite tree like the following:

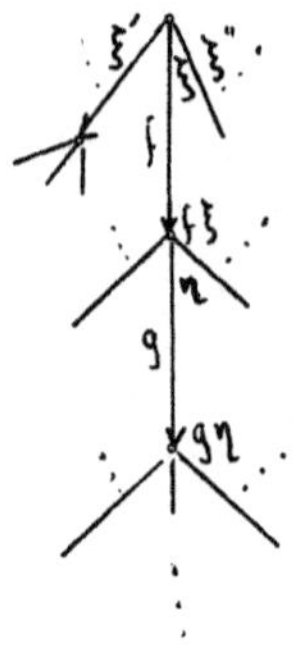

arcs in such a tree are either complete or incomplete:

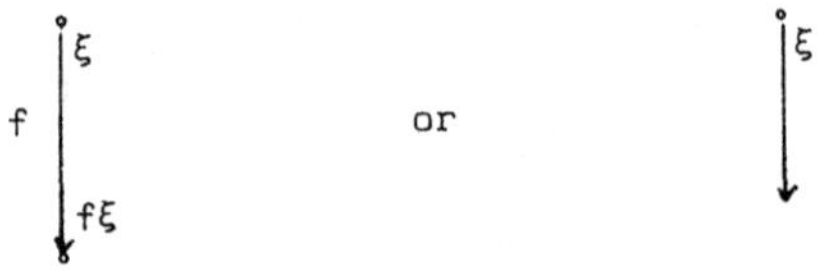

and, in the second case, do not lead to a target node (this corresponds to a null above). Thus, there may be finite and infinite paths in the tree. As defined above, our notion of action requires that there be an arc (complete or incomplete) from each node for each ξ; two arcs from one node with the ξ correspond to non-determinacy.

(Set-theoretic) formalization. Two possible set-theoretic formalizations of the notion of infinite tree considered would be: (1) tree = set of its paths; (2) tree = set of initial segments of its paths. We could define actions according to (1) or (2), but would have to add closure conditions on the corresponding sets: In both cases, the sets must allow "continuation for each ξ"; in case (1), the set must be closed against forming the limit of an ascending sequence of initial segments; in case (2), where we avoid infinite paths, the set must be closed against taking initial segments.

Finitely representable actions. Programming languages are, of course, concerned with finitely representable actions - in fact, a program is a finite representation of an action. The infinite-tree representation immediately suggests simplifications in the direction of finite representation, like the following: collecting identical continuations for different ξ into one (labelling the arc by the predicate characterizing those ξ); using graphs rather than trees; using labels for recurring subtrees. Examples (in notation which will be made precise below):

1. F = <u>if</u> p <u>then</u> <u>null</u> <u>else</u> (f;F)

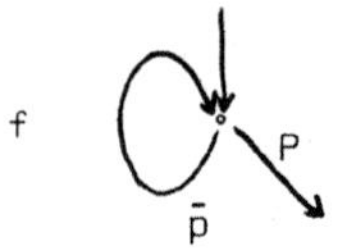

2. G = g <u>or</u> (h;G;k)

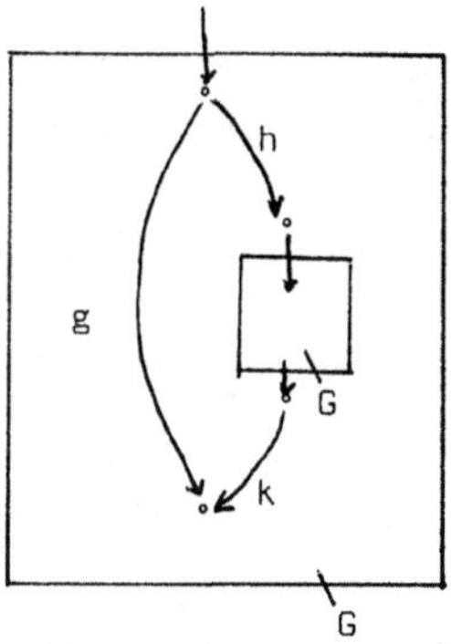

<u>Discussion, alternatives</u>. In chapter 2, we considered programs as functions from argument states to result states. A first step towards a more intensional notion would be to consider "derivations" of result states from argument states, i.e. <u>computations</u> of the following form:

$$\underset{\xi}{\bullet} \xrightarrow{\quad f \quad} \underset{f\xi}{\circ} \xrightarrow{\quad g \quad} \underset{g(f\xi)}{\circ} \xrightarrow{\quad h \quad} \quad \cdots$$

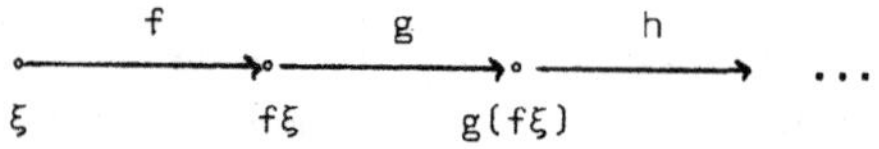

(where we admit also infinite computations). However, to identify a program with the set of computations that it performs is not sufficient: if we allow quasi-parallel computation, then the state fξ may have been changed by a second program before g is applied by the first. This leads to a notion of (what we call for the moment) <u>interrupted computation</u>, like

$$\underset{\xi}{\bullet} \xrightarrow{\quad f \quad} \underset{f\xi\ \eta}{\circ} \xrightarrow{\quad g \quad} \underset{gn\ \zeta}{\circ} \xrightarrow{\quad h \quad} \quad \cdots$$

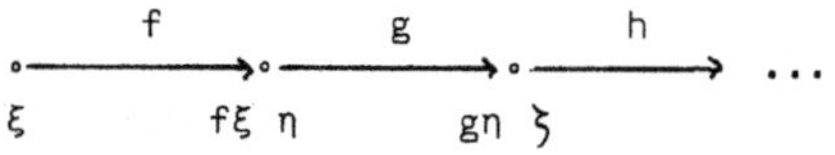

(and computations are the special case where η= fξ, ζ = gn, etc.) Actions (in the infinite form) arise by collecting interrupted computations into one picture; the - equivalent - definition in terms of next step and rest-action is more or less a formalization of the notion of "action" in /17/.

Variations of the notion of interrupted computation, and consequently of action, would result by (1) omitting the final label on each arc: this makes no real difference, since fξ can be obtained from f and ξ; or (2) omitting the middle label f, i.e.

"forgetting the operation that produced the next state"; in the definition of action, the pair (f,A') would be replaced by a pair (ξ',A'). - The requirements that A (as a function of ξ) and f be total functions could be relaxed (and effectively the first will be in 3.3 below).

3.2 Simple Action Compositions

Notation: To define actions as non-determinate functions, we need some notation for writing non-determinate expressions. In the definitions below, we use

a) an operator ⊔ , where the value of

$$e_1 \sqcup e_2$$

is either the value of e_1 or the value of e_2.

b) a cases-notation, where the value of

$$\begin{array}{ll} \underline{\text{cases}}\ e: & e_1 \to \dots \\ & e_2 \to \dots \\ & \dots \end{array}$$

is obtained by fixing a value of e and then using this value to run through the case distinctions. Of course, different choices of the value of e will, in general, lead to different values of the whole expression. (One possible formalization of non-determinate expressions would be as set-valued expressions: then ⊔ would become set-union ∪ , and cases e:... would become $\bigcup_{h \in e}$ (cases h:...).)

1. The null-action (which we denote by Null) gives null for every ξ:

$$\underline{\text{Null}}\ \xi = \underline{\text{null}}$$

2. The elementary action [f] consists of a single step f:X → X:

$$[f]\ \xi = f,\ \underline{\text{Null}}$$

3. Serial composition A; B of two actions A, B:

$$
\begin{aligned}
(A;B)\xi \;=\; & \underline{\text{cases}}\ A\xi: \\
& \qquad \underline{\text{null}} \rightarrow B\xi \\
& \qquad (f,A') \rightarrow f,(A';B)
\end{aligned}
$$

i.e. execute first A, then B.

4. Quasi-parallel (or "collateral") composition:

$$
\begin{aligned}
&(A \mathbin{//} B)\,\xi = \\
&\quad (\underline{\text{cases}}\ A\xi:\ \underline{\text{null}} \rightarrow B\xi \\
&\qquad\qquad\quad (f,A) \rightarrow f,(A' \mathbin{//} B)) \\
&\quad \sqcup \\
&\quad (\underline{\text{cases}}\ B\xi:\ \underline{\text{null}} \rightarrow A\xi \\
&\qquad\qquad\quad (g,B') \rightarrow g,(A \mathbin{//} B'))
\end{aligned}
$$

i.e. "unspecified merging" of the elementary steps of A and B, preserving the two individual orderings.

5. Choice:

$$(A\ \underline{\text{or}}\ B)\xi = A\xi \sqcup B\xi$$

i.e. execute either A or B.

6. Conditional:

$$
\begin{aligned}
&(\underline{\text{if}}\ p\ \underline{\text{then}}\ A\ \underline{\text{else}}\ B)\xi = \\
&\qquad p\xi \rightarrow A\xi,\ T \rightarrow B\xi
\end{aligned}
$$

where $p: X \rightarrow \{T,F\}$ is a predicate on states.

3.3 Recursion

Intuitively, it seems clear how "definitions" like

$$F = \underline{\text{if}}\ p\ \underline{\text{then}}\ \underline{\text{null}}\ \underline{\text{else}}\ (f;F)$$ see Fig.1 above

or

$$F = f\ \underline{\text{or}}\ (g;F;k)$$ see Fig.2 above

or

$$F = \underline{\text{if}}\ p\ \underline{\text{then}}\ A\ \underline{\text{else}}\ B \mathbin{//} (C;F;D)$$

are to be interpreted: in each case, the action F will be (represented by) an infinite tree that contains itself as a proper subtree. (For the first two examples, a finite representation of the tree has been shown in 3.1 above. Notation:Here, as already there, we write f instead of [f], when it is clear from context that the elementary action, not the state transformation, is meant).

Examples of "recursive" (or better: "self-referential") definitions like those above are familiar (as parameterless procedure declarations) from existing programming languages. But so are definitions like F = f;F or F = F;f or even F = F, where it is less clear what the intended action should be.

Recursively defined functions. The first of the examples above can also be read "extensionally", as defining a (partial) function $F:X \tilde{\rightarrow} X$ (namely the function while $\bar{p}$ repeat f). We briefly recall the theory of such recursive function definitions. One considers partial functions $f:X \tilde{\rightarrow} X$, and a (partial) ordering between such functions: $f \sqsubseteq g$ if f is "less defined than" g (or g is an "extension" of f), i.e. $g\xi$ is defined and equal to $f\xi$ whenever the latter is defined, but possibly defined also for other ξ. Next one observes that each ascending chain $f_1 \sqsubseteq f_2 \sqsubseteq \ldots$ has a limit, or least upper bound (with respect to $\sqsubseteq$): $\lim_{i\to\infty} f_i$ is the function f such that $f\xi$ is defined iff there exists a f_i for which $f_i\xi$ is defined, and then $f\xi = f_i\xi$. Given a "definition" like

$$F = \mathcal{F}\, F$$

where $\mathcal{F}$ is a functional, i.e. a transformation of partial functions, e.g. $\mathcal{F}\,F$ = if p then null else(f,F), one has to show that $\mathcal{F}$ is (monotone, i.e. preserves $\sqsubseteq$, and) continuous, i.e. preserves limits (in fact, the first property follows from the second). Then one can use a theorem stating that every such $\mathcal{F}$ has a least fixpoint, i.e. that there exists a least (in the sense of $\sqsubseteq$) function F such that $F = \mathcal{F}\,F$, and one can take that F as the function "defined" by the equation; moreover, one can show that F is the limit of an ascending sequence of functions:

$$F = \lim_{i\to\infty} \{F_i : F_0 = \emptyset \quad \text{(the totally undefined function)},$$
$$F_{i+1} = \mathcal{F}\,F_i \quad \}.$$

This latter representation of F corresponds to the way it is actually computed. Namely, we start with "no information about F", i.e. the totally undefined function F_0, and plug this into the defining equation to get the better approximation $F_1 = \mathcal{F}\,F_0$ to F, and so on. Conversely, to compute $F\xi$ for a ξ for which it exists, we actually compute $F_i\xi$ for some i.

Partial actions. We show how the same technique can be applied to deal with recursively defined actions, and have first to generalize actions to "partial" actions, corresponding to the transition from total to partial functions above. A partial action differs from the actions considered so far in that, at each stage, a special object $\underline{u}$ (for "undefined") may arise as result:

$$A\xi = \begin{cases} \underline{u} \\ \underline{\text{null}} \\ (f, A') \end{cases}$$

where now A' is again a partial action.

The reason why we model "undefined" as "(one of the values of) Aξ is $\underline{u}$" rather than "Aξ has no value" - a possibility which we exclude, but which would be naturally present in the notion of non-determinate function - is that we want to capture the situation that "some branches of a program yield undefined, whereas others don't", see also the examples below.

"Less defined than", limits. We say $A \sqsubseteq B$, or A is less defined than B, if B differs from A at most in that some paths in (the infinite tree representation of) A that run into $\underline{u}$ can be continued in B. It can be shown that an ascending chain $A_1 \sqsubseteq A_2 \sqsubseteq \ldots$ has a limit $\lim A_i$, i.e. a least upper bound with respect to $\sqsubseteq$ (see again the examples below).

Continuity. The operations on actions introduced in 3.2, like ";", and "//", can be extended to operations on partial actions. We will not give the extended definitions; the idea is, of course, that execution of an action runs into $\underline{u}$ whenever it requires execution of a subtraction that runs into $\underline{u}$. One would then have to prove (which we also will not do) that these operations are (monotone and) continuous in all their arguments.

Recursively defined actions; Examples. It follows that an equation $F = \mathcal{F}\,F$, where $\mathcal{F}\,F$ uses only the compositions defined in 3.2, has a least fixpoint that can be obtained by "infinite expansion", namely as the limit of the sequence $F_0 = \underline{U}$ (the totally undefined action, $\underline{U}\xi = \underline{u}$ for all ξ), $F_{i+1} = \mathcal{F}\,F_i$. In the examples that follow, we first study some "pathological" cases to see the role of $\underline{u}$.

1. $F = f;F$:

   We have $F_0 = \underline{U}$, $F_{i+1} = f;F_i$, $F = f;f;\ldots$ (which we might call f^{ω}):

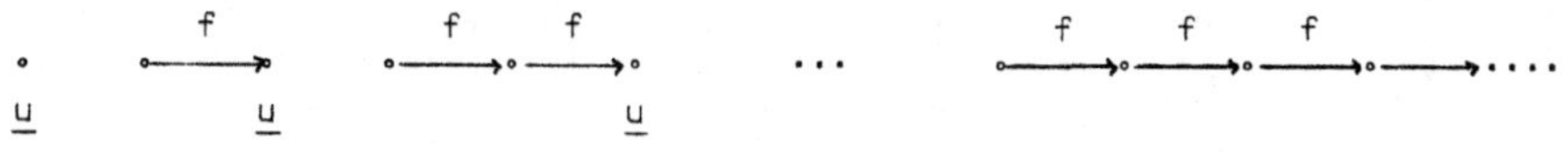

2. $F = F;f$:

$F_0 = \underline{u}$, $F_{i+1} = F_i;f$, hence $F_1 = \underline{u};f = \underline{u}$, $F_2 = \underline{u}$, ..., hence

$F = \underline{u}$:

Observe that $\underline{u}$ is not the only solution of the equation $F = F;f$ (though certainly the smallest): the f^ω above is another one. The difference between 1. and 2. corresponds to the usual understanding: in the one case, we get a definite (though non-terminating) computation, in the other, we get done nothing at all, having "first to do F which means first to do F which means ...".

3. $F = \underline{\text{Null}}\ \underline{\text{or}}\ (f;F)$

i.e. we get a set $f^* = \bigcup_i f^i$ of finite computations, but also the infinite computation f^ω. This shows that in the model where a tree is the set of its paths, lim is <u>not</u> set union $F_i = \bigcup_{j\leq i} f^j$, thus $\bigcup_i F_i = f^*$, but $\lim F_i = f^* \cup f^\omega$ - i.e. we have also to do "infinite completion". (On the other hand, lim <u>is</u> $\bigcup$ if we model a tree by the set of its initial segments).

4. $F = f \mathbin{//} F$:

i.e. $F = (f^*;\underline{u}) \cup f^\omega$. It is interesting to verify that this solution is in fact $\subsetneq f^\omega$ (which is another solution of $F = f \mathbin{//} F$): "taking away" $\underline{u}$ from a point that has already continuations makes an action "larger", because $\underline{u}$ is replaced by a continuation, albeit one already there.

5. $F = \underline{\text{if}}\ p\ \underline{\text{then}}\ \underline{\text{null}}\ \underline{\text{else}}\ (f;\ F)$:

6. $F = f$ or $(g;F;k)$:

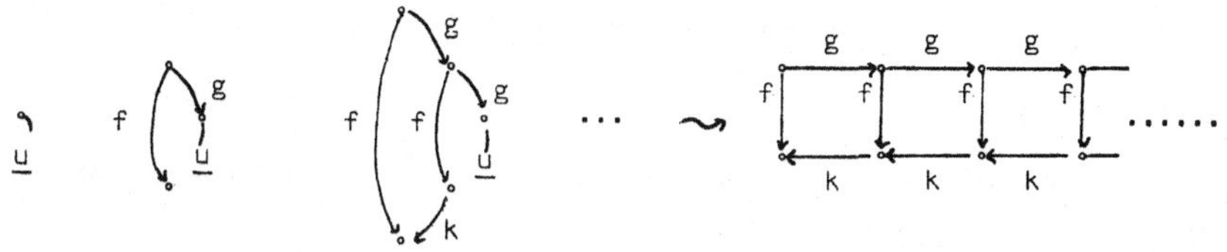

(for which a finite representation has been given in 3.1).

A note on the definition of action. As we have noted, the definition of action is itself self-referential: the set $\mathcal{A}$ of actions over X is "defined" by the equation

$$\mathcal{A} = X \times\!\!\to \{\underline{null}\} \cup (X \to X) \times \mathcal{A}$$

where $M \times\!\!\to N$ is the set of non-determinate functions from M to N, and $M \times N$ is the set of ordered pairs. Using the same technique, we can define

$$\mathcal{A}_0 = \{\underline{Null}\}$$

i.e. $\mathcal{A}_0 = X \to \{\underline{null}\}$ - the null-action is the only function in this set - and

$$\mathcal{A}_{i+1} = X \times\!\!\to \{\underline{null}\} \cup (X \to X) \times \mathcal{A}_i$$

The $\mathcal{A}_i$ are sets (of functions), and the ordering is now set inclusion $\subseteq$. (Strictly speaking, we do not have $\mathcal{A}_i \subseteq \mathcal{A}_{i+1}$: the next set does not contain more functions but different ones, because the range of the functions is larger and hence different. There is, however, an immediate notion of "embedding" the old functions in the new ones; or we define non-determinate function, i.e. correspondence, just as set of ordered pairs, ignoring domains and ranges.) Then the required $\mathcal{A}$ is $\bigcup_i \mathcal{A}_i$.

A further example of self-referential definitions is provided by definitions of functions on actions like ";" and "//" in 3.2 (or comp and res below), where, except in the case of res, the additional assumption is that the function to be defined is continuous; otherwise, e.g. the assumption that $f^\omega;B$ is undefined would be consistent with the definition of ";", whereas we want $f^\omega;B = f^\omega$.

3.4 Equivalence

We define two notions of equivalence between actions.

1. Computational equivalence. For an action A, the function comp A defined below gives "the computations of A on initial state ξ"; comp A is a (non-determinate) function from states to computations, i.e. to finite or infinite sequences of

the form

$$\overset{\circ}{\xi} \xrightarrow{\;f\;} \overset{\circ}{f\xi} \xrightarrow{\;g\;} \overset{\circ}{g(f\xi)} \longrightarrow \quad \cdots$$

(see 3.1; special case: a sequence $\overset{\circ}{\xi}$ with no arc); $\frown$ is concatenation of computations with "matching ends".

$(\text{comp } A)\xi =$

$\quad$ cases $A\xi$: null $\rightarrow \overset{\circ}{\xi}$

$$(f,A') \rightarrow \overset{\circ}{\xi} \xrightarrow{\;f\;} \overset{\circ}{f\xi} \frown (\text{comp } A')(f\xi)$$

Two actions are *computationally equivalent* if they yield the same computations:

$$A \underset{\text{comp}}{\sim} B = (\text{comp } A = \text{comp } B)$$

2. *Result equivalence*. For an action A, res A is the (non-determinate) mapping from states to states performed by A:

$(\text{res } A)\xi =$

$\quad$ cases $A\xi$: null $\rightarrow \xi$

$\qquad\qquad (f,A') \rightarrow (\text{res } A)(f\xi)$

Two actions are *result-equivalent*, if they compute the same results on the same states:

$$A \underset{\text{res}}{\sim} B = (\text{res } A = \text{res } B)$$

According to a remark made earlier, res is not a homomorphism: res (A//B) may depend on more than on res A and res B. Not even comp is a homomorphism, as is shown by the two actions

$$x := 0 \qquad \text{and} \qquad (1{:}x := o;\ \text{if } x \neq o \ \underline{\text{then}}\ \underline{\text{goto}}\ 1)$$

which are computationally equivalent (differing only by an unexecuted branch), but may behave differently when merged with a third action.

4. THE POLYADIC CASE

In this and the next chapter the paper will get rather sketchy, presenting ideas rather than worked-out solutions. The problem we want to consider in this chapter is the following: Programs not only contain "statements", but also "expressions" delivering intermediate results. The question arises where to "keep" those results; for example, in /16/ they appear in the "control", placed by the instructions that produce them into argument positions of instructions that will use them. Our present answer to the question is: intermediate results will appear in the computation, namely we will consider "polyadic" computations, that differ from the "monadic" computations considered so far by admitting "polyarcs", like

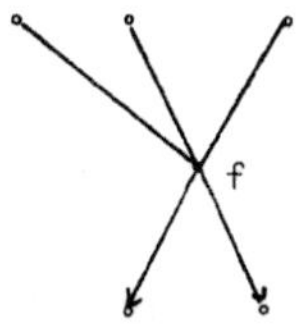

instead of just $\circ\xrightarrow{f}$.

4.1 Polyadic Actions

For simplicity of definition, we will keep actions "completely sequentialized", i.e. performing one step after one. This is unnecessary (and in fact undesirable), because there is no reason to impose an ordering on polyarcs working on disjoint sets of nodes. Also, in spite of polyarcs, we will continue to have only one state, i.e. the state will not be split into parts (see also 4.3).

A (polyadic) action A works on a tuple $\underline{v}$ of values and a state ξ:

$$A(\underline{v}\ ,\xi) \quad = \quad \begin{cases} \underline{\text{null}} \\ (a,A') \end{cases}$$

where A' is again a polyadic action; the next step a consists of a selector σ and a function f; a enlarges the computation produced so far by applying f to the σ-part of (v,ξ):

$a(\underline{v},\xi)$ =

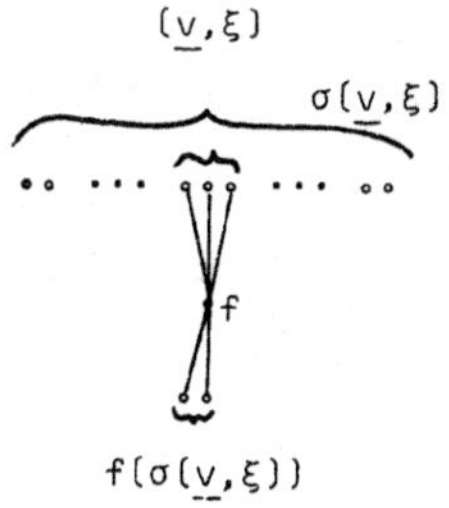

There are three types of f (for each choice of n, m $\geq$ o): $f: V^n \times X \rightarrow V^m \times X$ and the two types arising by omitting both factors X, or the right-hand factor X. The rest-action A' will operate on the typle that arises from $(\underline{v},\xi)$ by replacing $\sigma(\underline{v},\xi)$ by $f(\sigma(\underline{v},\xi))$, except that in the case $f: V^n \times X \rightarrow V^m$ the old ξ is also retained (i.e. several operations may "share" the same ξ-node as input); these remarks should be sufficient to indicate how to define comp A and res A.

4.2 Compositions

We assume that each action has a type $V^n \times X \Rightarrow V^m \times X$ (thus, in particular, all terminating paths of an action will produce results from the same set $V^m \times X$).

1. Elementary actions:

$$[f](\underline{v},\xi) \;=\; (I,f),\underline{\mathrm{Null}}$$

where I is the identity selector (for $f: V^n \times X \rightarrow V^m \times X$; no copy of ξ, resp. also no arm from ξ, for the other types; there is one $\underline{\mathrm{Null}}: V^n \times X \Rightarrow V^n \times X$ for each n).

2. Serial compositions:

$$\begin{aligned}
&(A;B)(\underline{v},\xi) \;=\\
&\quad \underline{\text{cases}}\ A(\underline{v},\xi):\ \underline{\text{null}} \;\rightarrow\; B(\underline{v},\xi)\\
&\qquad\qquad\qquad\quad (a,A') \;\rightarrow\; a,(A';B)
\end{aligned}$$

(for $A: V^n \times X \Rightarrow V^m \times X$, $B: V^m \times X \Rightarrow V^p \times X$); here, B works on the result $(\underline{v}',\xi')$ of A. Similarly, a serial composition $(A \,\ulcorner\!; B)(\underline{v},\underline{w},\xi)$ can be defined where A and B work on $\underline{V}$ and $\underline{w}$, respectively (and again B uses the result state ξ' of A).

3. Quasi-parallel composition:

$$\begin{aligned}
&(A \mathbin{//} B)(\underline{v},\underline{w},\xi) \;=\\
&\quad (\underline{\text{cases}}\ A(\underline{v},\xi):\ \underline{\text{null}} \;\rightarrow\; (\underline{\mathrm{Null}}\ulcorner B)(\underline{v},\underline{w},\xi)\\
&\qquad\qquad\qquad\quad (a,A') \;\rightarrow\; a\ulcorner\underline{\text{null}},A' \mathbin{//} B)\\
&\quad \sqcup\\
&\quad (\underline{\text{cases}}\ B(\underline{w},\xi):\ \underline{\text{null}} \;\rightarrow\; (A\ulcorner\underline{\mathrm{Null}})(\underline{v},\underline{w},\xi)\\
&\qquad\qquad\qquad\quad (b,B') \;\rightarrow\; \underline{\text{null}}\ulcorner b,\ A \mathbin{//} B')
\end{aligned}$$

where $\underline{\mathrm{Null}}\ulcorner$ and $\ulcorner\underline{\mathrm{Null}}$, resp. $\underline{\text{null}}\ulcorner$ and $\ulcorner\underline{\text{null}}$ enlarge the domain of an action resp. next step.

We can now express, for example, <u>normal argument evaluation</u> of operators: For $A_i : X \Rightarrow V \times X$ (say), $op : V^n \times X \Rightarrow V^m \times X$:

$$\underline{op}(A_1,\ldots,A_n) = A(A_1 \,//\, \ldots \,//\, A_n);op$$

i.e. the arguments are evaluated in parallel, and the operator op is applied to the results.

4. <u>Conditionals</u>

$(\underline{if}\ p\ \underline{then}\ A\ \underline{else}\ B)\xi =$
$p\xi \rightarrow A\xi,\ T \rightarrow B\xi$

(for $p:X \rightarrow \{T,F\}$);

$\underline{if}\ Q\ \underline{then}\ A\ \underline{else}\ B = Q;\ cond(A,B)$

where

$cond(A,B)(b,\xi) = b \rightarrow A\xi,\ T \rightarrow B\xi$

(for $Q:X \Longrightarrow \{T,F\} \times X$). (In the last case, some provision is needed for "ignoring the b":) $cond(A,B) \in \{T,F\} \times X \Rightarrow \ldots$, but $A \in X \Rightarrow \ldots$

5. <u>Application</u>

If the set V of values includes actions themselves (i.e. in conventional terminology, "procedures" or "routines", see 5.2), we may define

$$apply(A,\underline{v},\xi) = A(\underline{v},\xi)$$

(where again we have to "ignore the immediate result A")

$call\ (P,\ A_n,\ \ldots,\ A_n) = P \,//\, A \,//\, \ldots \,//\, A_n\ ;\ apply$
$(= apply\ \underline{(}P,\ A_n,\ \ldots,\ A_n\underline{)}\ )$

4.3 <u>Less Ordering Required</u>

The notion of polyadic action as defined above is a first attempt to deal with the problem and, additionally to lack of precision in the formal treatment, suffers from various inadequacies: 1) Each step works, in principle, on all intermediate results; also, $\underline{v}$ is private while ξ is shareable - this distinction is blurred by providing a next step for every choice of $\underline{v}$, ξ. 2) There is the problem of "dangling" intermediate results (as in the definition of cond and apply). 3) Most important, there is too much sequencing information retained; attempts towards "<u>the most parallel form of a computation</u>" would in particular be presented with the following problems:

a) To remove unnecessary ordering between operations on disjoint intermediate results; this will be further discussed below.

b) To remove unnecessary ordering between operations on disjoint parts of the state: this would require splitting up the state into parts - for an example see 6.4.

c) To disregard the identity of variables: because of quasi-parallel composition, this would go into a suitable notion of equivalence rather than into a refined notion of action.

Here, then, are a few remarks to deal with point a) (and also with points 1) and 2) above). A first guess might be to define polyadic actions as (certain) sets of (polyadic) interruptable computations - just as monadic actions can be considered as sets of monadic interruptable computations (see 3.1). An example of an interruptable computation (performed by the action c := a + b, where a, b, c are fixed locations and ca, cb, "c :=" are corresponding contents and store operations) would be

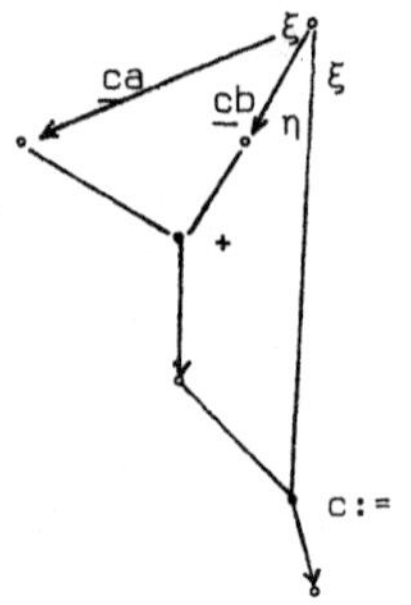

(where we have not shown computed results; for example, the resulting state would be ξ with the c-component changed to caξ + cbξ). But this example also shows that we have thrown away too much ordering (if in interrupted computations, like in computations, the only ordering is the one shown by the arrows): We can no longer mirror any ordering between ca and cb - although it would make a difference if other actions interfere. Also, we cannot mirror a situation where inspection of the state is required to determine a continuation which does not use a state.

This suggests a refinement of interruptable computations by introducing (1) non-dataflow arrows from nodes to sub-computations (which would also deal with point 2) above), and (2) the possibility of an ordering between the arrows leaving one state-node.

5. MORE COMPOSITIONS

In this chapter we present a few ideas on two more ways of action composition. The one is the use of labels and goto. The other is procedure definition and application which has already been mentioned in 4.2, but here we want to emphasize the fact that procedures usually are "non-stratified", i.e. that they may be arguments or results of themselves.

5.1 Labels and Goto

Several-entrance/exit actions. One way to deal with goto is to allow for actions that have more than one entrance and/or exit. For example

$$f;\ l{:}g$$

has two entrances and one exit; when entered at the standard entrance it "does" f;g, when entered at entrance l it does g, and in both cases leaves through the standard exit. Again,

$$l{:}\underline{goto}\ m$$

can be entered at either the standard entrance or l, and in both cases does nothing than leaving through exit m. We may now define a composition like $(l_1{:}A_1;\ l_2{:}A_2;\ \ldots;\ l_n{:}A_n)$ which "connects" exits with the corresponding entrances.

A possible variation would be to "remember" the l_i as entrances of the composed action. (The first possibility corresponds to the Algol 60 block, the second to the Algol 60 compound statement which can be "gone into" from outside); one-entrance actions are sufficient if we don't allow such a possibility).

There is no need to say what exits (or entrances) "are", except to make sure that they are "sufficiently different" from each other. This can be done by "disjoining" the sets of exits on action composition.

What is a label? A tempting answer would be: the action (or, in the extensional approach, the state-transformation) "yet to be performed". While this answer is sufficient for determining the meaning of the whole program, it is not sufficient if we want to keep the homomorphic approach (at least with our present notion of denotation). This is shown by an example like the following

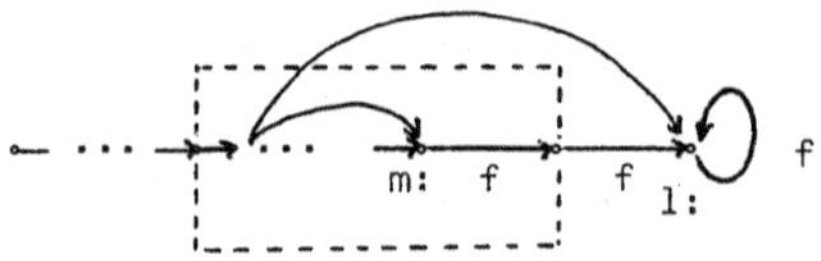

where the subprogram is to be terminated by goto l but not by goto m, and yet we would have $l = m = f^{\omega}$.

Statement = state transformation, given a continuation. Morris /9/ has shown that we can have label = state transformation and keep the homomorphic approach, if we complicate the denotations of statements: A statement is no longer a state transformation outright, but a function producing a state transformation given a continuation (i.e. another state transformation). Thus

$$(a := a + 1)\gamma = \gamma \cdot \sigma$$

(or, in our earlier notation, $\sigma;\gamma$), where σ is the state-transformation usually associated with a := a + 1. Again,

$$(s_1;\ s_2)\gamma = s_1(s_2\gamma)$$

i.e. to execute $s_1;s_2$ under continuation γ is to execute s_1 under the continuation which one gets by executing s_2 under continuation γ. Now a label l is a state transformation, and goto l executes l, disregarding any continuation:

$$(\underline{\text{goto}}\ l)\gamma = l\ .$$

A notation like $(l_1:s_1;\ \dots;\ l_n:s_n)$ can be defined as

$$\begin{aligned}(l_1:s_1;\ \dots;\ l_n:s_n)\gamma = \\ \underline{\text{let}}\ l_1 &= s_1 l_2 \\ l_2 &= s_2 l_3 \\ &\dots \\ l_n &= s_n\gamma\end{aligned}$$

5.2 Self-applicable, Self-returning Procedures

With the usual notion of function as a triple consisting of a set A, a set B, and a subset of A × B to define a function f:A → B, we first have to be given (or to define the sets A and B, and <u>then</u> can define the subset of A × B. This excludes self-applicable or self-returning functions, i.e. functions $f:A \rightarrow B$ such that $f \in A$ or $f \in B$; indeed, with the classical notion of function such a notion would be plainly circular.

On the other hand, in a language like Algol 60, there are two sources for "recursion", i.e. for a procedure to call itself: (1) self-referential definition of the procedure (with which, at least for the parameterless case, we have been dealing earlier), and (2) passing the procedure as a parameter to itself. Thus, there are procedures that can be applied to themselves, and similarly, in slightly more general languages, procedures that can return themselves.

Although the discussion also applies to actions - in the definition of <u>apply</u> in 4.2 we have assumed that (polyadic) actions may arise as values, which gives rise to precisely the kind of circularity being discussed now - it is independent of whether we interpret procedures as actions or, extensionally, as the transformations performed by them, and we will return therefore to the latter approach. In fact, the circularity has nothing to do with the "imperative" character of the languages being considered, but arises already in the "descriptive" part of Algol 60, or e.g. in the λ-calculus for the function $I = \lambda x.x$ we have $Ix = x$ for any object x (in the system) whatsoever, so in particular, $II = I$.

<u>A simple example</u>. There are easy examples of "circular" objects, like circular lists, or the "infinite" modes of Algol 68 (see Pair /10/ for a formal treatment of the latter). Take, for example, the three-element list

$$l = (a,l,b)$$

containing itself as second element. Viewing lists as functions (from natural numbers to elements), l is a function containing itself in its range; viewed as a set of pairs, this function is the set $\{(1,a), (2,l), (3,b)\}$, i.e. a <u>non-founded</u> set. In fact, we have encountered another example for this situation in the notion of (monadic) action: <u>A</u> as a function transforming ξ into <u>null</u> or (f,A') is non-founded. Here as there, we may consider two such functions as the same if their "infinite expansions" are the same, i.e. if they yield the same results under continued application.

<u>Scott's models of λ-calculus</u>. Scott /14/ has constructed extensional models for the λ-calculus by constructing a set D isomorphic to its own function space:

$$D \cong (D \rightarrow D).$$

The construction starts with a lattice D_0 and iterates the transition from D_i to $D_{i+1} = (D_i \rightarrow D_i)$, the lattice of continuous functions from D_i to D_i (see 3.3). There is a notion of "embedding" D_i in D_{i+1} and, conversely, "approximating" elements of D_{i+1} by elements of D_i; D is reached by a process of "infinite completion".

Another idea for modelling procedures. Here is an as yet rough idea for a model of procedures (as in a descriptive subset of Algol 60, say). How this idea relates to Scott's construction, I do not know.

1. Consider procedures as "parametric" graphs (i.e. "derivations", possibly infinite, of result values, possibly undefined, from argument values). These graphs will contain range-indicators, like real or proc, instead of actual ranges, associated with their parameters and results.

2. Associate with each graph P a mapping π from the tuple of its argument ranges (like reals, or graphs) to its result range.

3. Of course, the π's, as mappings, will in general contain P's in their domains and ranges. Eliminate the P's by "infinite expansion", i.e. by "transfinitely" identifying " with π. (Just as in the example above, l was "transfinitely identified" with (a,l,b) to get the infinite list).

6. APPLICATIONS

The aim of this chapter is not to present fully worked-out examples, but to provide evidence for the usefulness of the notions considered, namely a) a semantical approach to language design, and in particular, b) a structured and "detail-free" notion of process.

6.1 Examples from Language Design

In this section we consider two examples for the usefulness of semantical vs. (more or less) syntactical notions in deciding questions of language design.

1) "Right" vs. "wrong" recursion. It is understood as part of the block concept, that redeclaration of a non-local identifier of a procedure doesn't affect the meaning of that procedure. Thus, in

```
(real a; let Q = a:= a + 1; ...; (real a; ...; Q; ...) ...)
```

the call of Q in the inner block will act on the (location denoted by the) outer a. There is less agreement when the redeclaration is brought about dynamically, by a recursive activation of the block declaring Q, like in

```
let P(F) = (real a; let Q = a := a + 1; ...;
                              if p then F else P(Q); ...)
```

Assume an outer call P(N) running into the else-alternative, i.e. into an inner call P(Q); assume this inner call running into the then-alternative, which means calling F, i.e. Q. According to the right kind of recursion, Q will change the outer a, according to the wrong kind, the inner a.

The right recursion is understood in (informal) mathematics and in languages like Lisp, Algol 60, Algol 68, PL/I. The wrong recursion resulted from the (erroneous) formulation of the copy rules in the original Algol 60 Report, was present in (or at least implemented from) an early version of PL/I, and is still present in POP 2 and APL.

The informal argument for right recursion, that "identifiers mean something when you write them", is easily formalized in Mathematical Semantics: The call P(N) creates a new location α and defines Q as the transformation "augment contents of α by 1"; so there is nothing like "(the denotation of) q containing an identifier a"; in particular, that transformation cannot be affected by associating new meanings with the identifiers a and Q in the inner call. (In "mechanistic" definitions, this effect is usually brought about by "suitable systematic changes" of the redeclared identifiers).

Wrong recursion leads to "wrong" automatic variables: it is for precisely that reason that, under right recursion, automatic variables in PL/I are not the same as controlled variables with implied allocate/free statements at block begin/end.

2. Semantical scope of routines. Algol 68 allows for values of "higher types": procedures, or, as they are called there, routines, are values like any other and may, in particular, appear as arguments or results of other routines. It is therefore surprising that a definition like

$$f \circ g = \lambda x.f(g(x))$$

i.e. functional composition, cannot be (directly) expressed in Algol 68 (this was first discovered by P. Landin). Namely, a "call" of the operator $\circ$, say sin$\circ$cos, would return the routine $\lambda x.f(g(x))$; the information that f and g denote sin and cos would be present somewhere but the (perhaps "suitably changed") identifiers f and g are part of the routine. Now the scope, or dynamic life-time, of a routine is defined as the smallest among the scopes of its non-local identifiers, i.e. here as the activation of the declaration of "$\circ$" by the call sin$\circ$cos; for this call to return that routine would mean, therefore, to transport the latter outside its scope.

According to the semantical approach, on the other hand, the routine in question is the function sin$\circ$cos (or some action computing it), but it doesn't contain any longer the identifiers f and g. The difficulty disappears if the definition of scope of a routine is based on the scopes of the values denoted by its non-locals, rather than of the non-locals themselves. A corresponding proposal by the present author is considered for inclusion in a revision of Algol 68.

The present proposal is to be distinguished from the so-called "retention strategy", where program-created values, like locations α, are retained beyond their creating block. For example, the routine Q above could still not be transported, under the present proposal, outside its declaring block. The reason is that $\alpha := \alpha + 1$ refers to a program-created value, namely the location α, whose scope is that block, whereas $\sin \circ \cos$, or the function "add 3" denoted by the f(3) in

$$\underline{\text{let}}\ f(x) = \lambda y.x + y;\ f(3)$$

do not refer to any such values.

Implementation: Separation of E and ξ. The usual argument against the proposal is that it is difficult to implement, or at least that the programmer would have to pay for it even if he doesn't use it. The correct answer to that is that (alleged) difficulty of implementation shouldn't be used as an argument for restrictions that cannot even be formulated semantically (or, in other words, for banning "obviously meangingful" programs; in fact, the Algol 68 authors have not been aware of the restriction in the first place). The situation is somewhat reminiscent of the arguments against recursive procedures in the early days of Algol 60.

But there is perhaps also a more constructive answer. We have argued earlier that the environment E and the state ξ play quite different roles and should be separated on definitional grounds. Our discussion of scopes shows that they also behave quite differently as regards their dynamic life time. This suggests a separation of the two also in terms of implementation, i.e. to have association lists E pairing identifiers with the values denoted by them, and a store ξ pairing locations with their contents. The store ξ would be a stack, i.e. a pulsating list, whereas the system E of association lists would be a growing tree (whose paths correspond to what is usually known as "lexicographic chains"); segments of this tree can be deleted if they become unreferenceable, i.e. by the use of garbage collection techniques.

6.2 Formal Definition of Algol 68

One stimulus for the present work was provided by the language Algol 68 and the feeling that its description should and can be improved. We list some areas where further work needs to be done or has been done elsewhere (see also /2/).

Storage. Locations have associated with them "ranges" of values they can hold. Certain values, namely arrays ("multiple values") and structures ("structured values") are composed from other values; the structure of such values induces a corresponding structure on the location that holds the value. There are "flexible" locations where the structure depends on the current contents of the location. In /3/, storage, i.e. our state ξ, is described as a range-respecting structure-preserving mapping from locations to values. The treatment shows in particular the following simplifications in comparison to the official description:

(1) There is no need for "instances" of values (just as there is no need for "occurrences" of expressions).

(2) Flexibility is a property of ranges, hence of "names" (i.e. our locations), not of multiple values.

(3) There is no need to "linearize" more-dimensional multiple values.

Modes. There is, in particular, the problem of "infinite", i.e. self-referentially defined, modes like

mode person = struct (int age, ref person father)

(see Pair /10/). Whether one considers modes as indices of sets of values, or as the sets themselves, such infinite modes pose the problem of self-referentially defined sets of values, e.g. self-applicable procedures.

Scopes. To deal with scope checks, the store can be divided into segments which are created/deleted on block entrance/exit. A check can then be made that a value referring to a location α is not transported back beyond the segment that contains α in its domain.

Parallelism. We have dealt with "collateral", i.e. quasi-parallel, execution but the following features in connection with parallelism remain to be treated (see also 6.5 below):

- Halting and resuming an action, i.e. (in Algol 68) semaphores.
- Undefinedness of merging two actions "working on the same part of the state". (This arises because Algol 68 leaves it open which actions are elementary, i.e. uninterruptable).
- The implicit termination of all parallel branches caused by a goto out of one of them.

Coercion. There remain a number of questions which fall under Syntax, like context conditions, extended language, concrete representation. We mention in particular the problem of coercions, i.e. implied type conversion, because the coercion package is difficult to describe, to analyze, to prove unique (in fact, ambiguities continue to be found), and to modify. There are a number of trade-offs between coercions on the one hand and questions of concrete syntax and infinite modes on the other.

We list coercions under Syntax because one possible approach would be to translate the program into a fuller language which contains explicit symbols for the coercion operations. One of the first things to do would be to study the algebra of modes (under the coercion operations) and prove uniqueness of paths from one mode to another one to certain classes of other modes.

6.3 Correctness of Block Implementation

"Semantical" properties of programs may be formulated and proved as properties of the processes denoted by those programs. As an example, we consider the problem of proving correct the usual technique of implementing the block concept in languages like Algol 60 (see Jones and Lucas /6/). We can draw the following picture

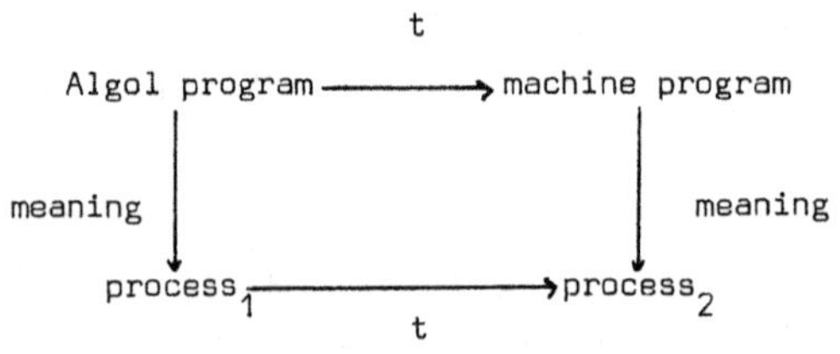

where we have three mappings: A mapping, called "meaning", from Algol programs to a set of processes; a mapping, also called "meaning", from machine programs to another set of processes; and the translation mapping t from Algol programs to machine programs. The lower t in the picture is the relation between the two sets of processes "induced" by the three mappings: $process_2$ is in relation t to $process_1$ if there exist two programs representing them such that the second is the translation of the first. It is a <u>relation</u> rather than a function, because $process_2$ will, in general, depend not only on $process_1$ but on the given Algol program representing it; for example, introducing "abbreviations" (non-recursive procedure declarations) like Q = a := a + 1 into the Algol program will not change $process_1$, but will lead to more organizational work done in $process_2$.

The main problem to be solved by block implementation is that, due to the translation of procedures into reentrant code, suitable state variables have to be introduced to ensure that the reentrant code "executes the right copy"; $process_2$, among other things, has to set, save, update and restore those state variables.

The aim is now to formulate and prove certain relationships between $process_1$ and $process_2$, like:

Under a certain mapping between the locations of the two processes (one-one on "coexisting" locations), $process_2$ "is essentially" $process_1$, more precisely: $process_1$, perhaps with additional ordering assumptions, can be embedded in $process_2$ such that the "remainder" of $process_2$ is only book-keeping.

The proof would proceed by defining a structure on each of the two sets of processes which is respected by t, and showing that the operations of the structure preserve the relation to be established. On the Algol side, the structure would consist of operations like "+", ";", "<u>if</u> ___ <u>then</u> ___ <u>else</u>"; on the machine side, there would be a much more basic structure to start with, in terms of which operations corresponding to those other ones could then be defined. (A first example for this appeared in /4/, where the basic structure is functional composition ";", and an operation like "+" is defined in terms of it as a + b = a;b;ADD).

Expected advantages of the method (whose feasibility has, of course, yet to be demonstrated by actually carrying out an example) would be that it is easier to formulate the desired correspondence; there is no need for introducing a concept like the twin-machine in /6/. Also, it seems easier to separate "interesting" from "uninteresting" information.

6.4 Expressing other Models

It may be interesting to study other proposed models of computation by trying to express them in terms of "actions" like the ones proposed here. The claim that our system might be particularly suited for the purpose is based on the very principle of its design: to include only "essential" information in it.

As a (not yet worked out) example, we consider the problem of describing the computations performed by the (interpreted) program schemata of Karp and Miller /7/. The state is split into parts, or locations. Each operation uses fixed argument and result locations and is performed in two parts: First, it copies its arguments from the state to "private" locations; then it uses the copy to compute the result and to place it into the state. The following example is written in Algol-like notation (using a, b, ... for shareable locations, and x, y ... for private locations; for simplicity, the operations f, g, ... are unary). We first associate with it a computation explicitly showing the copying:

<u>let</u> x = a
<u>let</u> y = b
b := fx
c := gy
<u>let</u> y' = b
<u>let</u> x' = a
a := hy'
b := kx'

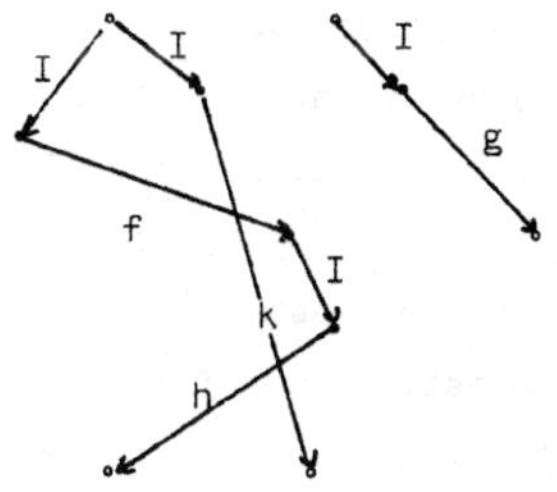

and then a more condensed form, omitting the copies

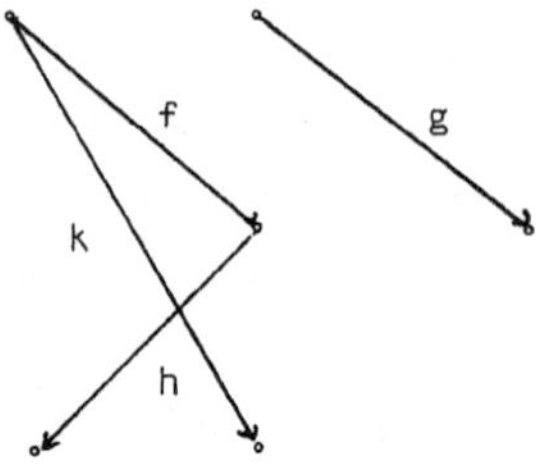

There is more ordering information needed than shown by the arrows: for every shareable location, there is always a "most recent" copy; this is shown in the two pictures by arranging copies of the same location in vertical columns. It is interesting to note that computations like the following

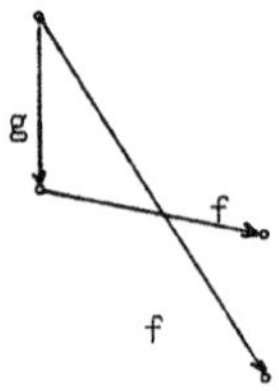

are not permitted - the copying and computing performed by two occurrences of the same operation has to be done in a first in - first out fashion. There does not seem to be a semantical reason for that restriction. (On the other hand, there may be reasons of implementation, or of ease of proof of equivalence. Also, the restriction allows a notation like $\bar{f}\ \bar{g}\ g_1\ f_1\ f_1$ for computations where $\bar{f}$ means "copy argument of f" and f_1 means "perform f with exit 1", see below).

Whether we want to associate with a program schema an action or (only) a set of computations, depends on whether we want to compose program schemata (and hence the associated actions) from given ones. In the first case, we need also an ordering between the arrows leaving one node (see also 4.3).

The "control" of a program schema allows, in particular, for decisions: the continuation of the computation may depend on the "exit" through which the last operation is left; the choice of exit will in general depend on the arguments on which the operation is performed. It seems possible to associate with any given control the set of computations (in the above sense), or, more generally, the action performed by it. The more interesting question is, of course, whether there is any simpler characterization of this set than the (usually rather implicit one) by the given control.

6.5 Language Features: a Philosophy

Language features are a difficult thing, both to discover and to judge for inclusion in any actual language. In this section we want to argue that the high-level approach to processes may provide us with a philosophy towards language features, and to illustrate the claim by an example from parallel programming: the problem of the mutual exclusion of critical sections. Consider first another example. It has been observed in /2/ that Algol 68 does not contain a return-statement of the following kind: in an expression like

(...) // (... return v)

if one of the parallel branches encounters a return v, then this will terminate also the other branch, and v will be returned as the value of the whole expression. This feature has not at all been discovered by systematic search, but by encountering two examples: the question whether Kleene's or-operator, which yields true if one argument is true even if the other is undefined, can be programmed in Algol 68; and the observation that a certain construction in the "extended" language of Algol 68, namely the conformity case clause, had an incredibly complicated expansion into the "strict" language, which turned out to be a consequence of the fact that an implicit termination effect of the kind required exists for termination of a branch via goto, but not for "normal" completion of a branch.

Process-oriented expression vs. programming with given primitives. In the first place we want to have a description of the required process in as "process-oriented" a way as possible, rather than to "program" the process in terms of a given set of primitives. For example, with the problem of the spaghetti eaters (see Hoare /5/), the most immediate description of the process required would be

$$\mathop{/\!/}_{i=1}^{5} \{\underline{\text{repeat}}(\ldots;\ \text{eat}_i;\ \ldots) \quad \text{eat}_i \text{ uninterruptable by eat}_{i\oplus 1}\}$$

i.e. the five philosophers may eat in parallel, except that no one may eat simultaneously with his neighbour. To program this in terms of semaphores is rather awkward, and it is difficult to discover the original structure in the resulting program. Semaphores are at too "low" a level also for another reason: It is possible to program the mutual exclusion problem in terms of them, but it is also possible to program a lot of nonsense.

Reasonable implementability. But a compromise is necessary. The means of expression we use must be "reasonably implementable", in particular:

- The feature must be implementable at all, i.e. there must be a corresponding algorithmic formulation. (Like of anything else, e.g. numbers, there are algorithmic and non-algorithmic descriptions of processes; implicit set notation, a mild form of which is used in the example above, is a good candidate for non-implementable description).
- The overhead, in the algorithmic formulation, of testing etc. over the process itself, i.e. the amount of "computation not doing anything", must be reasonably small.

Take as another example, a wait statement of the kind

wait p .

If we allow for p the general - even uncomputable - predicate p, the first postulate above is violated. Restriction to - arbitrary - computable p would still violate the second postulate: there would be too much too complicated testing.

The mutual exclusion problem. Why do we want certain "critical" program sections to be mutually uninterruptable? Because they use the same resources. We may as well request the programmer to make this explicit - i.e. mutual uninterruptibility of two processes will be expressed by explicitly associating the two processes with the same resource; this is precisely the idea behind the

with r do C

construction proposed by Hoare /5/. But the solution to the spaghetti problem in these terms is still rather complicated - we have to program now, not in terms of semaphores, but in terms of (a number of suitably introduced auxiliary) resources.

It was alright to use resources as "colours" to mark processes: processes with the same colour belong to one class of mutually uninterruptable processes. But why shouldn't a process have more than one colour, i.e. belong to more than one class? (For example, each philosopher has to use two forks, eachin common with one of his neighbours. Therefore we should generalize the construction to allow for

with r and s do C

similarly for more than two resources. Our spaghetti program now becomes

$$\mathop{//}_{i=1}^{5} \underline{\text{repeat}}(\ldots\ \underline{\text{with}}\ f_i\ \underline{\text{and}}\ f_{i\oplus 1}\ \underline{\text{do}}\ \text{eat}_i\ \ldots)\ .$$

Two remarks are necessary. First, we cannot replace "and" by nested use of "with": this would permit all philosophers to pick up their left fork simultaneously, and therefore finding their right forks occupied, and this situation might recur indefinitely. Second, some reasonable queuing discipline is needed for implementing the feature. A safe (tbugh probably not the most efficient) discipline would be to grant resources on a first in - first out basis, which may leave a requested resource unnecessarily unused, because the first user waiting for it also waits for some other resource. However, always preferring a later user in such a case would be no good - it would permit two philosophers to eat alternatively (with small overlaps) while the one in between them starves to death.

7. CONCLUSION

Starting from a "mathematical" approach to the semantics of programming languages, we have generalized it in the direction of more "intensional" meaning: programs denote processes, not (only) the functions computed by them. This led us to introduce "actions" as an explication of processes, and to define certain operations on them, like quasi-parallel composition of actions. One can note here a certain shift of emphasis: The original problem was to define the semantics of a (given) language; it turns out that it is much more interesting to study the semantical end of the correspondence, i.e. the algebra of processes, using suitable (informal, mathematical) notation as a metalanguage to talk about processes.

We have noted interesting theoretical problems, like the problem of self-applicable functions and a suggestion for a (more intuitive) model of λ-calculus. The proposed notion of action is by no means final: in particular, study towards a notion of action "exhibiting more parallelism" is required. Also, we have not even mentioned the problem of formulating or proving such properties as an action being determinate, or two actions working on disjoint parts of the state.

The approach also seems to hold promise for practical applications, although further work would be required to verify this in detail. We have mentioned in particular applications in the areas of language design, description of languages and their implementation, and correctness proofs.

REFERENCES

/1/ BEKIC, H.: On the Formal Definition of Programming Languages.- In: Proceedings of the International Computing Symposium, Bonn, 1970, to appear.

/2/ BEKIC, H.: An Introduction to Algol 68.- IBM Laboratory Vienna, Techn. Report TR 25.118, 1971.

/3/ BEKIC, H., WALK, K.: Formalization of Storage Properties.- In: Symposium on Semantics of Algorithmic Languages, (E. Engeler, ed.), Springer Lecture Notes, Vol. 188 (1971), pp. 28-61.

/4/ BURSTALL, R., LANDIN, P.: Programs and their Proofs: an Algebraic Approach.- In: Machine Intelligence 4, (D. Michie, ed.), Elsevier New York (1969) pp. 17-43.

/5/ HOARE, C.A.R.: Towards a Theory of Parallel Programming.- The Queen's University of Belfast, 1970.

/6/ JONES, C.B., LUCAS, P.: Proving Correctness of Implementation Techniques.- Springer Lecture Notes, Vol. 188 (1971), pp. 178-211.

/7/ KARP, R.M., MILLER, R.E.: Parallel Program Schemata.- J. of Computer and System Sciences, 3 (1969), pp. 147-195.

/8/ LANDIN, P.: A Program Machine Symmetric Automata Theory.- In: Machine Intelligence 5 (B. Meltzer, D. Michie, eds.), Elsevier New York (1970), pp. 99-120.

/9/ MORRIS, F.L.: The next 700 Formal Language Descriptions.- University of Essex, 1971.

/10/ PAIR, C.: Concerning the Syntax of Algol 68.- Algol Bulletin No. 31 (1970), pp. 16-27.

/11/ PETRI, C.A.: Kommunikation mit Automaten.- Schriften des Rheinisch-Westfälischen Institutes für Instrumentelle Mathematik, Bonn, 1962.

/12/ SCOTT, D.: Outline of a Mathematical Theory of Computation.- In: Proceedings of the Fourth Annual Princeton Conference on Information Sciences and Systems, 1970, pp.169-176.

/13/ SCOTT, D.: The Lattice of Flowdiagrams.- Springer Lecture Notes, 188 (1970), pp. 311-366.

/14/ SCOTT, D.: Lattice-theoretic Models for the λ-Calculus.- IFIP WG 2.2 Bulletin No.5, 1970.

/15/ SCOTT, D., STRACHEY, C.: Toward a Mathematical Semantics for Computer Languages.- In: Proceedings of the Symposium on Computers and Automata, Brooklyn, to appear.

/16/ WALK, K., et. al.: Abstract Syntax and Interpretation of PL/I.- IBM Laboratory Vienna, Techn. Report TR 25.098, 1969.

/17/ WIJNGAARDEN, A. van (ed.): Report on the Algorithmic Language Algol 68.- Num. Math. 14 (1969), pp.79-218.

ACKNOWLEDGEMENT

The work described in this report was carried out in the main while I worked for H. Izbicki. Early ideas on a more mathematical treatment of semantics gained substance through work with P. Landin and subsequent contact with Scott's work. The idea to extend Mathematical Semantics to deal with processes, and the particular notion of "action", seem to be new, although the latter was influenced by Algol 68 and by Landin's "polygraphs".

From comments

arising from a lecture in

Amsterdam, June 1972

This is a portion of a manuscript :
"Formal Semantics of P.L.'s: Theory and Applications"
Amsterdam, June 1972.

2. Actions

I think much confusion with my notion of "action" has been caused simply because I did not distinguish between an (infinite-depth, infinite-width) tree and the set of its paths.

The idea behind the definition of action as given in the paper is essentially the tree model. For each state ξ an action A tells you, possibly in a non-determinate way, the next step f (a state-transformation) to be performed now, and the rest A' (again an action) that remains to be done. Also, there must be some possibility of saying that an action has been finished, so one of the answers that A gives you for a given state ξ may be a special object null, rather than a pair (f,A'), telling you that nothing remains to be done.

According to that definition, the "logical" type of an action could be described as

$$\mathcal{A} = X \times\!\!\rightarrow \{\underline{\text{null}}\} \cup (X \rightarrow X) \times \mathcal{A}$$

where X is the set of states (hence X → X the set of state-transformations), and M ×→ N is the set of non-determinate functions from M to N. So, to make this precise, one would first of all have to make precise the notion of non-determinate function.

(The "justification" for this self-referential definition which I gave in my paper is wrong : the construction gives all the finite trees, but not the infinite ones. -On the other hand, the explication of $\mathcal{A}$ which Scott gave in his lecture does cover essentially the same informal notion, using a particular way of explaining non-determinate functions; it would be interesting to investigate whether other and perhaps more familiar ways of formalising M ×→ N, e.g. as relations M × N, or as set-valued functions M → subsets of N, would permit an analogous definition of $\mathcal{A}$. Apart from that question of how to deal with non-determinate functions, the two definitions differ only in details that could be adjusted either way : in Scott's model, an action gives null independent of ξ; also, only the result fξ, not the state-transformation f itself, is recorded.)

If we take the rest-action A' and a state N, we can again determine a next step g, etc. This leads to the idea of the infinite tree, where we just record the choice of next steps at each stage. (It's just like going from the (head, tail) representation of a list to the representation as a sequence of elements). But note that a certain amount of grouping is still there : the two trees

(representing the actions f;(g or h) and (f;g) or (f;h), respectively, where we don't show states in the picture which is alright as long as we have no decisions) are different.

In the paper I indicated two possible formalizations of infinite trees and hence of actions, but what the formalizations describe is really the set of paths of the tree, and this is definitely less information : the two different trees shown above have the same set of paths. Now there is of course much to be said for f and f or f being the same actions (which happens to be the case in my definition), and also for the two actions above to be the same (which happens to be not the case), but as we see now that would just require a different notion of action. Of course this other notion of action can perfectly well be formalized (e.g. as set of interrupted computations with certain closure conditions), and all the operations like ; and // and or can be defined on such i.c. sets. But the trouble arises when we come to actions defined by recursive equations. In the tree model, everything goes well. We can introduce partial trees, whose branches are allowed to run into u (= "undefined"), and we can define the relation $A \sqsubseteq B$ as "B is the same as A, except that it may sometimes offer a continuation to a branch which in A runs into u". This relation is a partial ordering, and there exist least upper bounds for ascending chains. So our equation systems do have well-defined minimal solutions.

Not so in the set-of-paths model! Not only (as Pair discovered) is the corresponding relation $\sqsubseteq$ on sets of paths not an ordering at all, but also there are examples (found by Engelfriet) where the limit construction does not yield what one would expect intuitively. Roughly speaking, $\lim_i$ (set of paths A_i) $\neq$ set of paths ($\lim_i A_i$), but we can't even state that precisely, because we have no general notion of limit in the set-of-paths model.

So do we have to use the tree model? But what about our desired identities, like the f; (g or h) = (f;g) or (f;h) above? I do not know, except for the following remark. In an implementation of procedures on a computer, a new call of a procedure causes some organizational steps to be performed corresponding to "opening a new level" etc. Suppose we were mirroring this in our model by introducing a special step ap ("apply"). Then left-recursive equations like F = F or F = f or F;f could have solutions that contain a path ap^{ω}, i.e. the infinite sequence of ap's. All the "pathological" equations seem to put the right solutions in this way. Of course we can then abstract by replacing any finite sequence ap^{n} by null and the infinite sequence ap^{ω} by u (only here do partial actions come in), but in constructing the limits we would need the ap's. While this seems to work (and to mirror the intuitive situation), it seems curious that one should have to introduce certain "ideal" elements (the actions containing ap) which are used only on the way and fall out in the end again. In other words : can one give a direct description of the solutions of equations in the set-of-path model, i.e. one not going via the ap-sequences?

Polyadic actions. Here, we would like even more to deal with sets of (polyadic) i.c.s, rather than with ways of producing them. To do this, we first would have to refine the notion of polyadic i.c. : replace the picture in [1], p.32, by

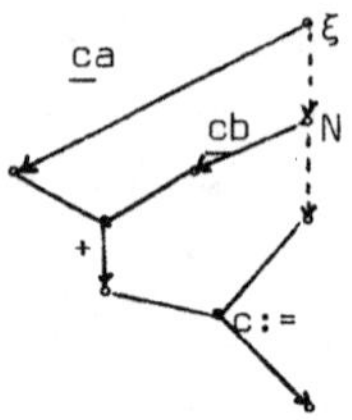

(so we can express now that location b is read after location a). Second, we get the same problems as in the monadic case by having just sets of i.c.s rather than some tree-like arrangement of the set; and may be ap (which comes in very nicely in the notation P() for calling a parameterless procedure) is again the right solution here.

(Ed: Letter written to)

1973.10.03

Mr. S. P. Carter
IBM Journal R. & D.

Dear Mr. Carter,

. . .

As to the changes I want to make, the most important one is concerned with recursion and non-determinacy: the relation "less-defined than", as defined on p.23, is not an ordering! So the question I want to spend some further thought on is: can it be made into an ordering, maybe by slight modification to the notion of action? A simple but less satisfactory solution (which I would take in lack of a better one) would be to modify action more drastically, recording choices as separate steps. (That the ordering presents a problem in the non-determinate case has been recognized by others, e.g. Manna and Milner. The usual way out, which is questionable even if one regards programs extensionally as non-determinate functions, is to consider programs equivalent which differ only by non-determinating paths.)

Section 4 on polyadic actions should be shortedned; the definition of polyadic action itself can also be simplified. The "explanation" of action given on p.25 is wrong but can easily be corrected. Also, I would reference, and maybe comment on, a recent paper by R. Milner (in: Congress on Theoretical Informatics, Pisa, 1973).

. . .

(Ed: Letter written to)

1974.05.27

Mr. S. P. Carter
IBM Journal Res. Dev.

Dear Mr. Carter,

. . .

As I wrote to you earlier and knew soon after I had completed the original TR, there was a problem with recursion in the non-deterministic case: the technique for solving recursive equations, which I had carried over straightaway from the deterministic case, does not work. Trying for months to solve this problem (with many interruptions, and mostly in my spare time), I came up with various ideas. Every one of these proved to need modification when I tried to apply it to another case (e.g. when I went from actions to polyadic actions, or when I tried the very similar situation of equations defining data types, where one of the type constructors is set union); also, none of these proposed solutions seemed to mirror exactly the intuitive picture I had of the process of solving such equations.

After another long week-end's work I finally seem to see how all these ideas interrelate and how they can be put together to solve the problem properly. Rather than complicate the objects themselves (like actions, types, etc.), one has to complicate, or better properly formalize, the notion of non-deterministic function. I have such a formalisation (as conventional function with an additional hidden parameter), and with it the known iterative process of solving recursive equations allows a nice generalisation to the non-deterministic case.

While this seems to work in all the situations I wanted to cover, there are still many things that have to be verified and many details that have to be filled in. After all the effort, I want to do this detailed work at a somewhat leisurely pace. Ideally, I would like to just work on it and send you the manuscript as soon as it is completed, without any prior commitment; let me indicate one month from now as a somewhat likely time.

. . .

(From a letter to Peter Lucas - written 1975.02.17)
(translated JJ)

I have altered my definition of "action" for the hundredth time: an action is now a set of interruptable computations (ic's), i.e. of normal computations except that the next step does not necessarily operate on the result of the previous step, but can operate on any state. (This is necessary in order to be able to combine the given action in parallel with another). Thus, these actions still contain enough information so that the normal operations (even, for instance, //) can be defined between them, but on the other hand little enough information to fulfil certain desirable equivalences, such as:

$$a;\underline{0} = a, \qquad a;(b;c) = (a;b);c, \qquad a//b = b//a \qquad \text{etc.}$$

A method for defining new actions from given ones is definition by recursive equations and the main problem (with the earlier and current actions) was that the usual method of solving such equations could not be used. Certainly it is easy to define an ordering $\alpha < \beta$ (α is less defined than β) between ic's, but it is not easy to promote this ordering to sets of ic's. Instead I introduce the concept of a "plan" $\hat{a}$ which contains more information than the action a and in which the ic's of a are still combined in a single tree and corresponding operations $\hat{a};\hat{b},\hat{a}||\hat{b}$ etc. between plans. In order to construct a from $\hat{a}$, I first define $\hat{a}[t,s]$ as that ic which is obtained if plan $\hat{a}$ is followed and then for each "choice" the next truth value is used from the sequence t; for each computation step the next state from the sequence s is taken as argument and then the construction

$$\hat{a} \to \{\hat{a}[t,s] \mid t \in B^{\omega},\ s \in B^{\omega}\}$$

is used (where $\hat{a}[t,s]$ should not be defined because t or s are too short - thus infinite or long enough sequences). The important property of this mapping $\Psi:\hat{A} \to A$ from plans on to actions is that it is compatible with a homomorphism i.e. with the operations ; , || . (Only when I tried to prove this did it become apparent that the earlier definition of action was inappropriate). To solve $x = F(x)$ over A I first solve $\hat{x} = F(\hat{x})$ over $\hat{A}$ (this is easy because the ordering $\hat{a} \leqslant \hat{b}$ is easy to define) and then take $x = \Psi\,\hat{x}$. Of course there is still a lot to do. Firstly I need a general technique for defining "infinite" objects: e.g. in the case that an ic can be an infinitely long sequence, an $\hat{a}$ be an infinitely deep tree, then equations like $T = [B\ T]$, $S = [X\ S]$ should define finite and infinite results in contrast to the identical BNF-equations. [It appears that all my definitions exist in a universe of (finite and) infinite trees; such a tree can of course contain itself as a sub-tree i.e. I may obtain a more "natural" model for self-applicable/returning functions]. Secondly I need a better proof technique (particularly combinations of induction with continuity - with induction alone I only get statements about finite objects), so as not to make proofs like the equivalence over $\hat{A}$ or the sentence over Ψ too extensive. Also I am not nearly as far as I thought I was in the original TR about actions (or e.g. so far as to be able to completely formalise Meta-IV), e.g. my actions are currently only sufficient for the type =>, not for V = > ω. Nevertheless I think I have enough material for an R and D paper (which will be fairly different from the TR).

THE SEMANTICS OF PARALLEL PROCESSING

H. Bekić

Rapporteurs: Mr. G. M. Arnold
Mr. I. King
Mr. P. M. Melliar-Smith

Summary

Dr. Hans Bekić developed a mathematical technique for formal definition of the semantics of combinations of elementary actions, and extended this to encompass parallelism by determining the fixed points of infinite sequences of such actions.

Dr. Bekić began by pointing out that, although IBM Vienna Laboratories was doing work on parallelism, he intended to cover aspects of the semantics of programming languages, but with some emphasis on parallel programs.

From the start of the work on programming language semantics, the main approach was the use of abstract machines in what was described as the "constructive way" of language definition. In this one considers the states of the language interpreting machine, where ξ_0 (the initial state) is determined by an abstract version of the program and its input data, and where the iterative application of the interpreting function yields successive states ξ_1, ξ_2 ... until either termination is reached or the computation proceeds forever. A particular feature of the PL/I definition is that the state transition function was allowed to be non-determinate, or, to express it in better understood terms, it is not a function from a set of states to a set of states but, rather, from a given state it produces a set of possible answers, and is thus a function from a set of states to a set of subsets of states.

Dr. Bekić continued by saying that since the above work his views of descriptional semantics had been much influenced by the work of Landin and of Scott, and that in his recent work he had moved in the direction of mathematical semantics. However the problem of non-deterministic programs remained and formed the basis of the material to be presented; namely, can one have a mathematical view of semantics, and can one deal with nondeterminate functions in a way that captures the underlying pragmatic notions.

Dr. Bekić first indicated briefly why the constructive technique of language definition failed to cover intuitive notions of associating meanings with expressions in a language. Drawing the simple analogy of a purely descriptive language of arithmetic expressions, one associates with each expression a certain value: thus, in a language which uses Roman numerals, the value of each numeral, V, X, I, is a number, 5, 10, 1.

Extend the language to include composite expressions, and write (in list notation)

$$+,(e_1,e_2)$$

then by associating values with the expressions e_1 and e_2, the resulting value is a function of those values. In particular, if the expressions e_1, e_2 involve identifiers, or are identifiers, then one must know from outside, or from context, what the values of these identifiers are going to be.

Thus is introduced the notion of environment, a function from identifiers to whatever one chooses as values. The interpreting function now takes not only an expression but also an environment, and yields a value. Although this is a trivial example, it indicates a difference in approach compared with the earlier work- there is no reason why the idea of environments giving meaning to identifiers cannot be carried over to algorithmic languages. Although expressions will denote either numbers, or more complicated things such as transformations of the machine state having more complicated values, the interpreting function will still take an expression, or statement, and an environment of the appropriate form, and will produce a value for the expression or a more complicated result for the statement.

It is necessary to distinguish between identifiers, which are associated with values, and denotations, which are the objects associated with programs or subprograms. As the programming language probably contains assignment statements, one has a notation of store, which maps storage locations to values and the denotation of an assignment statement will just be a transformation from stores to stores. Furthermore, one may arrange things in such a way that the denotation of composite statements depends only on the denotations of the simpler components. In this way one can represent the input-output behaviour of the program, and in so doing abstract from many things that might be considered irrelevant, so reducing the complexity of the machine state. However this also abstracts from details that for some purposes one might be interested in; in considering programs as expressions of algorithms, it may be essential to be able to analyse two different programs evaluating the same function using different algorithms. In other words there is a notion of denotation that covers more than just the function computed by an algorithm, namely the steps by which the function is computed.

When analysing Algol 68 using the denotational approach there is a problem that the "collateral composition" of functions does not yield a further function; that is, if states transformations are considered to be composed of several individually indivisible steps, the collateral composition of two such step sequences is a non-deterministic operation (if one merges the two sequences there may be many outcomes computed by the complete set of mergings). This complicates the chosen denotations in two ways. Firstly, rather than being simply state transforming functions they must be at least sequences of such functions. The second complication is that, due to the element of non-determinism, the denotation of a given expression might be a set of such sequences. Dr. Bekić added that in the latest definition of a large subset of PL/I in the "new style", the complications due to non-determinism and parallel interaction have been left untouched.

Denotation

The main purpose of the presentation by Dr. Bekić was to introduce the formal notations of denotation and to indicate how mathematical semantics can be employed, particularly for solving recursive equations for functions. In what follows, denotations are treated as if they are functions. Although such functions are state transformations, programs do not in general use a variable for the state. For instance, in serial composition

$$f \; ; \; g$$

the expansion of which is the function

$$\lambda \; \xi \; . \; g(f(\xi)) \quad ,$$

the variable ξ is never used in the program.

A useful combinator is that which besides changing the state also yields a value - in programming usually termed an "expression with side-effects". This is written

$$\underline{\text{let}} \; v \; : \; e \; ;$$
$$\ldots \; v \; ; \; \ldots$$

Here e is a state transformation which also yields a value, while v is just a state transformation

$$e \; : \; X \rightarrow V \times X$$
$$v \; : \; X \rightarrow X \; .$$

For this combination one may write

$$\lambda\xi . \; \underline{\text{let}} < v, \; \xi' > = e \; (\xi)$$
$$\ldots \; v \; (\xi)$$

which explains the combinators of simple let notation. To include combinators such as parallel composition

$$f \,||\, g$$

it is necessary to reinterpret all objects as more complex objects and reinterpret the combinators in terms of these more complex objects.

Such a language of combinators has proved to be quite convenient for representing given source language programs, so that from a PL/I or Algol 68 program one may derive a particular denotational expression using these combinators. This may be done by an extended version of the interpret function by which the semantic correspondence is defined. Such a derivation is a static process which, rather than executing the program, produces the corresponding meta-language program in terms of ";",":" and "let".

A more complicated notion of denotation is called "action", after a related notion defined in the Algol 68 report. Using the idea of "action" and the notion of "hand-translating" source programs into meta-language programs it is possible to formulate some notions of compiler correctness.

In the questions that followed, Dr. Bekić confirmed that his talks were covering the "new style" of language definition in which the new definition of PL/I had been carried out. He added that although there had been changes in the meta language, the most important change was away from the idea of an interactive machine and towards the association of meanings with expressions. Questioned about the example he had given of an expression with side effects, he said that the notation

$$\underline{\text{let}}\ v : e$$

described a declaration which allocated storage and returned the location for subsequent use; e is basically meant to return a value, but in doing so it changes the state. Following further questions he added that the "let" binds e and ξ to the body of the function associated with v.

Actions

In his second lecture Dr. Bekić introduced the more complicated notion of actions, went on to define certain compositions of actions, and finally dealt with the problem of solving recursive equations for actions.

Rather than considering simple state transitions, one must consider compositions of such transformations from others which may in some sense be considered to be indivisible or elemental. The notion of action is based on sequences of elementary transitions, but is more complicated in that an element in the sequence determines what is done next, but the next element may be dependent on the current state as well as on the continuation. Thus is obtained the following definition of an action:

Let X be the set of computational states, and
let ξ be a state value from the set.
$A = \underset{\sim}{0} + X \to ((X \to X) \times A)$

The action A is either the empty sequence $\underset{\sim}{0}$ or depends on the given state ξ. Thus there is a function from X, the set of states, to a pair. The first member of the pair is a state transformation of the set, and the second member is the remaining actions to be done. Thus, if α is an action, then apply α to the state ξ:

$$\alpha(\xi) = \langle f, \alpha' \rangle, \ f: X \to X$$

The action determines what happens next and what is left to be done. This definition of an action is similar to the head-tail definition of a list. It is also necessary to admit the possibility of infinite actions in the sense that the above lists may become infinite. The disjoining union sign is used here, although the sets are already disjoint, because the set is used as a definition in the same manner as Scott, in that there is an undefined element. This is still not enough, however, in non-deterministic programs, because of the possibility of choosing what to do next independently of the current state, since we may choose freely any one of several possibilities.

Deterministic Actions

Therefore, rename the set A to be the set of deterministic actions dA. An action then is just a set of deterministic actions, and the set of actions is a subset of the sets of deterministic actions.

A collection of actions can be built up from elementary items. So far, there is the null action. Let f be a state transformation which is an elementary action, then:

$$[f](\xi) = \langle f, \underset{\sim}{0} \rangle$$

Applying f to the state ξ gives a pair, namely f, as the step which is performed, and the remaining action which is null. Thus for each state transition there is a corresponding elementary action consisting of just that state transition.

Serial Composition

To define a Serial Composition of two actions, define operations on the superset of deterministic actions. Strictly, dA is not a subset of A because dA is essentially an element of A. However, elements may be identified between the sets and thus one may regard dA as a subset. Greek letters will be used for elements of dA and Latin letters for the more general actions.

The serial composition $\alpha;\beta$ of α and β devolves onto the restricted set dA. It is convenient here to picture actions as forming a rather complicated kind of tree. Complicated because there is a dependency on ξ at each node.

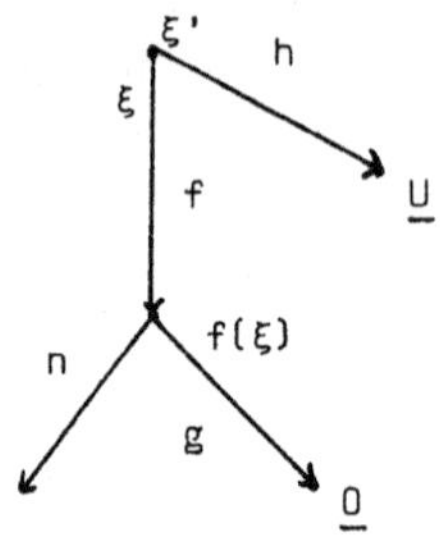

Choosing ξ as the current state, an action f can occur followed by a state to which action g can be applied. Eventually this process must terminate with the null action. Equally, from another state ξ' there might be the undefined action $\underline{U}$. Note that $\underline{U}$ is included implicitly as a starting element.

This gives a representation of the set dA. (A is just a set of such animals.) The inductive definition of serial composition is

$$
\begin{aligned}
\alpha;\beta = \; & (\alpha = \underline{U} \rightarrow \underline{U}, &) \\
& (\alpha = \underline{0} \rightarrow \beta, &) \\
& (T \rightarrow \lambda\xi.\text{let } \langle f,\alpha' \rangle = \alpha(\xi) \; \langle f,\alpha';\beta \rangle &)
\end{aligned}
$$

If the first element α is undefined, then so is the result, since there can be no continuation. If the first element is null then the composition consists of the second, and otherwise there is a function from states to pairs.

The gain here, is in the recursive definition. Since the domains involved are continuous, and the elementary objects like conditional expressions are continuous, such definitions can be used to derive a continuous function from an infinite sequence. The function to be defined is a serial composition of actions, not just deterministic actions, and this is given by:

$$a;b = \{\alpha;\beta \mid \alpha\varepsilon a, \beta\varepsilon b\}$$

the set of all compositions of deterministic actions.

One way to explain this is to choose an element of a and an element of b, and compose them, but that is not the way it is normally considered. One thinks of doing a, and, having done it, one of the many possibilities has been realised.

Parallel Composition

Consider first the parallel composition of deterministic actions:

$$\alpha \; || \; \beta$$

but the result of this must be a non-determinate action, and conditions will again be recursive. Postpone the problem of recursive definition of functions using sets, because of the ordering problems. It is not obvious how ordering relations are to be defined, so sets will not be introduced in this definition. Rather, let the definition depend on a third parameter, written as an index, giving a three case function, taking two deterministic actions and this hidden parameter. The hidden parameter can be an infinite tape of choice values: $t \in T$, $T = \{0,1\} \times T$.

Define next $(\alpha||\beta)_t$.

First the simple cases:-

$$\begin{aligned}(\alpha||\beta)_t = \; & (\alpha = \underline{0} \rightarrow \beta \quad) \\ & (\beta = \underline{0} \rightarrow \alpha \quad) \\ & (\alpha = \beta = \underline{U} \rightarrow \underline{U}\;)\end{aligned}$$

If the first action is null then the composition comprises only the second, and vice versa. If both are undefined, so is the result.

This is compatible with the previous definition. Moreover if α is undefined and β is not, commencing with α stops with an undefined outcome. However, commencing with β may make it possible to continue. Only when α is performed is the action undefinable. This is where the choice parameter is used. If the next token on the tape U_t is zero, continue with the next part of α and only then go on with parallel composition. Introducing a new operation here, $\alpha\rceil|\beta$ "left parallel" indicating that, without choice, the first step of α is executed first, the definition is completed with

$$T \rightarrow (U_t = 0 \rightarrow (\alpha\rceil|\beta)_{t1t}, \; U_t = 1 \rightarrow (\beta\rceil|\alpha)_{t1t}))$$

where U_t signifies the use of the tail of the choice value tape.

$(\alpha\rceil|\beta)_t$ is defined as follows:

$$\begin{aligned}(\alpha\rceil|\beta)_t = \; & (\alpha = \underline{0} \rightarrow \beta \quad) \\ & (\alpha = \underline{U} \rightarrow \underline{U} \quad) \\ & (T \rightarrow \lambda\xi.\text{let } \langle f,\alpha' \rangle = \alpha(\xi) \; \langle f,(\alpha'||\beta)_{t1t} \rangle \;)\end{aligned}$$

Thus when α is not null or undefined, the composition is a more complicated action, namely a function transforming ξ the current state into a pair, the result of the first step of α, and the parallel composition of the remainder of α with β under the tape, having used the first token on the tape.

This definition is still very restricted compared to that in existing programming languages; namely a state is indivisible, a single entity, and it is known of the functions only that they transform that entity. There is no notion of parts of a state. If there was such a notion, then parallel composition could be defined in a more direct way, without trying to mix or describe all possible sequences produce the same effect. Even with such more complicated states, there will also be parallel compositions which act on a part of the state, and it will still be necessary to decide on their meanings.

The operation $a||b$ can now be specified as the set of all $(\alpha||\beta)$ over T.

$$a||b = \{(\alpha||\beta)_t \mid \alpha\varepsilon a,\ \beta\varepsilon b,\ t\varepsilon T\}.$$

Consider further two very simple, compositions:

$$a \ \underline{\text{or}}\ b$$

Since the actions are defined as sets. This is just set-union

$$a \ \underline{\text{or}}\ b = a \cup b.$$

Also, a conditional,

$\underline{\text{if}}$ p $\underline{\text{then}}$ a $\underline{\text{else}}$ b, where p is a predicate on states, To show the testing of p as a separate step, define it as follows:

$$\underline{\text{if}}\ p\ \underline{\text{then}}\ a\ \underline{\text{else}}\ b = \{\lambda\xi.\langle I,(p(\xi) \to \alpha, T\to\beta)\rangle \mid \alpha\varepsilon a,\ \beta\varepsilon b\}$$
$$\text{and } p : X \to \{T,F\}$$

It is an action of functional type, and its first component is the identity function, the next step being either a or b depending on the state.

Recursive Definitions

Define an action by

$$a = \underline{\text{if}}\ p\ \underline{\text{then}}\ \underline{0}\ \underline{\text{else}}\ f;\ a$$

or by $a = f \vee (g;a;k)$.

The usual technique for solving such equations is to start with a as undefined, and in the general case a = F(a). Thus, starting from $\underline{U}$ and iterating F, we form a limit to the sequence obtained. Since the objects which are obtained are sets of determinate actions an ordering between such sets is needed. It is easy to define an ordering on determinate actions. If the branch of the action tree for one action α ends in undefined whereas for another action β at that point there is a continuation possible, then β is more defined than α, written $\alpha \sqsubseteq \beta$

This relation could be extended to sets, to introduce

$$a \sqsubseteq b = \forall \alpha \varepsilon a \ni \beta \varepsilon b \quad \alpha \sqsubseteq \beta$$

and conversely. Thus, a is less defined than b if for all α in a and β in b α is less defined than β, and conversely, for all β there is an α less defined than β. Then considering the case a = {α,γ} and b = {α,β,γ}, suppose $\alpha \sqsubseteq \beta \sqsubseteq \gamma$. Then if $a \sqsubseteq b$ there is a continuation β as a continuation of α. But equally, if $b \sqsubseteq a$ there is a continuation, since β and α may continue to γ. Thus the relation is not an ordering.

Thus the whole idea of using sets as the universe over which to solve the recursive equations is wrong.

An alternative approach uses elements and the notion of the hidden parameter. Consider the following examples. Take

$$a = (f \vee g) || h; a.$$

This example has no conditionals, and thus the determinate actions can be considered as sequences of functions. Starting with $\underline{U}$ and applying F(a) to it as above gives a whole set of possibilities, and thus a whole family of functions dependent on hidden parameters. Given any deterministic action α, and taking the right hand side above, first prefix it by an h and insert an f or a g at some point. (That point might be infinitely distant, since it cannot be assumed that in parallel execution either one of the two actions is necessarily performed within any specific period of time. One of the two actions may be repeated for ever.) This gives the following family of functions:

$$F_{\emptyset}^{n}(\alpha) \quad \emptyset \in \{f,g\},\ 0 \leqslant n \leqslant \omega$$

Ø is either f or g, and n ranges from zero to ω. For a given n and Ø, F is defined as follows:-

$$F_{\emptyset}^{n}(\alpha) = h;\alpha \quad \text{with } \emptyset \text{ inserted after } n \text{ elements.}$$

Consider the restricted case of actions as sequences of functions, then, given an n and Ø. this definition is not complete. Some provision must be made for n larger than the length of the sequence. The undefined case needs to be corrected. Thus the insertion is not made after the nth element, but after min(n,l(h;a)) elements if possible where l(h;a) is the length of the sequence. Anything that would have been inserted after undefined will not be inserted because sequences ending in undefined are neutral over composition. This ad hoc definition of a family of functions, covers all possibilities of non-deterministic operations.

The finding of a fixed point of the original equation can now be approached, in the deterministic case, by applying functions iteratively. Since there is a choice of which functions to apply, consider sequences of the form

$$F_{\emptyset_1}^{n_1} (\underline{U})$$

and replace $\underline{U}$ by the application of further such functions forming

$$F_{\emptyset_2}^{n_2} (\underline{U}) \quad \ldots \quad F_{\emptyset_k}^{n_k} (\underline{U}).$$

Then form the limit of that sequence:

$$\operatorname*{Lt}_{k\to\infty} \; F_{\emptyset_1}^{n1} \; (F_{\emptyset_2}^{n2} \; (F(\ldots\ldots(F_{\emptyset_k}^{n_k} \; (\underline{U})))))$$

Now that limit is for a given sequence of n, Ø values.

i.e. $\langle n_1\emptyset_1\rangle, \langle n_2\emptyset_2\rangle \ldots \qquad (\overline{N}_o \times \{f,g\}^{\omega})$

where $\overline{N}$ is the set of numbers between zero and ω. Thus, the choice tapes may be considered as presenting n,Ø pairs instead of truth values, in order to determine the choice of function.

These generate a set, a, of all infinite sequences of elements h,f,g.

$$a = \{h,f,g\}^{\omega} | \; \#f+\#g \leqslant \# \, h+1\}$$

Each time an f is applied, it is certainly prefixed with an h, and there may or may not be one more f or g inserted, thus forming all sequences having for every subsequence the number of f's plus the number of g's, less than or equal to one more than the number of h's.

Actions with Choice Nodes

Rather than prove the above example either that the set of limits really gives the required set a, or that the construction really solves the original equation, it is of more interest to know for a certain class function F, how generally, one can devise such a family of non-deterministic functions and use this same method.

To do this, introduce another space of objects, called actions with choice nodes. Above, a tree represented actions of a certain kind. Now introduce a more complex tree in which branches are labelled with zeros and ones to denote possible alternatives at each choice. Thus all possible paths are contained in the one tree.

The equation for this set will be :-

$$A = \underline{0}\ (x \rightarrow x) \times \hat{A}\ ) + \{0,1\} \rightarrow \hat{A}$$

and again compositions similar to those above can be defined, for example $\hat{a};\hat{b}$ in which the second tree can be appended to any end of the first. In the case of $\hat{a}||\hat{b}$ there are the same trivial cases for null or undefined, but in the other case, a new tree forms dependent upon the choice of zero or one. In the case of one, take the next step of $\hat{b}$.

Define a function "range of"

$$r : \hat{A} \rightarrow A$$

$\hat{A}$ gives all the possibilities required, and in addition to A gives the labelling of particular subtrees with zeros and ones. What is needed is to leave out the labelling information, so the range of $\hat{A}$, r, is the set of paths in the tree disregarding labels. This rather imprecise definition, could be given a precise inductive form. The crucial property of r is that it is not a continuous function, since there are no continuous functions from elements to sets, but it has the useful property of compatibility with the various compositions. For example

$$r\ (\hat{a};\hat{b}) = r(\hat{a});r(\hat{b})$$

This allows, given some equation a=F(a), the forming of the corresponding equation on the set $\hat{a}$, $\hat{a} = \hat{F}(\hat{a})$, which can be solved because the $\hat{F}$'s are continuous and so are their compositions. The fixed point may be formed by the usual construction $\hat{a} = Y\ \hat{F}$ and a step made into the other space using $a = r\hat{a}$ where a solves the original equation

$$F(\underline{r}\ \hat{a}) = \underline{r}(\hat{F}\ \hat{a}) = \underline{r\hat{a}}$$

and because $\hat{F}$ is compatible with all the functions and therefore with their composition F, and of course $\hat{a}$ is the fixed point of $\hat{F}$.

An Example

For his third lecture, Dr. Bekić considered the example of a very simple equation for an action a:

a is the effect of an action f in parallel with a

$$a = f \,||\, a$$

Certainly this is not deterministic. Using the technique above he introduced a family of functions F_n of a deterministic action α which insert f after the n'th position, with a qualification on the insertion that f cannot be inserted beyond the undefined symbol regardless of n.

The limit of the elements of a is the set of limits $F_{n_1}, F_{n_2} \ldots F_{n_k}$ of u, where these run over all infinite sequences of the modified integers containing the element ω as above.

F_0 is the operation of inserting f at the beginning of the sequence. An infinite number of such operations causes an infinite number of fs. In all other cases the sequence will be terminated by the undefined symbol, as in the sequences:

$$\underline{\underline{u}}$$
$$f\,\underline{\underline{u}}$$
$$f^2\underline{\underline{u}}$$
$$\vdots$$

and also the sequence f^{ω}

Then Dr. Bekić introduced an alternative approach to the definition of the semantics of such parallel processing making use of the set $\hat{A}$ of actions with choice nodes and with trees in which these choices are recorded. The choice tree can be applied to a particular tape to obtain family of actions.

$$\underline{ap}: \; \hat{A} \times T \rightarrow dA$$

$\underline{ap}(\hat{a},t)$ selects a subtree of $\hat{a}$, according to the tape t, by deleting edges from the tree.

The function $\underline{r}\,(\hat{a}) = \{\underline{ap}\,(\hat{a},t) \mid t \in T\}$
yields all possible values of applying all different tapes.

Dr. Bekić further considered the equation

$$a = F(a)$$

to define the family of functions F_t.

$$F_t : \underline{\hat{A}} \to dA$$

$$Ft : [dA\ \underline{c}]\ \hat{A} \to dA$$

F_t of $\hat{a}$ is the result of the operation on the choice tree producing a further choice tree which can be applied to a given tape. Thus the type of the function is a choice tree to a family of functions. The determinate actions are themselves a subset of the choice trees, so that although F_t is a function over $\hat{A}$ it is certainly a function over a subset.

In the case of this particular example

$$F(a) = \{F_t(\alpha) \mid t \in T,\ \alpha \in a\}$$

Thus $f||a$ here is just the operation already discussed of $(f||\alpha)_t$. The definition of parallel composition already required a corresponding additional parameter, and the expansion of this determines valid conditions for $f||a$ to have a meaning. The functions F_n, F_t are therefore the same but indexed differently, one by tapes and the other by integers, and the function F_t can be used to form the set of limits.

Dr. Bekič demonstrated that this simple relationship between F and F_t does not hold even for the restricted class of functions formed by compositions of primitive combinators. Consider an equation formed from the combinators but with a present more than once, say k times.

$$a = F(a) = G(a, \ldots. a)$$

Assume that G satisfies a similar equation

$$G(a_1, \ldots. a_k) = G_t(\alpha_1 \ldots., \alpha_k) \;\Big|\; \begin{array}{l} t \in T \\ \alpha_i \in a_i \end{array}$$

Then the relationship is not true because different α_i could appear for different occurrences of α.

Representable Functions

However the relation is valid for functions which are just compositions of the functions defined with the combinators. For such functions a family of functions G can be derived

$$G\,(\hat{a}_1,\ldots\hat{a}_k) = \underline{ap}\,(\hat{G}(\hat{a}_1,\ldots,\hat{a}_k),\ t)$$

obtained by first applying $\hat{G}$ to the choice trees and then applying the result to t. To solve this equation, we must take not an infinite sequence of t's, but a tree of t's. Start with t, and if that t has two arguments, take two additional t's, and so on. These infinite trees must be approximated by finite trees which have undefined to terminate each branch.

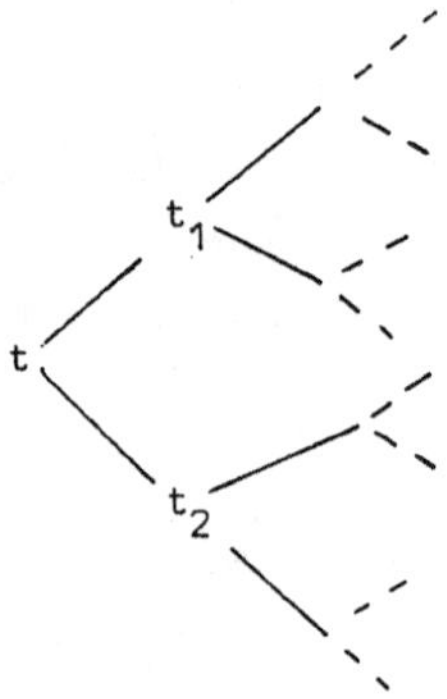

Then

$$a = \Big\{ \lim \quad G_t\,(G_{t_1}\,(\ldots(\underline{u})\ldots),G_{t_2}\,(\ldots(\underline{u})\ldots))$$

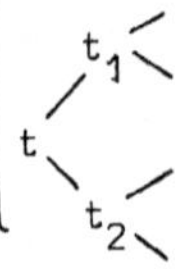

where

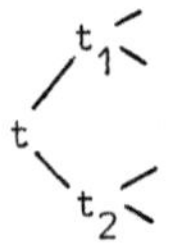

$\in T \Big\}$

There is no proof yet that the fixed point of this construction is the same as the fixed point $\sim(\gamma\hat{F})$ derived above. To derive such a proof it would be necessary to use the fact that instead of using just one tape, the tape can be split up and different parts used for different portions of the evaluation, and that conversely the different portions of the tape represent a pattern that exists on the whole tape.

A more interesting question relates to what is it that makes the function F have a fixed point.

For a deterministic function, the function just has to be continuous, but for a non-deterministic function there can be no notion of continuity.

If $F{:}A \to A$ has a representation like

$$f(a) = \{G_t(\alpha_1,\ldots,a_k) \mid t \in T, \alpha_1 \in a_1\}$$

If there is one fixed point of F

$$a = \mathrm{fix}\ F = \left\{ \begin{array}{l} \lim G_t\ (G_{t_1}\ (\ldots),\ G_{t_2}\ (\ldots)) \\ \qquad \diagup \\ \quad\ t_1 \diagup\!\!\!\diagdown \\ \ \diagup \\ t \\ \ \diagdown \\ \quad\ t_2 \diagup\!\!\!\diagdown \end{array} \right\}$$

then we can call such a function a representable function. It can be shown that parallel composition, serial composition, and the OR operation are representable and that their compositions are again representable, so that this class of functions is closed against arbitrary substitution. It is closed against fixed points.

NONDETERMINISTIC FUNCTIONS AND THE SEMANTICS OF CSP

Hans Bekić (Wien)

Nondeterministic functions are defined as functions mapping elements into indexed sets of elements, also called multisets. Operations on such functions are defined, like serial composition, nondeterministic choice, and definition by recursion. A notion of equivalence is introduced which abstracts from any particular indexing and which is shown to be preserved by the operations on functions.

This method of modelling nondeterminism is used to define a domain of actions which can serve as denotations of CSP-like constructs [1]. In particular, the difference between internal, i.e. environment-independent, and external choice is made explicit. Operations on actions include those corresponding to the ones on functions, but also restriction and parallel composition. Again, a notion of equivalence is defined that is intended to be compatible with the operations.

Reference:

[1] C. A. R. Hoare, "Communicating sequential processes". CACM 21, 8, 1978.

Non-deterministic Functions

and

the Semantics of CSP

1. A "new" notion of non-det. function

2. Apply this to outline a denotational semantics of CSP

HB 17 Mar 81

Why not $P(X)$?

if s infinite, must contain $\bot$

fairness ?

$a^* \cup \bot$ vs. $a^* \cup a^\omega$

$\{a,c\} = \{a,b,c\}$ for $a \sqsubseteq b \sqsubseteq c$

Back's example : R. J. Back, LNCS 85

```
while x≠0 do (x>0 → x:=x-1,
              x<0 → x:= some x≥0)
```

$\forall k. f_k(-1)$ can be $\bot$ (choose some $x \geq k$)

yet $f(-1)$ always $= 0$.

Instead of $P(X)$, use

$M(X)$ ("Multisets over X"):

$M(X)$ = index-sets $\rightarrow$ X

With that, define

$F(X) = X \rightarrow M(X)$ ... n.d. functions over X

operations on $F(X)$: ; , $[p_1 \rightarrow f_1 \,[\!]\, \dots \,[\!]\, p_n \rightarrow f_n]$, *

$f \sim g$ equivalence, to abstract from particular indexing

show opn's preserve $\sim$.

Multisets

c.p.o. $\mathcal{I}$ of indices : (at least) countable, containing $\mathcal{I} \times \mathcal{I}$ as subdomain.
Say $\mathcal{I} \cong N_\perp + \mathcal{I} \times \mathcal{I}$

Index-sets : $\quad i \not\uparrow j =_{Df} \neg\exists k.\ i \sqsubseteq k \ \&\ j \sqsubseteq k$

$\mathcal{J} = \{\text{nonempty } I \subseteq \mathcal{I} \mid \forall i,j\ I.\, i \neq j \supset i \not\uparrow j\}$,

ordered by

$$I \sqsubseteq I' =_{Df} (\forall i\varepsilon I.\exists i'\varepsilon I' \ \&\ \forall i'\varepsilon I'.\exists i\varepsilon I).\, i \sqsubseteq i'$$

Fact : $(\mathcal{J}, \sqsubseteq)$ is a c.p.o.

Opn on index-sets : $\quad$ for I and the $\mathcal{J}_i$, $i\varepsilon I$, index sets,

$$\sum_{i\varepsilon I} \mathcal{J}_i = \bigcup_{i\varepsilon I} \{(i,j) \mid j\varepsilon \mathcal{J}_i\}$$

is again an index-set.

Multisets over X :

$$M(X) =_{Df} \bigcup_{I\varepsilon\mathcal{J}} (I \to X), \qquad \text{ordered by}$$

$$m \sqsubseteq m' =_{Df} \forall i\varepsilon \mathrm{dom}\, m,\ i'\varepsilon \mathrm{dom}\, m'.\, i \sqsubseteq i' \supset mi \sqsubseteq m'i'$$

$(M(X), \sqsubseteq)$ is a domain.

$$\sum_{i\varepsilon I} m_i =_{Df} \bigcup_{i\varepsilon I} [(i,t) \mapsto m_i t \mid t\varepsilon \mathrm{dom}\, m_i]$$

N.d. functions

$\mathcal{F}(X) = X \to \mathcal{M}(X)$

Operations on $\mathcal{F}(X)$

composition : $f;g = \lambda x. \sum_{t \in \mathrm{dom} fx} g(fxt)$

n.d. conditional :

$$[p_1 \to' f_1 \,\square\, \dots \,\square\, p_n \to' f_n] = \sum_{\pi \in \Pi(n)}' (p_{\pi 1} \to' f_{\pi 1}, \dots, p_{\pi n} \to' f_{\pi n})$$

$$= \lambda x. \sum_{\pi \in \Pi(n)} (p_{\pi 1}x \to f_{\pi 1}x, \dots, p_{\pi n}x \to f_{\pi n}x)$$

n.d. iteration :

$$[p_1 \to' f_1 \,\square\, \dots \,\square\, p_n \to' f_n]^* =$$

$$\mu F. \sum_{\pi \in \Pi(n)}' (p_{\pi 1} \to' f_{\pi 1};F, \dots, p_{\pi n} \to' f_{\pi n};F, \text{else} \to' \underline{0})$$

identity : $\underline{0} = \lambda x.\lambda\bot.x = \lambda x.ux$

(primitive) det. functions :

for $a: X \to X$: $a' = \lambda x.\lambda\bot.ax$

$= \lambda x.\mathbf{u}(ax)$

"$\mu F. ..$" = "$Y\lambda F. ...$" works because the constructions used, like Σ, $\to$, application, are continuous.

Equivalence

$\mathcal{C} = \bigcup_{I,J \varepsilon \mathcal{J}} (I \to J)$ ... correspondences between index-sets

$\varphi : I \to J \sqsubseteq \varphi' : I' \to J' \;=_{Df}$

$I \sqsubseteq I' \;\&\; J \sqsubseteq J' \;\&\; \forall i \varepsilon I, i' \varepsilon I'.\; i \sqsubseteq i' \supset \varphi i \sqsubseteq \varphi' i'$

containment by φ :

for $:X \to \;:$ $\quad f \overset{<}{\sim} f' \;=_{Df}\; \forall x.\; fx = f'x \circ x$,

i.e.

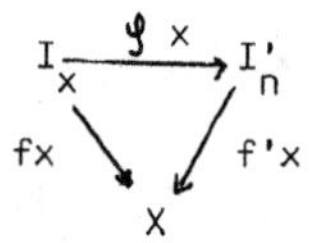

commutes.

Theorem. Opn's preserve $\lesssim$ continuously, i.e.

if $f_1 \overset{<}{\underset{\varphi_1}{\sim}} f'_1, \ldots, f_n \overset{<}{\underset{\varphi_n}{\sim}} f'_n$, then

$$op\,(f_1, \ldots, f_n) \overset{<}{\underset{\varphi}{\sim}} op\,(f'_n, \ldots, f'_n)$$

where φ varies continuously in the f_i and φ_i.

Proof:: 1. Show for Σ on multisets, hence for ; Σ' $\to'$, by explicit construction of φ from the φ_i .

2. For μ : use fact that $f \overset{<}{\underset{\varphi}{\sim}} f'$ is directed- complete to go from a chain of relations to its limit.

Equivalence : $\quad f \sim f' \;=_{Df}\; \exists \varphi, \psi.\; f \overset{<}{\underset{\varphi}{\sim}} f' \;\&\; f' \overset{<}{\underset{\psi}{\sim}} f$

$\leadsto$ Opn's preserve $\sim$.

Example

"<u>while</u> x≠0 <u>do</u> (x>0→x:=x-1, x<0→x:= <u>some</u> x≥0)"

$$f = (pos \to' decr,\ neg \to' anynonneg)^*$$
where $pos = \lambda x.x>0,\ neg = \lambda x.x<0,$
$decr = (\lambda x.x-1)',\ anynonneg = \lambda x.\lambda i\varepsilon N.i$

$$f_o = \bot_F = \lambda x.\lambda\bot.\bot$$

$$f_{k+1} = (pos \to' decr;f_k,\ neg \to' anynonneg;f_k,\ \underline{else} \to' \underline{0})$$
$$= \lambda x.(x>0 \to \lambda(\bot,t_k\ \varepsilon\ dom\ f_k\ (x-1)).\ f_k(x-1)\ t_k\ ,$$
$$x<0 \to \lambda(i\ \varepsilon\ N,\ t_k\ \varepsilon\ dom\ f_k\ (i)).\ f_k\ (i)\ t_k\ ,$$
$$x = 0 \to \lambda\bot.0\qquad)$$

<u>n ≥ 0</u> :
$$k\leq n \to f_k(n)\bot^{k+1} = f_{k-1}\ (n-1)\bot^k = \ldots = f_o\ (n-k)\bot = \bot\ ,$$
$$k>n \to f_k(n)\bot^{n+1} = f_{k-1}\ (n-1)\bot^n = \ldots = f_{k-n}\ (0)\bot = 0\ .$$

<u>n < 0</u> :
$$k\leq i+1 \to f_k(n)(i,\bot^{k+1}) = f_{k-1}\ (i)\bot^k = \bot\ ,$$
$$k>i+1 \to f_k(n)(i,\bot^{i+1}) = f_{k-1}\ (i)\bot^{i+1} = 0$$

$$f(n) = (n\geq 0 \to \lambda\bot^{n+1}.0,\ n\leq 0 \to \lambda(i,\bot^{i+1}).\ 0)$$

A domain of Actions

Separating "internal" and "external" choices :

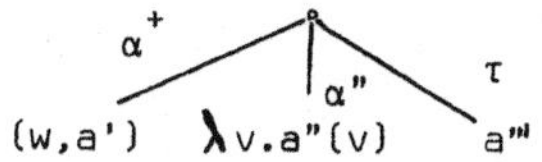

$$\Rightarrow \lambda C \subseteq C_o .\ (\alpha \in C \to [1 \overset{\alpha^+}{\mapsto} (w,a''),\ 2 \overset{\alpha''}{\mapsto} \lambda v.a''(v),\ 3 \mapsto a''C],\ \alpha \notin C \to [3 \to a''C]\ )$$

C_o ... (finite) set of channels

$C \subseteq C_o$ ... "live" channels

Actions over C_o :

$$A\ (C_o) \cong \prod_{C \subseteq C_o} M\ (\underline{0} + \sum_{\alpha\in C} V_\alpha \times A\ (C) + \sum_{\alpha\in C} (V_\alpha \to A\ (C)))$$

This models :

value passing along channels

termination : $\underline{0}$

non-termination : $\perp$

Might want to add :

input (read-only) variables

value-returning

Operations

"restriction" : $a_C = \lambda C' \subseteq C.aC'$ (for $C \subseteq C_0$)

$\underline{null} = \lambda C.u\underline{0}$

$$a;b = \lambda C.\Sigma i \varepsilon dom\ aC.\ \underline{cases}\ aCi:$$

$$(\underline{0} \to bC,\ (\alpha^+,\ (v,a') \to u(\alpha^+,\ (v,a;b_C))\ ,$$

$$(\alpha^-,\ \lambda v.a'(v)) \to u(\alpha^-,\lambda v.a'(v);b_C))$$

$$[\ldots \square \left\{\begin{matrix}\alpha^+ \to (v,a') \\ \alpha^- \to \lambda v.a'v\end{matrix}\right\} \square \ldots] = \lambda C.\lambda \pi \varepsilon \Pi(n).\ (\ldots,\ \alpha \varepsilon C \to \left\{\begin{matrix}(\alpha^+,\ (v,a'_C)) \\ (\alpha^-,\lambda v.(a'v)_C)\end{matrix}\right\},\ \ldots)$$

$$[\ldots \square \{---\} \square \ldots\ \underline{else}\ b] = \lambda C.\Sigma \pi \varepsilon \Pi(n).\ (\ldots,\ \alpha \varepsilon C \to u\{---\},\ \ldots\ \underline{else}\ bC)$$

$$[\ldots \square \{---\} \square \ldots]^* = \mu A.\ [\ldots \square \left\{\begin{matrix}\alpha^+ \to (v,a;A) \\ \alpha^- \to \lambda v.a'v;A\end{matrix}\right\} \square \ldots\ \underline{else}\ \underline{null}]$$

$$a//b = \lambda C.\ \Sigma i \varepsilon dom\ aC.\ \underline{cases}\ aCi.$$

$$(\underline{0} \to bC,\ (\alpha^+,\ (v,a')) \to u\ (\alpha^+,\ (v,a'//b_C))\ ,$$

$$(\alpha^-,\lambda v.a'v) \to (\alpha^-,\lambda v.a'//b_C))$$

$$+\ \Sigma j \varepsilon dom\ bC.\ \underline{cases}\ bCj.$$

-- mutatis mutandis --

$$+\ \Sigma\{(i,j)\ \varepsilon\ dom\ aC_0 x dom\ bC\ \mid$$

aC_0i and bC_0j indexed by compl'ary labels}.

$$\underline{cases}\ aC_0 i,\ bC_0 j\ :$$

$$(\alpha^+,\ (w,a')),\ (\alpha^-,\lambda v.b'v) \to (a'//b'w)C\ ,$$

$$(\alpha^-,\lambda v.a'v),\ (\alpha^+,\ (w,b')) \to (a'w//b')C$$

Equivalence

A "correspondence" between $\underline{a}$ and $\underline{a}'$ must provide an index mapping wherever $\underline{a}$ allows for choice. Therefore, the domain $\phi(C_o)$ has an equation somewhat similar to that for $A(C_o)$ itself :

$$\phi(C_o) \cong \prod_{C \subseteq C_o} \mathcal{C} \times (\underline{0} + \sum_{\alpha \in C} (V_\alpha \to \phi(C)) + \phi(C))$$

$a \underset{\varphi}{\lesssim} a' = \forall C \subseteq C_o.$ let $(k, \rho) = \varphi C$

$\forall i \varepsilon \text{dom} aC.$

aCi and a'C (ki) must

both be $\underline{0}$

or have parts that are $\lesssim$ by

corr'ing parts of φ

$a \sim a' = \exists \varphi, \Psi.\ a \underset{\varphi}{\lesssim} a' \underset{\Psi}{\lesssim} a$

Again should be ablve to prove :

1. opn's preserve $\lesssim$ continuously

2. therefore, opn's preserve $\sim$.

Nondeterministic Programs : An Example

Hans Bekić, Wien

March 1982

Corrections May 1982

1. Introduction

There have been many attempts to give a denotational semantics for nondeterministic and parallel programs. Most of these approaches are based on the notion of power domain [1,2], i.e. the domain of subsets, or certain equivalence classes of subsets, of a given domain. There are some well-known problems with the notion of power domain : the need to consider equivalence classes does not come primarily from the intended applications, but is forced by the desire to make the set of all subsets into a domain. As a consequence, certain concepts arising in the applications, like unbounded nondeterminism or fair merging, present difficulties in this approach.

In [3], a different approach has been outlined which seems to be able to overcome these difficulties. It is based on the use of indexed sets, rather than just subsets. The purpose of the present Note is to illustrate the theory on a small but typical example involving unbounded nondeterminism. An attempt has been made to make this Note self-contained by including enough, but only as much, theory as needed for the example. (The general theory can also be applied to asynchronous communication; it allows an equivalence to be defined which abstracts from any particular indexing; it requires diagrams, e.g. $\begin{matrix} a_{11} & \rightarrow & a_{12} \\ \downarrow & & \downarrow \\ a_{21} & \rightarrow & a_{22} \end{matrix}$, rather than partial orders $a_1 \rightarrow a_2$.)

The example, informal (suggested to the author by E. Astesiano). Informally, the example can be described by the following flowchart :

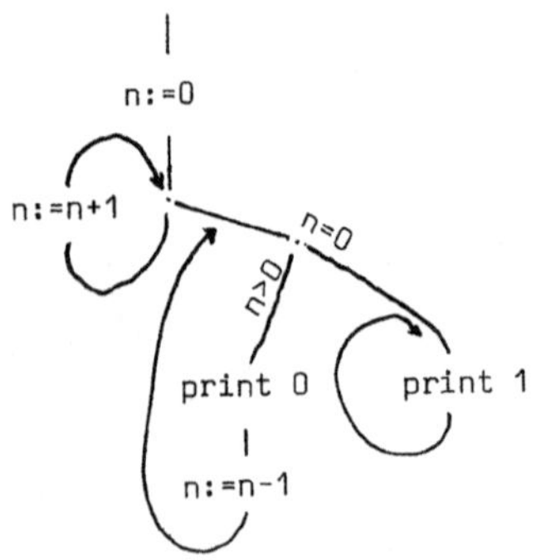

A little informal analysis shows that the program either loops forever without printing anything, or prints k zeroes followed by an infinite number of one's. Thus, the program may be said to denote the set of possible outcomes

$$F = \{\bot\} \cup \{0^k 1^\omega \mid k \in N\} .$$

What makes examples like this difficult in the framework of power domains is the fact that the set F is not prefix-closed : for every k, 0^k is prefix of some sequence in F, yet the limit 0^ω is not prefix of any sequence in F.

2. Domains

We start with domains that are complete partial orders (c.p.o.'s) with a least element $\perp$. Standard operations on domains (even on p.o.'s) are

$X + Y$	...	disjoint sum
$X \times Y$	...	Cartesian product

Since X + Y introduces a new $\perp$, it is a domain even if X and/or Y are c.p.o.'s only. In general, domains will be structures $(D, \sqsubseteq, \bigsqcup)$ where $\sqsubseteq$ is a p.o. and $\bigsqcup$ is a limit operation on chains, not necessarily l.u.b.; c.p.o.'s are a special case.

The domain of outputs. We are concerned with programs producing sequences of 0's and 1's. The domain S of these sequences can be defined by

$$S \cong \{\bullet\} + \{0,1\} \times S$$

where "$\bullet$" is a special element, the null sequence. Some elements of S are :

$011\bullet$	more precisely : $(0,(1,(1,\bullet)))$ - a finite complete sequence
$011\perp$	a finite incomplete sequence
01111...	an infinite sequence.

(The difference between $011\bullet$ and $011\perp$ corresponds to the difference between a program that has produced 011 and then stops, and a program that has produced 011 so far but may go on running).

Some operations on sequences are :

$$s\hat{\ }t =_{Df} \underline{\text{cases}}\ s\colon (\bullet \rightarrow t,\ bs' \rightarrow b(s'\hat{\ }t)) \qquad \text{(concatenation)},$$

$$s^0 =_{Df} \bullet, \quad s^{k+1} =_{Df} s\hat{\ }s^k \qquad \text{(finite powers } s^k\text{)},$$

$$s^\omega =_{Df} Y\lambda x.\ s\hat{\ }x = \bigsqcup_k s^k\hat{\ }\perp \qquad \text{(infinite power } s^\omega\text{)}.$$

(This uses the convention that "$\perp \rightarrow \perp$" can be omitted in a cases-clause. Thus $\perp\hat{\ }t = \perp$ for all t).

3. Primitive functions, combinators

Our program may be viewed as computing elements of S, but it also has an internal state variable n ranging over the natural numbers N. Thus, if we consider parts of the program, the appropriate type of objects are functions in $N \to N \times S$*) (at least for deterministic functions; this will be extended to nondeterministic functions presently).

Functions over N : A function $a: N \to N$ can be considered as a function $\hat{a}: N \to N \times S$ printing nothing :

$$\hat{a} \;=_{Df}\; \lambda n.(an,\bullet)$$

Printing 0 or 1 : For $b \in \{0,1\}$, we define print b : $N \to N \times S$ as

$$\text{print } b \;=_{Df}\; \lambda n.(n, b\bullet)$$

Serial composition : For f and g : $N \to N \times S$, we define $f;g : N \to N \times S$:

$$f;g \;=_{Df}\; \lambda n.\ \underline{\text{let}}\ n',s' = fn\ \underline{\text{in}}\ \underline{\text{let}}\ n'',s'' = gn'\ \underline{\text{in}}\ (n'', s'^\frown s'').$$

4. Nondeterministic functions

The following summarises the relevant notions from [3].

Indices, the domain of index sets, the domain $\mathcal{J}(X)$ of indexed sets over X. The idea is to model nondeterminism by indexed sets so that, for example, a nondeterministic function from X to Y becomes a (conventional) function in $X \to \mathcal{J}(Y)$, where $\mathcal{J}(Y)$ is a domain whose elements are (suitably) indexed sets with elements in Y. To start with, we need an universe I to choose indices from; since functional composition leads to "multiplication" of choices, I should be closed against forming pairs. We take

$$I \cong \{\bullet\} + N + I \times I$$

so that I contains a countable set of indices (the natural numbers) to start with. (The special index • is added for convenience only). Next, we define which subsets of I we are going to admit as index sets, and an ordering between index sets :

*), The context of domains, N stands for the domain of natural numbers with an added bottom element $\perp$.

$$\text{Indexsets} =_{Df} \{I \subseteq \mathcal{I} \mid I \neq \emptyset \text{ and } \forall i,j\varepsilon I, i\neq j \supset \neg \exists k\varepsilon \mathcal{I}, i\sqsubseteq k \,\&\, j\sqsubseteq k\}$$

with an ordering

$$I \sqsubseteq I' =_{Df} (\forall i\varepsilon I.\ \exists i'\varepsilon I'.\ i \sqsubseteq i') \ \&\ (\forall i'\varepsilon I'.\ \exists i\varepsilon I.\ i \sqsubseteq i') \ .$$

and a limit operation for chains : $\bigsqcup_n I_n =_{Df} \{(\bigsqcup_n i_n) \mid \forall_n . i_n \varepsilon I_n \ \&\ i_n \sqsubseteq i_{n+1}\}$.

($\bigsqcup$ is a minimal u.b., but, in general, there are no l.u.b.'s). (The restriction on I says that different elements in I must have no common upper bound in $\mathcal{I}$; without the restriction, $\sqsubseteq$ would not be an ordering). Finally, given a domain X, we can define the domain $\mathcal{J}(X)$ of <u>indexed sets over X</u> by

$$\mathcal{J}(X) =_{Df} \bigcup \{(I \to X) \mid I \ \varepsilon \ \text{Indexsets}\}$$

with

$$m:I\to X \sqsubseteq m':I'\to X \quad =_{Df} \quad I \sqsubseteq I' \ \&\ \forall i\varepsilon I,\ i'\varepsilon I'.\ i \sqsubseteq i' \supset mi \sqsubseteq m'i' \ .$$

and $\bigsqcup_n (m_n : I_n \to X) =_{Df} m:(\bigsqcup_n I_n)\to X,\ \ mi = \bigsqcup_n m_n i_n,$ where i_n = <u>the</u> $i_n \varepsilon I_n$ <u>s.t.</u> $i_n \sqsubseteq i$.

(The example will illustrate the working of $\sqsubseteq$ and $\bigsqcup$).

<u>Notation</u>: For $m:I\to X$, let $\underline{D}m = I$, $\underline{R}m = \{mi \mid i\varepsilon I\}$.

Nondeterministic functions from X to Y, then, are elements of the domain $X\to\mathcal{J}(Y)$, with $\sqsubseteq$ and $\bigsqcup$ defined component-wise.

<u>Primitive nondeterministic functions</u> : A function $f:X\to Y$ can be viewed as a n.d. function $\tilde{f}:X\to\mathcal{J}(Y)$ with a singleton choice :

$$\tilde{f}x: \{\bullet\}\to Y, \qquad \tilde{f}x\bullet =_{Df} fx \ .$$

<u>Nondeterministic choice</u> : For index sets I and $\mathcal{J}$, let

$$I+\mathcal{J} = \{(0,i) \mid i\varepsilon I\} \cup \{(1,j) \mid j\varepsilon \mathcal{J}\}$$

(disjoint sum of index sets). Then, for $f,g \ \varepsilon\ X\to\mathcal{J}(Y)$, define $f\vee g:X\to\mathcal{J}(Y)$ as

$$(f\vee g)x =_{Df} \lambda c\varepsilon\ \underline{D}f + \underline{D}g.$$
$$\underline{\text{cases}}\ c:\big((0,c') \to fxc',\ (1,c'') \to gxc''\big) \ .$$

(fvg may be viewed as "f or g"; it uses as index set a set of pairs; the first member of a pair determines whether f or g is applied).

Serial composition. Considering, more specifically, functions in $N \to \mathcal{J}(N \times S)$, we can generalise the definition of ";" in 3 above to apply to nondeterministic functions. For the example, the following case is sufficient : for $a:N \to N \times S$, $g:N \to \mathcal{J}(N \times S)$ define $a;g \in N \to \mathcal{J}(N \times S)$ as

$$
\begin{aligned}
(a;g)n \ =_{Df}\ & \underline{let}\ n',s' = an\ \underline{in} \\
& \lambda\, d \in \underline{D}(gn'): \\
& \quad \underline{let}\ n'',s'' = gn'd\ \underline{in}\ (n'',s'{}^\frown s'') .
\end{aligned}
$$

(For the general case f;g with f and g in $N \to \mathcal{J}(N \times S)$, we would use indices (c,d) with c used for fn and d used for gn', and "sum" over c :

$$
\begin{aligned}
(f;g)n \ =_{Df}\ & \Sigma c \in \underline{D}(fn) : \\
& \underline{let}\ n',s' = fnc\ \underline{in} \\
& \lambda d \in \underline{D}(gn'), \\
& \quad \underline{let}\ n'',s'' = gn'd\ \underline{in}\ (n'',s'{}^\frown s'')
\end{aligned}
$$

where $\sum_{i \in I} m_i = \bigcup_{i \in I} [(i,j) \mapsto m_i j \mid j \in \underline{D} m_i]$ is the disjoint sum of a system of indexed sets).

Output of a program : Given a function $f:N \to \mathcal{J}(N \times S)$ (representing the whole program) and an initial value $n_0 \in N$, we finally want to define the output of f under n_0 : OUTPUT f $n_0 \in \mathcal{J}(S)$,

$$
\text{OUTPUT } f\ n_0 \ =_{Df}\ \lambda c \in \underline{D}(fn_0).\underline{let}\ (n',s) = fn_0 c\ \underline{in}\ s \quad .
$$

5. The example, definition

Using the combinators above, we can transcribe the flowchart given in the Introduction :

$$
\begin{aligned}
f &= (incr;f) \ \vee\ g \ , \\
g &= (pos \to' (print0;\ decr;\ g)\ , \qquad else \to' h) \ , \\
h &= print1;\ h\ , \\
F &= \text{OUTPUT } f\ 0
\end{aligned}
$$

with

$$
iner = \lambda n.n+1, \quad decr = \lambda n.n-1, \quad pos = \lambda n.n>0,
$$

$$
(p \to' f, \ldots) \ = \ \lambda n\,.\,(pn \to fn, \ldots\ )
$$

(In this definition we have left implicit the "conversions" $a \mapsto \hat{a}$ for $a \in N \to N$ and $f \to \tilde{f}$ for $f \in N \to N \times S$. The implied use of $Y\lambda f$, $Y\lambda g$, $Y\lambda h$ will be made explicit in the computation of f,g,h below.)

6. Calculating g,h

The only nondeterminism is in the equation for f, so, for g and h, we can work in the domain $N \to N \times S$. Making recursion explicit, we have

$$h = \bigsqcup_k h_k, \text{ with :}$$

$$h_0 n = \bot,$$

$$h_{k+1} n = (\lambda n', s'. (n', 1s'))\ (h_k n)\ .$$

A little induction on k gives

$$h_k n = (\lambda n', s'. (n', 1^k s'))\ (h_0 n) = (\bot, 1^k \bot)$$

thus

$$hn = (\bot, 1^\omega)\ .$$

Similarly, we have for g :

$$g = \bigsqcup_k g_k, \text{ with :}$$

$$g_0 n = \bot,$$

$$g_{k+1} n = (n>0 \to (\lambda n', s'. (\ n', s'. (n', 0s'))\ (g_k(n-1)), \text{ else} \to hn\ )$$

Using again induction, we get, for k>n :

$$g_k n = (\lambda n', s'. (n', 0^n s'))\ (g_{k-n}\ 0)$$

$$= (\lambda n', s'. (n', 0^n s'))\ (h\ 0)$$

$$= (\bot, 0^n 1^\omega)$$

hence

$$gn = (\bot, 0^n 1^\omega)\ .$$

7. Calculating f

Working now in the domain $N \to \mathcal{J}(N \times S)$ and introducing names C_k for $\underline{D}(f_k n)$, we have

$$f = \bigsqcup_k f_k, \quad \text{with}$$

$$f_o n = \lambda c \varepsilon C_o . \bot, \qquad C_o = \{\bot\}$$

$$f_{k+1} b = \lambda c \varepsilon C_{k+1} . \ \underline{\text{cases}}\ c : ((0,c') \to f_k(n+1)c',\ (1,\bullet) \to \tilde{g}n\bullet),$$

$$C_{k+1} = C_k + \{\bullet\} .$$

For the C_k, we obtain

$$C_o = \{\bot\}$$

$$C_1 = \{0\bot,\ 1\bullet\}$$

$$C_2 = \{0^2\bot,\ 01\bullet,\ 1\bullet\}$$

$$\cdots$$

$$C_k = \{0^k\bot,\ 0^{k-1}1\bullet,\ \ldots,\ 0^2 1\bullet,\ 01\bullet,\ 1\bullet\}$$

$$\cdots$$

thus $C_k = \{0^k\bot\} \cup \{0^i 1\bullet \mid 0 \leqslant i < k\}$. For f_k, we have

$$f_k n(1\bullet) = \tilde{g}n\bullet = gn \qquad (k \geqslant 1)$$

$$f_k n(0c') = f_{k-1}(n+1)c' \qquad (k \geqslant 1) ,$$

thus

$$f_k n(0^k\bot) = f_{k-1}(n+1)\ (0^{k-1}\bot) = \ldots = f_o(n+k)\bot = \bot,$$

$$f_k(n)(0^i 1\bullet) = f_{k-1}(n+1)\ (0^{i-1}1\bullet) = \ldots = f_{k-i}(n+i)\ (1\bullet) = g(n+i) \qquad (k>i) .$$

For $f = \bigsqcup_k f_k$ we have $fn: C \to (N \times S)$ with

$$C = \bigsqcup_k C_k = \{\bigsqcup_k 0^k\bot\} \cup \{(\bigsqcup_{k>i} 0^i 1\bullet) \mid 0 \leqslant i < \infty\} = \{0^\omega\} \cup \{0^i 1\bullet \mid i \geqslant 0\},$$

$$f_n 0^\omega = \bigsqcup_k f_k n(0^k\bot) = \bot,$$

$$fn(0^i 1\bullet) = \bigsqcup_{k>i} f_k n(0^i 1\bullet) = g(n+i) = (\bot, 0^{n+i}1^\omega)$$

i.e. fn is the indexed set

$$fn = [0^{\omega} \to \bot] \cup [0^{i}1 \bullet \to (\bot, 0^{n+i}1^{\omega}) \mid i \geq 0] \quad .$$

Finally, for F = OUTPUT f0, we obtain

$$F = [0^{\omega} \to \bot] \cup [0^{i}1 \bullet \to 0^{i}1^{\omega} \mid i \geq 0] \quad .$$

The range of values in F is $\underline{R}F = \{\bot\} \cup \{0^{i}1^{\omega} \mid i \geq 0\}$, which coincides with the set of outputs informally associated with the program in the Introduction.

References

[1] G. D. Plotkin : A powerdomain construction. - SIAM Journal on Computing, Vol.5, No.3, 1976.

[2] M. Smyth : Powerdomains. - JCSS, Vol.16, No.1, 1978.

[3] H. Bekić : Nondeterministic functions and the semantics of CSP.- Presentation at 2nd Workshop on the Semantics of Programming Languages, Bad Honnef 1981. (Full paper under preparation).

A MODEL OF NONDETERMINISM:

INDEXED SETS AND THEIR EQUIVALENCE

H. Bekić, Wien

Work in (slow) progress :

"Theory of Processes" IBM TR 25.125

Indexed sets of interleaved computations, functions with choice parameters

Struggle with CSP

$\mathcal{J}(X)$: systematic use of indexed sets

Objective :

algebra of nondeterministic functions/processes

"fully abstract"

avoid ad-hoc identifications/restrictions

Contents :

use $\mathcal{J}(X)$ instead of $P(X)$

↳ = domain of indexed sets over X

use $x \xrightarrow[\varphi]{} x'$ to abstract from indexing

↳ "x is mapped into x' by φ "

<u>Some dissatisfaction with P(X)</u> :

$\{a,c\} = \{a,b,c\}$ for $a \sqsubset b \sqsubset c$

$\{1,2,3,\ldots\} \notin P(N_{\perp})$

$\{0^k \mid k \in N\} \notin P(\{0,1\}^{\omega})$

<u>Introducing $\mathcal{J}$(X)</u> :

= indexed sets over X, using "certain" indexings

1.

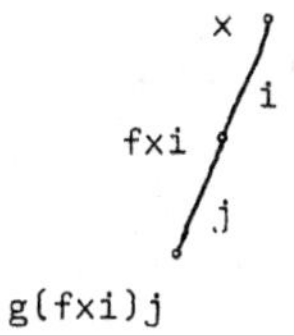

$(f;g)\ x\ \underbrace{(i,j)} = g\ (fxi)j$

<u>pairs</u> of indices

2.

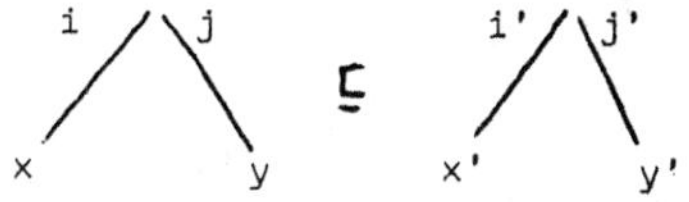

:

i', j' should again be different

→ $i,j \in I$ & $i \neq j$ ⊃ i and j are <u>joinless</u>

Indices :

$$I \cong \{\bullet\} + N + I \times I \quad .$$

Index sets :

$$\mathfrak{I} =_{Df} \{I \subseteq I \mid I \neq \emptyset \ \& \ \forall i,j \varepsilon I. \ i \neq j \supset \neg \exists k \varepsilon I. \ i \sqsubseteq k \& j \sqsubseteq k\} \quad ,$$

$$I \sqsubseteq I' =_{Df} (\forall i \varepsilon I. \exists i' \varepsilon I'. i \sqsubseteq i') \ \& \ (\forall i' \varepsilon I'. \exists i \varepsilon I. i \sqsubseteq i') \quad ,$$

$$\bigsqcup_n I_n =_{Df} \{(\bigsqcup_n i_n) \mid \forall n. i_n \varepsilon I_n \ \& \ i_n \sqsubseteq i_{n+1}\}$$

for chains $\langle I_n \mid n \varepsilon N \rangle$.

Indexed sets over X :

$$J(X) =_{Df} \bigcup_{I \varepsilon \mathfrak{I}} (I \to X) \quad ,$$

$$m: I \to X \sqsubseteq m': I' \to X' =_{Df}$$

$$I \sqsubseteq I' \ \& \ \forall i \varepsilon I, i' \varepsilon I'. \ i \sqsubseteq i' \supset mi \sqsubseteq m'i' \quad ,$$

$$\bigsqcup_n (m_n : I_n \to X) =_{Df} m: (\bigsqcup_n I_n) \to X \ ,$$

$$mi =_{Df} \bigsqcup_n m_n i_n$$

where i_n is <u>the</u> $i_n \varepsilon I_n$ s.t. $i_n \sqsubseteq i$.

Two (unpleasant) properties of $\mathfrak{J}$, $J(X)$, ... :

1. $\mathfrak{J}$ is not a c.p.o. :

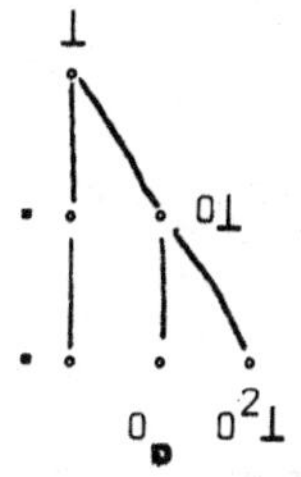

$$\bigsqcup_n I_n = \{0^k\cdot \mid k \in N\} \cup \{0^\omega\} .$$

(under $\{0^k\cdot \mid k \in N\}$:) but this is another minimal u.b.

2.
$$\begin{array}{ccccccc} I_{11} & \sqsubseteq & I_{12} & \sqsubseteq & I_{13} & \sqsubseteq & \dots \\ \sqsubseteq & & & & & & \\ I_{21} & \sqsubseteq & I_{22} & \sqsubseteq & I_{23} & \sqsubseteq & \dots \end{array}$$

does not imply $\bigsqcup_n I_{1n} \sqsubseteq \bigsqcup_n I_{2n}$:

$$\begin{array}{ccc} i_{11} & \sqsubseteq & i_{13} \\ \sqsubseteq & & \sqsubseteq \\ i_{21} & \sqsubseteq & ? \end{array}$$

$\leadsto$ we need diagrams, e.g.
$$\begin{array}{ccc} I_{11} & \rightarrow & I_{12} \\ \downarrow & & \downarrow \\ I_{21} & \rightarrow & I_{22} \end{array}$$
, which is

stronger than
$$\begin{array}{ccc} I_{11} & \sqsubseteq & I_{12} \\ \sqsubseteq & & \sqsubseteq \\ I_{21} & \sqsubseteq & I_{22} \end{array}$$
, and can be defined

similarly to $\sqsubseteq$, which becomes $I_1 \rightarrow I_2$.

$\bigsqcup$ also becomes a special case by admitting diagrams over $N \cup \{\omega\}$.

n.d. functions

$\mathcal{F}(X) \;=\; X \rightarrow \mathcal{J}(X)$

Operations on $\mathcal{F}(X)$.

composition : $f;g = \lambda x.\ \sum_{t \in \mathrm{dom} fx} g(fxt)$, where

$$\sum_{i \in I} m_i =_{Df} \bigcup_{i \in I} [(i,j) \rightarrow m_{ij} \mid j \in \mathrm{dom}\ m_i]$$

n.d. conditional :

$$[p_1 \rightarrow' f_1 \,\square\, \ldots \,\square\, p_n \rightarrow' f_n] = \sum_{\pi \in \Pi(n)}{}' (p_{\pi 1} \rightarrow' f_{\pi 1}, \ldots, p_{\pi n} \rightarrow' f_{\pi n})$$

$$= \lambda x.\ \sum_{\pi \in \Pi(n)} (p_{\pi 1}x \rightarrow f_{\pi 1}x, \ldots, p_{\pi n}x \rightarrow f_{\pi n}x)$$

n.d. iteration :

$$[p_1 \rightarrow' f_1 \,\square\, \ldots \,\square\, p_n \rightarrow' f_n]^* =$$

$$\mu F.\ \sum_{\pi \in \Pi(n)} (p_{\pi 1} \rightarrow' f_{\pi 1};F, \ldots, p_{\pi n} \rightarrow' f_{\pi n};F, \text{else} \rightarrow' \underline{0})$$

identity : $\underline{0} = \lambda x.\lambda\bot.x = \lambda x.\underline{u}x$ $\qquad \underline{u}x = [\cdot \rightarrow x]$

(primitive) det. functions :

for $a: X \rightarrow X$: $a' =$ ~~$\lambda x.\ .ax$~~
$= \lambda x.\underline{u}(ax)$

"$\mu F.\ \ldots$" = "$Y\lambda F.\ \ldots$" works because the constructions used, like Σ, $\rightarrow$, application, are continuous.

Equivalence

$\mathcal{C} = \bigcup_{I, J \varepsilon \mathcal{J}} (I \to J)$ ... correspondences between index-sets

$\varphi : I \to J \sqsubseteq \varphi' : I' \to J' =_{Df}$

$I \sqsubseteq I' \ \& \ J \sqsubseteq J' \ \& \ \forall i \varepsilon I, i' \varepsilon I'.\ i \sqsubseteq i' \supset \varphi i \sqsubseteq \varphi' i'$

$\bigsqcup_n \varphi_n = \ldots$

<u>containment by φ :</u>

for $\varphi : X \to \mathcal{C}$: $\quad f \underset{\varphi}{\leqslant} f' =_{Df} \quad \forall x.\ fx = f'x \circ \varphi x$,

i.e. $\forall x$: $\quad I_x \xrightarrow{\varphi x} I'_n$, $\quad fx : I_x \to X$, $\quad f'x : I'_n \to X$ $\quad$ commutes.

<u>Theorem.</u> Opn's preserve $\leqslant$ continuously, i.e.

if $f_1 \underset{1}{\leqslant} f'_1, \ldots, f_n \underset{n}{\leqslant} f'_n$, then

$$op\,(f_1, \ldots, f_n) \leqslant op\,(f'_1, \ldots, f'_n)$$

where φ varies continuously in the f_i and φ_i .

<u>Proof</u> : 1. Show for Σ on indexedsets, hence for ; Σ' →', by explicit construction of φ from the φ_i .

2. For : use fact that $f \underset{\varphi}{\leqslant} f'$ is directed - complete to go from a chain of relations to its limit.

<u>Equivalence</u> : $f \sim f' =_{Df} \exists \varphi, \psi.\ f \underset{\varphi}{\leqslant} f' \ \& \ f' \underset{\psi}{\leqslant} f$

⇝ Opn's preserve $\sim$.

Outlook :

Domain equations :

e.g. $A \cong \{\underline{0}\} + (X \to \mathcal{J}(X \times A))$

$\mathcal{J}$, +, x, $\to$ are domain transformers, working on/producing domains and retractions

$$A \underset{\Psi}{\overset{\Phi}{\rightleftarrows}} A$$

between them. A retraction between domains is a functor, accepting/producing objects and morphisms

$$a \underset{\varphi}{\to} a'$$

between them. In this way, the equation can be used to define both objects and morphisms.

"External choice" in CSP :

"α?", "α!" in guards is "α∈C",

where C = channels still alive.

All other choices modelled by $\mathcal{J}(\ )$.